WHAT
CAN
A MAN
DO?

WHAT CAN A MAN DO?

BY
MILTON MAYER

A SELECTION
OF HIS
MOST
CHALLENGING
WRITINGS

EDITED BY
W. ERIC GUSTAFSON

THE UNIVERSITY OF CHICAGO PRESS
CHICAGO AND LONDON

Library of Congress Catalog Card Number: 64-15801

THE UNIVERSITY OF CHICAGO PRESS, CHICAGO & LONDON

The University of Toronto Press, Toronto 5, Canada

TO
THE
MEMORY
OF

Rabbi Emil G. Hirsch of Sinai Congregation, an Amos in Chicago, who looked (*I* thought) like Michelangelo's Moses (who in turn looked like God); and

Mrs. Florence F. B. Manley of Englewood High School in Chicago, who taught me Latin and tried to teach me that decency was more important than Latin,

this book is dedicated in the awe
that only childhood
knows enough to know.

It was one of the few days which really stick in my memory, the day in October, 1951, that I met Milton Mayer for the first time in Zagreb at a peace conference of which the Yugoslav government was host and sponsor. There he appeared — a truly human being, not just a part of a homogeneous flock, not just a member of a political, social, cultural, or religious group, but a human person, interested in all questions, sharing in all problems, trying hard to find out what might be done to overcome the stalemate of humanity and to save mankind from the devastating and drowning flood of inhumanity that rose in the wake of the Second World War.

As visiting research professor at Frankfurt University after the war, Milton Mayer was to investigate the rise of National Socialism, and there he discovered his real mission — to live with the German people, to listen, to help, and to heal. From this experience his memorable book, *They Thought They Were Free* (Chicago: University of Chicago Press, 1955) originated, and from it, too, he gained new friends for himself and his country among Germans of all kinds (even among former Nazis). He did not blame nor did he accuse, as he — a Jew — might have been expected to. His own spirit became alarmed and sorely troubled; he wanted to know and to understand, not what the Germans, or some of them, had done and been, but what man had done and been and what might be and do.

So, in the tumultuous years since then, he has become a leading figure in the reconciliation of "West" and "East," and he is now claimed by friends in Europe — on both sides of the "Iron Curtain" — as much as he is in his own country. And with him always his good wife Jane.

I value Milton Mayer first as a person and only then as a writer, first as a friend, and only then as a journalist and essayist. Without any doubt he is an eminent and remarkable analyst of enduring influence, and this collection of his shorter works is a most significant contribution to our time and to times to come. But I shall always think of him as a person and as a dear personal friend, when I remember Zagreb and Prague and Moscow, Marburg and Stockholm and Geneva.

He wants to be a Christian, a real Christian, in this world where it is hard to be a Christian; and he is. And therefore he is as controversial as anyone would be who asks his question, "What can a man do in order to be human?" This is the great question in the social order everywhere. Of the few who dare ask it, Milton Mayer surely is one of the most competent, for the genuine and true answer is granted, not where we rely on our reflective intellect alone, but where we "apply our hearts unto wisdom" (Psalms 90:12).

Martin Niemöller

Wiesbaden, Germany

CONTENTS

SWING
LOWER
SWEET
CHARIOT

Once in the dear dead days almost, I am glad to say, beyond recall, and before everyone wondered how soon life would end all at once, a literary con man, or fourflusher, leapt aboard the Dale Carnegie gravy train with a book called *Life Begins at 40*. Like all sweet deceits, this one sold a lot of copies. But not to me; I have never been one to be diddled by the Diddlers of the Masses; I would wait until I was forty and life began, and see for myself; meanwhile I would save my money.

Age forty came and went. I waited and waited for life to begin. It didn't. Things went on, or didn't go on, pretty much as they had. In my fortieth year I thought I was just about where I was in my thirty-ninth; I was wrong, of course, because the man who thinks he is just about where he was a year ago didn't know where he was a year ago either. I was maybe a wee bit worse in my fortieth year than I was in my thirty-ninth — just a wee; just enough to make my fortieth year a landmark.

Landmarks are hard to discern anyway. This little life flies by so fast, and a fellow has all he can do to hold on to its tail feathers. Under the circumstances he mistakes one landmark for another (or a divot for a landmark) and some, lying lower along the horizon, he does not discern at all. So flies this little life, and a fellow with it, away.

An old friend, who shall, or should, be nameless, and I were fishing up at Mud Lake once, using an empty bottle for a float. "How old are you?" said my friend, who thought he had just snagged a pike but turned out to have snagged a pikestaff and had grown pensive. "Forty," I said. My friend, who was a couple of years younger than I (and, indeed, still is), whistled. "You'd better get going," he said. "Where?" I said. "*Some*where," he said. "I've been there," I said, "and it's a sell." "You're approaching your prime," he said. "The next ten years will tell the story." "I'm retreating," I said, "and

From the *Progressive*, June, 1959.

there isn't any story." "They ought," he said, "to be the best ten years of your life."

And so they have been, like every ten years before them. But nothing decisive happened, and not much even indecisive. I waited and waited for life to begin at. It never did. Things are great, even peachy, but they always were. I'm just about the same, except for my hair, or, as I am now able to say, my hairs, as I was at Mud Lake.

A couple of months ago I was in Europe saving my money and trying to drum up a little business— I'm still there, and still trying— and I got a letter from my friend. "How old are you?" he wrote. "Fifty," I wrote back, "and don't tell me I'd better get going. I'm gone." "Do you know," he wrote back, "what I want you to do? I want you to write your reflections on being fifty. You must have some. *Fifty*," and he whistled into the mail box.

I know what moves my friend to keep after me decade after decade. He is right behind me on the unlighted path of life. He looks behind him and around him, and it is dark unto ebon. He wants to know if I see anything up ahead. He wants to know when life begins. *Hélas!* my friend — never.

There is, of course, the grace of God. This, when it comes over a man, at fifty, forty, or eighty, is said to be a beginning. I wouldn't know, but I can imagine. One day, as he weeps in the garden, he hears a voice as of an angel saying: "Take up and read." And he takes up, and the book falls open, and he reads: "Let us walk honestly, as in the day; not in rioting and drunkenness, not in chambering, and wantonness, not in strife and envying. But put ye on the Lord." And he whistles a beatific whistle and sells what he has and gives it to the poor; and signing no more petitions, writing no more inspirational essays, running for no more offices in which he may serve his fellow citizens, and selling no more soul for no more money, he walks into a monastery (like the young man who bombed Hiroshima) and escapes at last (like the young man in Stendhal who went to join Napoleon) the sorrows that are poisoning his life, especially on Sundays. Thus, it would seem, and only thus, life begins. Anything less and he is about the same this year as last — a little seedier, a little greedier, a little timider. He says, and he thinks, that he means to change; but what he really wants is *to be changed,* but he has not come to the right Party.

Fifty. I whistle up the Urals.

Where have I been all my life?

It's funny. The less a man has to lose, the less he is willing to risk; the worse the bargain, the tighter he hugs it. I remember the first time I heard myself saying that Socrates' choice was no mystery: by being noble, and taking death instead of dishonor, he simply traded in a couple of years of life for immortality. "He was an old man, anyway," I said. "He didn't mind dying." "Young man," said an old man in the group, "you have never been an old man."

I remember the time a vicar in the town of Wakefield was quoted as telling his son that a man must never choose the lesser evil in the hope that he might, thereby, survive to do good. "The evil he chooses, my son," said the vicar, "he must do today. The good for which he chooses it he will do tomorrow. But before tomorrow comes the book of his life may be closed, and then the evil he did will be written in it, and the good he would do — " I remember the time I read of the man who ate, drank, and was merry, instead of building a barn for his goods, and then resolved that he would positively build the barn tomorrow, when he heard a voice saying, "Fool, this night thy soul shall be required of thee."

So fast flies this little life away. I remember a tale out of school, and what a school. I was sitting in the office of the president of the school, admiring his one hundred fifty million dollars. I had my feet on his desk. He kicked them off and told me some of his troubles. "What you need," I said, "is time off, to think." "If I had time to think," he said, "I would have to think about why I am not a socialist, a pacifist, and a Christian. Thanks just the same." Me, too. So fast flies this life, and lest we have time to think, we fly it faster.

Fifty. At fifty Jesus and Alexander had each been dead seventeen years, each having overcome the world, in his own way, at thirty-three; Mozart at thirty-five; Michelangelo had finished the Sistine ceiling fifteen years earlier, and his back still ached, and Leonardo had learned enough about Woman to paint her picture; and Napoleon had had four years on St. Helena to think about why he was not a socialist, a pacifist, and a Christian. At fifty Marshall Field II had, by pluck and luck, accumulated seventy-five million dollars; in the year 1900 Andrew Carnegie made twenty-three million dollars and paid no income tax, and his workers' wages averaged four hundred dollars a year. At fifty Hitler attacked everybody, and at fifty Alfred Krupp, who owned a hundred companies at thirty and was a war criminal at forty, owned a hundred companies again. Me — at fifty I have overcome no worlds, painted no ceilings, learned nothing about women, and accumulated between twenty-three and seventy-five million dollars worth of grocery bills. True, I have attacked everybody, I am a war criminal, and my back aches. True, too, I have managed not to have time to think about why I am not a socialist, a pacifist, and a Christian.

At fifty I'm winded. But I always was. At fifteen Coach Rosie Rosenbaum of the Englewood High School track team put me in against De Paul in the two-mile run. "But I'm a miler," I said. You're neither a miler nor a two-miler," said Rosie, "but there are only two men entered, and if you finish, we pick up a point. You'll get your second wind at the end of the first mile. If you don't, keep going anyway." I finished late that night, and Englewood won the meet by one point and, with it, the city championship. I never got my second wind.

I never will. I'll keep going anyway until they repeal Newton's first law of motion. It's the end of the first mile and the beginning of the last; there's a reflection at fifty for you, friend. The long pull, and all pull now. At twenty-five I held down three jobs and wrote nights. At fifty I hold down no jobs and write days — some days. No wind. At twenty-five Bill Benton held down three jobs and wrote nights; at fifty he held down six jobs and wrote twice as much nights; and at sixty he holds down nine jobs and writes three times as much nights. Third wind. Paul Geheeb, the greatest educator in Europe, is out mountain-climbing in the Berner Oberland at eighty-nine; when he took off, he reminded me that Sophocles hadn't hit his stride until he was ninety.

Me — I was superannuated at fifteen; never picked up a point again. The Bentons, Geheebs, and Sophocleses live forever. Me — I die forever. I feel as heavy as yonder stone.

It isn't bad. I lived long enough to hear of what the old Chassid said of the man who foreknew in his lifetime that for him there was to be no heaven: "What a unique and enviable chance that man had of doing right without fear of reward!" I lived long enough, too, to hear A. J. Muste say, "If I can't love Hitler, I can't love at all." It isn't bad, to have lived long enough to hear the Word, even on the fly.

At fifty the devil takes over, if, indeed, he has bided his time that long. He inflates a fellow's ego as a defense against being passed by by the world and the new generations indifferent to what a fellow knows and thinks and is. Kids who once wanted advice are giving it now. A fellow is ever more isolated; he has to fight now for a hearing; his gray hairs command the disrespect of the young. It's the space age, and he hasn't found out yet how to use the space he already had.

But his friends grow old with him, and, growing old all of them together in lockstep, they are always young and fair (or fair to middling) to one another. So they maintain the hallucination; they go on dancing, or drinking, or walking, or whatever they always did, with one another. Ah, but then their ranks (if not they individually) begin to thin. An old friend moves away, and that's a betrayal. An old friend dies — if you haven't died at fifty nowadays, you never will — and that's a greater betrayal. They leave you there alone, with strangers, who do not care what happens to you because they themselves are beset, like you, with their responsibilities and their betrayal and (finally, when you and they are both very old) their bitterness. A very old man — I know some great men who are very old — is either a bore or suspects that he is. None of his virtues, wisdom included, offsets his one unforgivable vice of being old. "Here comes old man Mayer again. Quick, turn off the lights and we'll pretend we're in bed. I haven't got time to listen to him. I wish he'd find something to do."

You will be old and resent every thing new — plastics and light metals, calculators and computers, ranch houses, clutchless cars frozen foods, picture windows, and turnpikes. You will know, the day it's discovered, what television is going to be and do, because you saw radio do it. Unless you're a fool clear out to the rind, you have long since discovered that there is no progress. And if you, my friend, think, you and your campaigns to change the world, that you will not leave the world and yourself a little worse than you found them, you're crazy. If you think that ontogeny does not recapitulate phylogeny — still more so, philogyny — you're out of your head.

Among the new things a fellow resents, at fifty, are his children, as his parents resented him, and with reason. What right has my Little Julie to sell a story for $350? Who taught her to write? Who's the writer in this family? Who changed her diapers and washed them and wiped her little nose and held her while she took her medicine and sat her on the toilet and wrapped her pink blanket around her to keep her warm? Confound it, I haven't seen $350 in one piece in twenty years. I don't want her $350; I don't even want her not to have it; what I want is for her not to have sold a story for $350. But she will always pretend that all that she is today she owes to her darling father; they all will, the little hypocrites.

It's other people's daughters who rowel me, not my own. Peaches-and-cream little girls — past their teens now; little girls who take me for their uncle, who no longer look at me on the street car or crowd over to me at parties or after lectures or receptions. To thine worst enemy, the mirror, friend! It will lie to thee and tell thee that thou hast twenty-thirty good years yet! If thou wast not handsome then, hast thou changed? Not at all, says the mirror; oh, a wee bit, but only a wee — dimples to creases and creases to ruts; a hair here and there gone, another here and there discolored, gray with the dust of life's dusty road. What right have *they* to take you for their uncle, to go out with you, unafraid, after dark?

Recollected in no tranquility the first love; rapture and agony; never anything else, and neither of them recollectable now except by analogy. Now you begin to fill up with wistfulness. Everything — a lilac bush, a sidewalk crack, an ice cream cone — bespeaks wistfulness. It will burst you unless you work or play harder to shrivel it; in which case work or play will burst you, and the wistfulness of a sprig of mignonette, of a ribbon, of a glove or a garter, will come seeping back anyway and fill you up; if you work and play by day and by evening, then by night.

But you're too tired to work and play, too tired to withstand the wistfulness. Maybe your raptures (when the dentist stops drilling) and your agonies (when he starts) will distract you. You are coming apart now. In another ten years, fifteen anyway and maybe five, you will be coming apart full-time. When you were little and you had your toy hook-and-ladder, you were doctored and dentisted and dieted all the time, and you had to leave your hook-and-ladder for them. There followed the years (when life first flew fast away and you never noticed) of no doctor, no dentist, no diet, the years you did as you pleased, the years you balanced on ladders and then the years you played with hooks. Now at fifty you must leave them and go back to being doctored, dentisted, dieted, opticianed, vitamined, and arch-supported. There are twenty-thirty years in you yet, but don't call them good years; call them good days. Not yet — but soon.

In the fall an old man's fancy turns to death. Let it turn lightly, friend; if I see darkness ahead, what see you behind except darkness? I see that the road ahead is longer than the road behind; if God exists, nothing else is important, simply because the road ahead is longer than the road behind; nothing else, then, is important except whether God exists. I don't try to tell you He does; death is wasted on the old. *Your* death — reflect at fifty, friend — means nothing except to you. Nobody will miss you; see all the relicts, a few months afterward adjusted, a few years afterward happy as birds. Let your death mean nothing to you, and it will mean nothing to anybody. Who sees the sparrow fall?

It isn't death, but dying that bothers you is it? Ah, yes, because of all the things you intended to do. But if you were to live ten minutes less than forever, that would still be the case. The only thing you can count on doing forever is busying yourself being dust. You remember the Roman's question: "What are you busy *about*?" You remember the Carthaginian — Augie of Hippo, they called him — who despaired because children wasted their time in aimless play and then despaired the more when he considered that men wasted their time in things that were worse because they were aimed in the wrong direction. Consider how your light is not spent but thrown away. If you have an affair, put your affair in order. Fool, this night. . . .

"I will restore to you," the Lord promised me through his prophet Joel, "the years that the locust hath eaten." *That's* the kind of talk. But not yet. The locust will eat yet awhile. Now just what are the things you intend to do, friend? Cut yourself down to size and them with you, or you will be miserable when you have lived ten minutes less than forever. Reflect at fifty. If you will avoid misery, reflect. You must have a fixed hierarchy of things you intend to do and steer yourself by it, for he who will not answer to the rudder will answer to the rock. And you must establish your hierarchy in terms of two separate and co-ordinate principles; first, in terms of the things that are good in themselves, such as changing the world, and second, in terms of the things that are within your own power, such as changing yourself.

I tell you that these separate principles are not only co-ordinate but co-operative: you will change the world in so far, and only in so far, as you change yourself, for, as the men are, so will the world be, and you, though you would never know it to look at you, are a man. You insist that you would do more — maybe remake America — but America is remaking you faster than you will be able to remake it. Bite off more than you can chew — sure — but not so much that you choke on it. Hierarchy, hierarchy. It's a great life only if you weaken, and this is the Hot Gospel, the Law and the Prophets, the Medes and the Persians, and the Real Gazookus.

In my fiftieth year I have learned to play chess. A little child of mine led me and beat the pants off me. Then I taught the companion of my sorrows (and the cause of most of them) and now she beats the pants off me. Chess is the ultimate form of supraverbal communication. Now, as I totter around Russia and parts farther still, I need not learn the language; chess is the universal language. Brother Ziak, the vice-president of the Czechoslovakian People's Republic, beat the pants off me; I'm challenging Brother Mao. Maybe I'll change the world; if I do, it will be because I changed myself into a chess player. I have spent maybe a fourth of my fiftieth year playing chess with the companion o. m. s. (a. t. c. o. m. o. t). What a waste! But how have you spent a fourth of yours, my friend — deciding that to go to war with the Democrats is a lesser evil than going to war with the Republicans?

In my fiftieth year I have learned to sleep on straw in *youth* hostels at a dime a night. In an Italian hostel a Greek standing next to me in the washroom said, "You are the first American boy I have met in a hostel." *Boy*. In my fiftieth year I have learned, in a word, to punish myself a little, knowing that at fifty the devil's whisper is always, "Why punish yourself?" and that the masochist answer is the only right one, "Because I enjoy it." I have learned to live on a *little less* money, a *little* less fame, and a *little* less power than I lived on twenty years ago, knowing that at fifty the devil's whisper is always, "All these may be yours." I know the devil — I guess I ought to; we've been traveling companions for fifty years — and I know his name. It is Ego. Against him, at fifty, I make war. I am losing the war — winning a skirmish here and there, but losing the war — but at least I am losing the right war. Are you sure, my friend, that you are not winning the wrong one? Are you even sure you are winning it?

Twenty years ago I was an eagle flying high in Bombay. Money, fame, and power were a dime a dozen, but many an eye had a cinder in it. The devil took me up to the covers of the slick magazines and watched me jump off and split his sides as I screamed going down. But at least I don't have to go up there any more. I'm losing the war, but at least I don't have to go up there any more. I remember the mountain top and *its* raptures and *its* agonies and how little time it left me to think about why I wasn't a socialist, a pacifist, and a Christian, and I don't have to go up there any more.

All the breaks. Nothing but breaks. The first fifty years have been a toboggan ride, a two-mile jog. If, fool, this night my soul is required of me, my regret is that I owe the world a living and I haven't had time to pay anything on the debt. I've been intending to pay — a *little* something, anyway — but the road to good intentions, my friend, is paved with hell. I may never get it paid off, but at least I won't welsh.

Nothing but breaks. Through no virtue of my own, I'm a free

enterpriser, and therefore, a free man *in posse*. Nobody can fire me; still better, nobody can pension me; best of all, nobody can retire me with a blue-plate dinner and a gold watch (which turns out to be plated) for fifty years of faithful service to — what? I was reading in the paper, and *only* the other day, that the Essex Universal Corporation, which makes missile control systems, has acquired William Gluckin & Company, makers of corsets and brassieres, and that Wilson Brothers, men's underwear and shirt makers, have absorbed the Sciafe Company, producing missile equipment. I was reading in the paper, only the other year, that sixty-five scientists who made the atomic bomb for Mr. Roosevelt petitioned Mr. Truman, on July 15, 1945, not to use it. When I go back into faithful service — if ever — I'm going to take the light yoke, and you know Whose that is, friend. Meanwhile, I am my own man and my own fool and not, like Mr. Henderson, somebody else's.

And who, did you say, is Mr. Henderson? Why, Mr. Henderson is Loy Henderson of the Dulles-Acheson-Stevenson State Department. And in Karachi a month or two ago Mr. Henderson, as head of the American observer delegation to the Bagdad Pact Ministerial Council, informed the Council, as per Dulles, Acheson, and Stevenson, that "the free nations recognize that survival requires concrete measures to meet the threat of international communism. The Bagdad Pact is playing a significant role in this effort. The American government and people have unstintingly supported the Pact. We will continue to support it and its objectives." I may squander my life at chess, but at least I don't have to tell the Ministerial Council that the American people support the Bagdad Pact — or that they know what it is.

God heard me scream when I jumped down from the mountain top. He picked me up and threw me into good company and let me see Red Schaal of the American Friends Service Committee bent in half carrying suitcases full of books through the railroad station so that the two-bit tip would go instead, into a bottle of milk for a kid somewhere far away. Then He wised me up by letting me hear the Chassid, the vicar of Wakefield, and A. J. Muste. Then He gave me the gift of prophecy, so that I knew before every brave new war began that the winners would be the buzzards and the sharks and so that

I would never make an unholy chump of myself by saying, like Franklin D. Roosevelt, that the aim of the peace-loving peoples was to get rid of German militarism forever, "the cancer which for generations has produced only misery and pain for the whole world." He even saved me from saying, like the *New York Times* the day after the Nazi murderers were murdered at Nürnberg, that "mankind has entered a new era of international morality." He kept calling my attention to little items like that — always little items — like the little item from Tokyo that reported that sixty Japanese (sixty *known*) had died in the year 1958 — you heard me, 1958—of radiation incurred in Hiroshima and Nagasaki in the year 1945.

And after doing all that for me, He crowned His free and unmerited gifts by letting me grow old without growing up. Everything is said to be easy for Him, but this was pie. All He had to do was direct my attention to the merchant prince's unbuttoned button, to the judge's cuspidor, and to the wisp of straw sticking out of the statesman's shirt. What Lucian, Cervantes, Swift, and Rabelais saw and articulated, He taught me to see and left me inarticulate lest I let the devil take me up to the mountain top again. I don't mean that He left me illiterate. He taught me to read straight, so that when I read the words, "Forgive us our trespasses, as we forgive those who trespass aginst us," I knew that the important word was "as," and I realized I'd better get going. He taught me that, when I read the words He spoke to the prophet Isaiah, "Cease to do evil, learn to do good," He did not mean "do good" but "learn to do good."

"Learn to do good." To your homework, friend, and I, at fifty, to mine. No use stalling around and waiting for life to begin, because it won't, not ever, not even if you live to be fifty. But maybe it won't ever end either.

Don't get excited; I only said "maybe."

PART
ONE

IF YOU
DON'T
LIKE IT
HERE

THE
SUN
NEVER
SETS

It was the dimmest of dawns, but my eyes, at that dim hour, were dimmer yet. "There," said the Captain of the "Kristina Thorden," "is your kingdom," and he pointed off to the starboard at nothing at all. "I don't see it," I said, "do you?" "Yes," said the Captain, who, unlike me, was not wearing glasses, "but I'm accustomed to seeing it. Come on inside and I'll show you a picture of it." He turned on the radar, and the sweep went around, picking up nothing at all except the undulation of the sea around us. Then, as it went by the starboard scope, a little green blip came into view and went out again. "That's your kingdom," said the Captain. "It doesn't look like much from here," I said. "It doesn't look like much from anywhere," said the captain, "except from below. From below it's one hundred fifty miles long. But it's only eighty-three feet in diameter at its base on the surface, and it rises almost sheer. But it's yours — all yours."

Rockall — a Gaelic word meaning "the spiked rocks" — is its name. The Captain had shown it to me on the chart the night before. As he described it, it is almost perfectly conical, except for a six-foot ledge that runs halfway around it, about thirty feet from the summit. The summit is a peak, seventy feet above the surface of the North Atlantic at low tide. Rockall's location is N. Lat. 57° 36″, W. Long. 13° 41″, two hundred miles west of the Outer Hebrides and two hundred fifty miles northwest of Ireland. It had never been claimed by anybody; it was the last no man's land on earth. "I'll take it," I said. "I'll have a look at it tomorrow, but I'll take it sight un-

From the *Progressive*, February, 1956.

17

seen. I'll build on the ledge." "Not so fast," said the Captain. "In the first place, you won't take much of a look at it tomorrow because we're forbidden to come that close. It has no light, no horn, nothing. A Norwegian ship foundered on it — radar and all — and now we keep a good twenty-five miles off it, to the port; more, in heavy weather like this. It's a regular devil. It's on a submarine plateau (which, oddly enough, is part of the American landmass geologically), and the reefs have never been fully sounded. I'll take you as close as prudence and the Company will let me."

The Captain knew all there was to know about Rockall. We Swedes — he was a Swede, like me — are a dour people. Our winters are long and dark, and our summers, in which we work from dawn until ten at night, are short; and our character is consequently affected. We go from long glooms to short ecstasies and, like our seasons, quickly back again. We live ten miles from our nearest neighbor, but misanthropy besets us in the long gloom and we wish we lived a thousand. It is then that we think of islands like Rockall, but, according to the Captain, nobody had thought of it yet. It was mine.

"I'll log your claim," said the Captain, "but you'll have to do more than sit in an overstuffed chair, drinking the Company's *aquavit*, to establish it. You'll have to enforce it against all comers. That, when you stop to think of it, is how the rest of the world was divvied up."

"But," I said, "I have no army and navy."

"Then," said the Captain, "you may encounter difficulties."

"But," I said, "there wouldn't be room for them anyway. You yourself said that there's only room for one man on that ledge."

"One or two," said the Captain, "and two would be enough to present difficulties. Besides, it might be fought for on the sea or in the air."

"But," I said, "you told me nobody wanted it."

"No," said the Captain, "I told you nobody wanted it *up to now*. As soon as you want it, somebody else will want it."

"But," I said, "it's worthless."

"True," said the Captain, "but who will believe it? People will say, 'If it were worthless, Mayer wouldn't want it; we know Mayer. Therefore it must be valuable. Let's go and get it.'"

"Captain," I said, "what do you advise?"

"I advise you," he said, "to land there, if you can, and cement a plaque on the face of the rock and hoist a flag."

"What flag?" I said.

"Your own," he said. "You will have to think one up, maybe with a lion-and-lamb motif, or a heart with an arrow through it, anything you like. You should fire some sort of salute and have a ceremony, with newsreel cameras present, perhaps offshore with long-range cameras, and make a speech. Then you will have to prepare to hold it against, as I say, all comers. This will not be difficult during the winter, since the summit is often awash; if you chain yourself to the ledge, you will be all right, except, of course, you will have to prepare for invasion."

"By whom?"

"By the Russians or the Americans, unless, like the Egyptians and the Yugoslavs and the Indians, you are able to persuade both of them each to offer you aid against the other. But," the Captain went on, "as a Swede you ought to know that that is a dangerous game. Rockall is, if I may say so, in a tactically exposed position. One false step, and you are lost, your rule replaced by a puppet (always to be found among the natives or, if, as on Rockall, there are no natives, to be imported), your people enslaved and exploited, your farms and industries expropriated, and the Voice of America and the Voice of Moscow jamming each other in your ears. Think it over."

"I'm thinking it over," I said. "There are no people or farms or industries on Rockall."

"That doesn't matter," said the Captain. "After it has been liberated, by either the Russians or the Americans, or by both in turn, they will immediately resettle it. The fact that it wasn't settled in the first place will not occur to anybody. It must be protected by reliable, peace-loving people."

"Against whom?"

"Potential aggressors."

"Well," I said, "I'll protect it myself."

"They won't let you," said the Captain. "They won't believe you are strong enough. After all, the Russians have 169 fully armed divisions and the Americans 168.2 and the French .8. What could you do to protect yourself against either one of them? They will insist upon giving you aid. Have another *Schluckchen* of the Company's *aquavit*."

"What about the Spirit of Geneva?" I said. The Swedish for "spirit" — we were speaking Swedish, naturally — is *spoke*. It also means "ghost."

"*Spoke* is right," said the Captain, in Swedish.

The next morning, after I had seen my kingdom on the radar screen, the Captain said he had thought of another difficulty. If I succeeded in establishing my claim to the satisfaction of other sovereigns, they would insist upon recognition and the exchange of legations. Whose would I recognize as the government of China — Mao's or Chiang's? What about Franco Spain? Outer Mongolia? Would I court Afghanistan, and, if I did, wouldn't Russia court me, and then what would the Americans do? Would I — or wouldn't I — exchange diplomatic missions with our glorious democratic ally, the emperor of Abyssinia, in whose democratic land human slavery is still practiced outright?

"No entangling alliances," I said.

"You will practice isolation?" asked the Captain.

"That's why I'm going to Rockall in the first place."

"But," said the Captain, "you will have commercial responsibilities, and these will lead to political responsibilities. The North Atlantic Conference —"

"I will not join NATO," I said.

"I am not talking about NATO," said the Captain. "The North Atlantic Conference is a shipping organization. When you have established your claim, it will compel you to maintain a light, and perhaps a foghorn, to protect shipping."

"Let them protect their own shipping," I said.

"Then they will have to take over part of your ledge — the greater part, I fear — as an international light, and you will find yourself in politics. Not to mention the offshore fishing rights. The Rockall submarine plateau is one of the finest fishing grounds in the world Cod, hake, haddock, and halibut abound (if I may use the term) on the banks. And many a war — the Russo-Japanese of the last century, for example — has begun over fishing rights."

"But," I said, "Rockall rises almost sheer from the water, and if only I can succeed in landing on it, I ought to be able to prevent my enemies from landing. Has anyone ever landed on it?"

"Yes," said the Captain, reaching for his *Lippincott Gazetteer*. "Four landings have been made — the first in 1810 — and many more have been tried unsuccessfully. In 1896 the Royal Irish Academy sent a scientific expedition which failed to land after two desperate attempts. And in 1949 James Fischer, the eminent English ornithologist, sailed to Rockall with H. G. Hasler on the latter's yacht 'Petula' in the hope of landing there and determining whether or not it is actually a breeding place (or only a resting place) for shearwaters and fulmars, but the landing attempt failed. The first landing party, in 1810, by the H.M.S. 'Endymion,' Captain Basil Hall, Commander, succeeded in climbing to the peak of the rock, a feat which has never been repeated. If you can take it, you ought to be able to hold it."

"I can but try," I said, thinking of Captain Basil Hall.

"You will, of course, have to have a considerable store of supplies," said the Captain, "because it may be another ten or twenty years before the weather conditions are appropriate for another landing. And the island is solid rock, a three-mineral granite quartz to which the name of the island has given the name 'rockallite,' so you'd better take a few bushels of dirt with you for gardening."

"I can but try," I said and returned to the bridge to gaze through the lifting mist in the direction (general, to be sure) of my kingdom. The swell of the winter sea was immense; the troughs were canyons. I brushed the ice from my beard and my eyelashes, moistened my salted lips, and wiped them instantly with my sleeve before they froze. Emperor of Rockall.

A few weeks later I meandered through Stockholm — whither I had come with my little brood to discover what a century of peace and prosperity had done for the Swedes — to the British Information Service, which, like the American Information Service, allows an item or two of actual interest to be sandwiched in among the propaganda materials, and I went idly through my favorite newspaper, the *Times* of London, which has the want ads on the front page and the news at the back. In the edition of September 22, 1955 — more than a month before we had sailed from New York on the "Kristina Thorden" — there appeared a column-long article which left only five lines at the bottom of the page for an item about a man who had murdered all six of his wives the evening before. The column-long article was headed, "Annexation of Islet," and began:

The Admiralty announced yesterday the annexation of the islet of Rockall in the North Atlantic, 200 miles west of the Outer Hebrides, has been carried out in the name of the Crown by a landing party from the H.M.S. "Vidal," 2000-ton survey ship under the command of Commander R. H. McConnell, R.N. The landing party of four was lowered by helicopter to the six-foot ledge on the steep face of the hitherto unclaimed rock, where, after a plaque was cemented, the Union Jack hoisted, and a 21-gun salute fired from the "Vidal," Rockall was established as one of the Realms and Territories of Her Majesty.

The Admiralty explained that Rockall had never been claimed by any nation and that the Crown was formally claiming it now to eliminate the possibility of embarrassing counter-claims once the Hebridian guided missile project was under way. The official absorption of Rockall was not unexpected, in view of its location in the approximate firing channel for rockets from the island of South Uist in the Hebrides. Rockall is little known apart from the sonorous reference in the B.B.C. weather reports to "Bailey, Rockall, and Shannon."

In the same edition of the *Times* there appeared a Letter to the Editor from Marshall of the Royal Air Force J. C. Slessor. It began:

All who, like myself, know and love the Hebrides, must be deeply disturbed by the proposal to put a guided missile range on South Uist, not only on account of the threat to sport and bird life on the island, the last breeding place of the greyleg goose, whose feathers winged our arrows at Crecy. . . .

THE VIEW
FROM THE
METROPOL
WINDOW

A year or so ago a couple of fun-loving East Texans tanked up on beer and gas and decided to do a little crow-shooting as they tore through Niggertown. They got their crow through a window — a sixteen-year-old boy. They pleaded guilty, with extenuating circumstances: they were young (in their twenties), full of beer, going fast, and without personal malice toward the boy they killed. The East Texas jury gave them a five-year suspended sentence.

Leaving Russia the other day, by way of Leningrad, I met an East Texan. I asked him how he'd liked Russia, and he said, "All I can say is thank God that I'm on my way back to God's country." The Texan was, I think, simply venting the common persuasion — from which the tumbleweed itself may not be exempt — that it is better to be one place than another. He did not mean that East Texas was a good place to be or a bad one but that he had always been there. You will not be amazed to learn that there are Russians who have always been in Russia and who, after seeing East Texas (or the Bowery, or Shantytown, Pa.), thank Lenin that they are back in Godlessness' country.

I went to Russia because I never knew what to say when people got up in the audience and said, "If you don't like it here, why don't you go to Russia?" Now I can say, "I did go to Russia, and I didn't like it there, either. Besides, I like it here. I like it there, too, as a matter of fact. Some of my best friends are Russians. Others are East Texans."

You bring your Russia to Russia with you, and the Russia you brought with you is the Russia you take home. The Russia I brought

From the *Progressive*, October 1958.

with me was wonderful, and it's the Russia I take home. We are all walking bundles of preconceptions. Mine were formed by Russian literature and by the idea of Christian communism (Acts 4: 32-35), which, disused by the Christians, was being misused, but at least used, by the anti-Christians. These preconceptions rested in turn upon my dissatisfaction with the popular, or Bad Man, theory of history. This dissatisfaction is, I hope, a manifestation of the faith that there is that of God in every man, even in Stalin and me; but it may be nothing but perversity.

Perversity, or cussedness, can come in useful in this life. When *Time* magazine celebrated the death of Stalin with the caption, "Killer of the Masses," and at the same time estimated that several million Russians went weeping past his bier, perversity suggested to me that by "Masses" was meant "Luces," Perversity likewise warned me, while all the *Times* in America were celebrating Khrushchev's obliteration of Stalin, that I should not be surprised to go to Russia three years later and find the pictures of Lenin and Stalin, and of them alone, still hanging in every post office and their busts still standing in the lobbies of public buildings, and Stalin still holding down his half of the box in the Holy of Holies outside the Kremlin wall. Never having been a left or right deviationist, never having bought the Worker's Paradise abroad or the White Man's Paradise at home, the perverse fellow can afford to blow himself to a chuckle at the sight of the purged Molotov toddling nattily around Moscow, like the purged Brownell around Washington, and I should have been no more surprised or unhappy to see Malenkov in for a quick visit, and a couple of shows, from the Urals than to see Herbert Hoover in from the Coast Range to get his high collar vulcanized on Fifth Avenue. While perversity, unlike flattery, will get you nowhere, it does keep you from believing what you read, or write, in the newspapers.

I knew I should find it easy to love the Russians. I already loved those I knew; there was something nutty, or strictly American, about them. They were no more open-minded than the Americans and just as open-hearted. The writer Sergei Michalkow, when I first met him in the Tyrolean Alps in the dead of winter, was wearing an Argentine polo cap; and this summer he and I had a bucket of tea together in Moscow, and he suggested — in German, the only language we have in common — that we should go to China together and write a book about it. Who but an American or a Russian clowns around like that?

I found it just a wee bit hard after the war (as before) to love the Germans. But after I'd lived in Germany (with my wife and little ones) and I wanted to live in Russia (again with my wife and little ones), I asked Martin Niemöller whether he thought we could bear it, and he said, "Anybody who can live with the Germans can live a lot easier with the Russians. As long as you don't expect them to be good Americans — they're Russians, you know — you'll love them."

They *are* Russians, you know. We spent some time with two groups of American students on their way home, one from Cornell and vicinity and the other from Whittier College in California, and when we asked them what they liked best about Russia, they all hollered in ecstatic chorus, "The people," and when we asked them if they really liked Communists, they said that, although the people they liked were Communists, that was not what they meant. The students, like all students, could teach their elders something. A few years ago, when I'd sat three days in the Soviet Embassy in Berlin without seeing anybody and I complained (to Pastor Grüber of Berlin) that the Communists are slow, he said, "That's the *whole* trouble with the Americans. They think they're dealing with Communists, and they forget that they're dealing with Russians." So I was prepared to go overboard, in Russia, and overboard I went. I didn't see Russia or the Russians in a month there, but neither did John Gunther; the view from the window of the Metropol Hotel is uninstructive, and so are the canned interviews with the officials. But the streets and the buses and the shops and the cheap cafeterias are instructive, and I came to Russia to be instructed.

My instruction began my first morning in Moscow. Our tourist group was scheduled to go with our girl guide to meet a stuffed shirt. I wanted, instead, to go to the Finnish Embassy, and I asked the guide if I might go alone. "Of course," she said. "Just take a taxi," "I wanna walk," I said. "You'll get lost,' she said. "I wanna get lost," I said. "Then walk," she said, and she showed me Kropotkin Street on my map. "That's not where the Finnish Embassy is, she said. "It's in *Little* Kropotkin Street, which is not on the map. But it must be somewhere around Kropotkin Street. And if you get hopelessly lost, just go into any bookshop. They won't be able to tell you where it is, but they'll give you some books in English to read, and when it's lunchtime just show people this" — she gave me the name of the hotel on a slip of paper — "and go where they point."

I did get lost, and I got back through a maze of railroad tracks and construction projects, and I kept getting lost for a month. You don't have to know the language to find your way home; all you have to know is that you don't know your way home, and two hundred million Russians will show you. When our group left Moscow for the south, my wife and I wanted to stay on in Moscow, and we asked the guide if we might. She explained that the whole group had one guide, so we'd have to stay on alone and find our own way around. We did, and our instruction proceeded, and myth after myth fell apart, beginning with the myth that spies are fastened on tourists as guides.

Without the language, nobody ever yet got to know anything about a country and its people, and Russian is a difficult language because it's so rich and an impossible language (for newcomers) because of its alphabet. It's *you* who insist on the guide — or interpreter, or spy. Without her you die, because without her you can not read the word for bread (much less know that it means bread or ask for bread). That's why the question, "Do they let you travel around Russia alone?" is a laugh. Let you? — They couldn't *make* you. Two of the American Quakers who went to Russia in 1954 went all the way across Russia alone, to Tashkent; but one of them, Bill Edgerton, is a professor of Russian at Columbia. It's like this: When you see the word "Paris" on a French railroad station, you've got at least a Free Chinaman's chance of knowing where you are, but you'll never get off the train at Leningrad alone (or the Moscow subway at Leningrad Station) because the sign, which says "Leningrad" to a Russian, says gibberish to you and, without your guide, you panic.

The man in the street — the man you wanted to meet and pretend to have met — speaks his native language, in Russia as everywhere else. He is the Russian and the only Russian. The natives you really meet (like the few multilingual native Americans you meet at home) are the cosmopolites. You never meet the man in the street, but if you stay in the street, and out of the ministries and the universities and the hotels and the restaurants, you meet his eyes, and his meet yours. You show him on your map where you want to go, and he insists (the spy!) on going with you to make sure you get there, and when you get where you're going and you make the mistake of offering him a cigarette, he declines, or insists on your taking a more expensive Russian cigarette from him in exchange. The Russian dialectical materialist is the first non-materialistic man, as a whole people, you have ever met. He expects, and will accept, none of the customary contemptuous gratuities that, at home or abroad, you toss to the servile. The Swiss — says the German — lives off the world's tips; not the Russian. There's no "Service 15%," no "Kurtaxe," no "Imposta di soggiorno," no headwaiter's petty panhandling. A day's wages — low — for a day's work. The Russian who does you a personal service and smiles, smiles because he wants to. Does it take an inhuman dictatorship to restore personal sentiment to personal relations? Heaven forfend.

You have been instructed, the first morning you were out on the street. You have learned that this Russian "slave" is a man of more dignity than you are accustomed to meeting abroad or at home. You reserve your astonishment, mistrusting your morning's experience. At the end of a month on the streets, your experience unvaried, your astonishment is complete. Your experience has extended to the kids you met at the Kremlin, who offer you Russian lapel pins of all sorts; what they want in exchange is an American (that is, a foreign) coin or stamp (of any denomination), and when your supply is exhausted and you offer a kid Russian money for a pin you want, he refuses it; and if you have some way of letting him know how badly you want that pin, your chances of his giving it to you are good.

This is the Russian, who, your first morning out on the street, seemed to you to carry himself in a manner that reminded you of someone you had seen before — but of whom? Your third morning out you know: the Russian carries himself exactly like the jaunty, self-confident, and unself-conscious Yank, the "outgoing man" of the sociologist's jargon, not the salesman, the panhandler, or the pusher, but the man who knows who and what and where he is, where he is going and why, and what he's about, and is ready to make friends for no other reason than friendship's. Your eyes — and the Russian's — did not deceive you. He doesn't know he's a slave, and it is his view of his situation, not yours, that's decisive. You have not persuaded him that he is oppressed; maybe because he has always been oppressed; but in that case, where is the hang-dog grin, the bowing and scraping, the "Yas-*suh*, boss" of the long oppressed who always mean "No-*suh*" and always say "Yas-*suh*"? This slave (as you call him) acts as if he owns the place. Maybe he does.

There used to be a sign in the corner saloon that said, "If You Spit on the Floor at Home, Spit on the Floor Here." There are no "No Smoking" signs in the rococo subway stations of Moscow and Leningrad, and nobody smokes. Nobody. In our cities at home are "Help Keep Our City Clean" signs on the trash receptacles on the sidewalks, and nobody helps keep our city clean; in cities in Russia there are no signs on the receptacles, and everybody helps keep the city spotlessly clean. Can it be because they really, in their socialized innocence, lap up that "*Our* City" stuff? Or are they afraid? And of what, or whom? Nowhere outside America have I seen so few policemen or so many citizens arguing with the policeman who bawls them out for parking wrong. Nowhere outside America have I seen jaywalking so universally practiced. Nowhere, inside or outside America, have I felt so secure from pickpocketing as in a Russian crowd, so secure from thuggery as in a Russian alley, so secure from holdup in a deserted midnight street as in a Russian city, so secure from a Russian drunk. I don't need to wonder if the Soviet crime statistics are phony; I've been there, and I've been in Chicago.

Where there are no juveniles, there is no juvenile delinquency. Where are the juveniles? Our friend Lois Hogle, who wanted to see Russian children, decided, her first day in Moscow, that there are no Russian children. They're not in the streets after school; they're in sports clubs. And in the summer they're not in the city at all; they're in the Young Pioneer camps in the country. I've been there, too, and I know that their parents send them voluntarily — some stay home to work or study — at irresistibly low fees. And are the little ones blotting up Communist propaganda at camps? You bet they are. We wouldn't do that in America, but we might give them a few wholesome talks on Americanism.

Are these people, who seem, on the street, so unafraid, in fact afraid, and of what, or whom? I didn't see them being afraid of the boss — though I'm sure they are — because I didn't see them being bossed. You ask a clerk at a crowded counter in one of the ubiquitous state resale or secondhand stores if she has an old chess set. (You've learned to say *shahkhmahti* by this time.) She hasn't, as it happens, but now wait — where did she or somebody else see one recently? She asks the other clerks, who abandon their customers to consider the matter. All this is voluble, so voluble that the abandoned customers overhear. They cluster around, and everybody, clerks and customers, gets into the consideration. Where did somebody see an old chess set recently? On and on it goes. The boss is not to be seen, to hustle the clerks back to work, nor, quite obviously, is there among the happily abandoned customers a government spy who is going to report the laxity. Laxity! the bellhops in the hotel, between hops, untie their neckties and drop off to immediate sleep in the biggest chair in the lobby. Where is the manager to fire them or at least whip them? The waiters in the restaurant are engaged in the most animated possible jabber, while the customers strangely uncomplaining, are neglected and themselves engage in animated jabber. There's the head waiter; why doesn't he jack up the service or send the offenders to Siberia? The young lady elevator operator is reading her book — usually a foreign language textbook — while the customers stand woodenly (wooden Americans among them) in the car, and there's the chief operator, seeing it all and doing nothing about it. Laxity! What they need is an iron hand. Where is it?

What are they afraid of, or whom? We scurried around for a month looking for the terror. I'm still sure it is there, but where? There must be plenty of terror; think of the slave labor camps. Of course we don't believe them when they say there are no slave labor camps, and (would you believe it?) they don't believe us when we say there are no chain gangs. People who are terrified do not tell strangers that they are terrified, so maybe the Russians are terrified. In all our scurrying, we found two who showed signs of terror. One, obviously a student, followed us around a corner and accosted us and kept pulling us around still another corner whenever somebody approached. He said, in English, without our asking him, that we hadn't seen the real Russia. We said we'd like to, and how about it, and just then somebody approached and he beat it. We couldn't find him again. I may be dead wrong, but on the basis of our eccentric contact I should not be sure that he, any more than we, knew where the real Russia was. The other was a lady who told us, first, that her whole family had been killed in the war, except for her oldest beloved brother, who had gone to New York forty years ago. Her brother owned a chain of stores in America but never wrote her or sent her anything, presumably because he was afraid to. (The lady spoke to us in a European language.) She had to support herself, she said, on four hundred rubles a month, a fourth of which went for rent. She seemed to be terrified. I asked her (we were alone) why she didn't write to her wealthy brother, and she looked around furtively and shook her head and said she couldn't. So I said, "How about writing him and giving me the letter to take with me?" She said she would, but she didn't, although I saw her several times, and then I asked her for the letter, and she said she was afraid to write. So I said she should give me her brother's full name, and I would find him in New York, and she said she would, but she didn't, although I saw her several times after that. And then I told her we were leaving and to give me her brother's name, and she said she would, and then she said again that she had to support herself on four hundred rumbles a month, a fourth of which went for rent, and she did not know what she would do if it were not for the kindness of Americans she met. But she did not give me her brother's name, though I saw her again, and then I met a Frenchman who said, "Oh — that one. If you've got anything to sell on the black market, she'll handle it. She told me about her rich brother in Paris."

They may still be terrified, all of them, without looking, walking, talking, or acting terrified. But of whom, and of what? The government? The dictatorship? But what if they believe — and don't merely say — that their government is representative and that they obey their government's laws with no more or less terror than we do ours? What then? The Russians I talked to, all of them, seemed to believe that when they said it. And when I said "Beria," they said "Rosenberg," and when I said "Hungary," they said "Lebanon" and even "Guatemala," and so it went. And when they said "Free elections" and I said, "But all the candidates have to be Communists," they said, "And in America all the candidates have to be anti-Communists."

They seem to have no real sense of political liberty, no awareness at all of the right of fundamental dissent as the very first principle of social organization. Within the system they wrangle furiously: the last parliamentary debate over the decentralization of the tractor collectives, for instance. *But always within the system.* And in the area of foreign affairs — which for forty years has had the character of national emergency — the uniformity of press and people is very depressing. Here, above all, one concludes tentatively but forcibly that these intelligent, if long isolated, people are convinced that neither they themselves nor their elected representatives have competence and that the executive elite always rules right. The contrast with, say, France or Italy, where every third man is a revolutionary, rejecting the system itself, is more acute. There, one says instantly, is liberty, and the only liberty the Soviet system does not allow; the liberty to reject the system. But is the comparison with the United States — especially in the light of our pretension to the love of liberty — as unflattering to the Russians? We Americans are at liberty, if we are rich, to buy this car or that, to move to this town or that one (if we are either rich or jobless), to send out children to private or public schools. But I do not see that we are much better off than the Russians in terms of the liberty to attack the system itself and campaign for its overthrow, the exception being except for a minuscule and detested section of our press (though that is certainly something).

I argued with the Russians I met — not, remember, with the man in the street. They gave me a very hard time. But the hardest time of all was given me by young Mr. Vassiliev, who interviewed me for the Moscow *Literary Gazette*. I spoke my piece freely and fully, and Mr. Vassiliev said nothing. But the next day he telephoned to ask when I was leaving Moscow, because, he said, he would arrange to have my fee paid if I were leaving right away. In a couple of days, I said; and the next day he arrived with five hundred rubles. Now five hundred rubles buys an old *shahkhmahti*, and five hundred rubles, at the blocked rate for tourists, cost $50, which I did not have to spend. But the five hundred rubles, since I could not take them out of Russia in cash, or get dollars for them, I could spend on an old *shahkhmahti* in as good conscience as anyone can ever have buying an old *shahkhmahti*. Mr. Vassiliev laid the rubles on the line and asked me to sign the *Gazette's* receipt for the fee. I told him that in America interviews were never paid for; he told me that in Russia they always are. Then I told him I had a problem.

"My problem," I said, "is this. What I said here, I would say in America, with, however, more difficulty in getting it published. But what I have said here will not be published until next week, when I am gone, and you have already told me that you may have to cut the interview, because of length. But in cutting it somebody — not you — may cut what I said about Hungary, for instance. Now I know you have promised me that that would not happen, but interviewers for the *Chicago Tribune* have made me the same promise and their superiors broke it for them."

"Then," said Mr. Vassiliev, speaking for the first time, "you do not have an exactly free press in America."

"Not an exactly," I said, "but let me go on. If — just *if*, mind you — that happened here, and I was accused in America of having given you an interview in which I condemned American practices without condemning Russian practices, I could defend myself by saying that the *Literary Gazette* had committed the *Chicago Tribune*'s habitual crime of contextomy against me. But if I am accused, in addition, of having taken Moscow gold for the interview, I would be in terrible trouble," and I sighed.

"With whom?" said Mr. Vassiliev.

"With Senator McCarthy," I said.

"But I thought that Senator McCarthy was dead," said Mr. Vassiliev.

"He is," I said, "but his soul goes marching on."

"Mr. Mayer," said Mr. Vassiliev, after a pause, "you said in your interview that you were an American liberal."

"I am," I said.

"Then," said Mr. Vassiliev, with a question mark, "the liberals in America are also afraid of Senator McCarthy?"

Those were Mr. Vassiliev's words, and those were mine, and you ought to see my old *shahkhmahti*.

The Russians I met simply can not, I think, bring themselves to think very much about personal political liberty — and, if not the cosmopolitan Russians, certainly not the uncosmopolitan. I don't suppose that they ever have, on the whole, except for liberty from shoelessness. I don't know how much we Americans think about liberty these days. We talk about it, I know; and the Russians talk about peace, and I don't know how much they think about peace. I know that the Russians grumble; some of them grumbled to me. They grumble about bureaucracy, and about shortages, and about prices, wages, hours, and working conditions. And the farmers — just imagine! — grumble. But I couldn't get them to grumble about liberty, the few I met, not even to defend its restriction (as they might have, had they wanted a rationale) on the ground of national emergency, which President Eisenhower so recently argued in defense of the restriction of the right of Americans to travel. Maybe there is fundamental dissent among as many as 1 per cent of the Russians, or of the Americans; but I doubt it. Maybe, praising communism so effusively as in itself to make a sophisticated American suspicious of their earnestness, or at least of their sophistication, they dispraise it in their hearts. Maybe the counterrevolution, for which we waited from 1918 to 1935 and for which we thereafter prayed in some of our churches, is brewing in secret. I doubt it. I saw no signs — not even secondary signs. Forty years is a long time. There are not many old Bolsheviks left, and still fewer old anti-Bolsheviks.

Naziism was a hideous affair, no more in practice than in theory, and its theory, the theory of *natural* slavery, is much more popular in the United States than it is in the Soviet Union. Decent Germans should have resisted Naziism on its theory alone. But, on the whole, they didn't, any more than decent Americans, on the whole, do. Naziism promised and delivered bread and work, and when, after the war, I pointed out to a very simple-minded ex-Nazi that he had had no free speech, he said, "Who wants to make a speech?"

Who wants to make a speech? Not many Germans. Not many Americans. And not, I suppose, many Russians. If they find the theory of communism much less hideous than the Germans should have found the theory of Naziism, and if, in practice, they have bread and work, I can imagine that like other people, they do not see why they should assassinate their rulers, who walk much more freely and unguarded among them than ours walk among us.

The Russians I looked at seem to be cheerful, the most cheerful people I have ever seen, and not, like the Germans under Hitler, euphoric. And while a couple of thousand is not a couple of hundred millon, I cannot believe, would I want to, that a whole people in the town, in the country, can look like what they are not; no government that ever was or will be can make people smile. When we met a troupe of fifth-graders with their teacher, and they clustered around us and danced and jabbered and said, "I — talk — the — English," A. J. Muste said what the rest of us thought: "These are beautiful, natural, happy children. To associate *this* spectacle with repression, inhibition, fear, and dictatorship is impossible."

Anomaly? Plenty of anomaly; profound anomaly, as, I dare say, a foreigner finds in America, the land of the free, with unfreedom practiced and even principled. The colossal anomaly is everywhere and instantly apparent: On the one hand, the whole behavior of these people conspires to convince the visitor that they are individualistic by temperament to the point of anarchy, self-standing, self-assured, self-minded; and, on the other, they respond, adequately and contentedly, though with never a goose step, to a collectivism incongruous to that temperament. The lady bus conductor on Line 63 in Moscow takes a snooze in the back seat at the end of the line, awakening only when the bus jerks into motion; her indifference to authority (if there is any authority), to the bus line inspector who might come along, is unmistakable; but she will stand, or sit, for hours on end in a government anteroom, a vaccination queue, a union meeting, or a market, moving, writing, speaking, and, I suppose, voting exactly as she is told to (or more likely, exactly as she is expected to, without having to be told).

Maybe they're unafraid, independent, and happy; maybe not. How would I know? Or anyone else leaning out of the Metropol window? I've never been a Russian. I'm never going to be one. How, then, would I, or anyone else in the Metropol (or the Waldorf-Astoria) know what it is to be a Russian in Russia, or whether or why another people are happy or unhappy, or what they believe in, or what they oppose? And the Russian expatriates in America, our Russian experts, who tell us what to think about Russia, do they know what it is to be a Russian in Russia, these ex-princes of blood or caste or money or Trotskyism? Does an American Communist know what it is to be an American, or only what it is to be an alienated American? Does Lucius Beebe know what it is to be an American, or only what it is to be a rich American?

St. Thomas said something about God — he said several things about God — that comes back to me. He said that getting to know God is like getting to know a country — you have got to live there. Maps and guide books and treatises, sermons, interviews, tours, and translations are not enough. You have got to live there. And St. Francis said something about poverty — he said several things about poverty — that comes to me. He said that to know poverty one must be poor. The Russians were poor and terrified of poverty. Maybe no other terror, now that they're no longer poor, terrifies them. I don't know. I can't compare. I am one of the rich. And you're another.

"You know what I always say," I said. "I always say, '*Principiis obsta.*'"

"That could become monotonous," said Ulrich, "but I think I know what you mean. I think you mean, 'Resist the beginnings.'"

"Exactly," I said.

"That is a very good saying of yours," said Ulrich, "and you say it very nicely, for an American. But it has difficulties."

"*Par exemple?*"

"For example," said Ulrich, "it does not tell you what the beginnings are."

"But any fool knows the beginnings when he sees them," I said. "You fools certainly knew them when you saw them in Germany."

"And when was this?" said Ulrich.

"Why, when Hitler was coming to power."

"But that was many years, maybe many decades, maybe many centuries," said Ulrich, "and there were many beginnings. But to know the beginning for certain, I think it is necessary first to know the end."

"Ah," said I, "*Finem respice.*"

"You always say that, too?" said Ulrich; "you are perhaps an old Roman?"

"A middle-aged Roman."

"Well, those are very good middle-aged Roman sayings, but now we can see that though the Romans said 'Resist the beginnings' and 'Envisage the end,' they were ruined because it is impossible, in worldly matters, to know the end in time to recognize the beginnings and resist them."

"Then it's always impossible to recognize the beginnings?"

From the *Progressive*, January, 1950.

"Not, perhaps, impossible, but very difficult for most of us, because most of us think naturally only of the moment."

"That," I said, "is what de Tocqueville always said. He always said —"

"That the mind of man runs to the immediate."

"But that's in English," I said.

"So much the better," said Ulrich.

"*Tant mieux*," I said.

"I think now," said Ulrich, "that I can recognize one very important beginning in the ruin of Germany. At the time I did not recognize it, at least not so sharply."

"And what was that?"

"That," said Ulrich, "was in 1937. I had a young student at the university. His father was dead, and the family had had a very hard time. And like so many poor people — and like so many rich people — they had become Nazis. But they were not the type to have murder and pogroms. They were simple and they wanted to believe in something, and of these people there were many, in the beginning, who became Nazis. In the end, most (I cannot say all) knew better.

"I made a point of talking with this student because I, like you, never tired of wanting to learn how otherwise decent people could become Nazis. And I learned, in these talks, something that I think now was one of the beginnings of the ruin of Germany. I learned that these poor people ate crusts of bread in order to save money to give to the poor. And this was one of the beginnings. Now you will say, 'What's that?' "

"*Quid hoc sibi vult?*"

"Yes, and now let me explain. These people ate crusts to give to the poor, or, rather, they shared what they had with the other poor. And they had always done this. But before the Nazis, they had done this directly and in person, and now they did it through the Nazis' relief organization, the *Nationalsocialistische Volkswohlfahrt*. When I asked which poor persons received this bread, my student said he didn't know. The government agency distributed it. He was proud to say it was given and received anonymously."

"But," said I, "I would say that this was one of the few decent things the Nazis did, assuming they didn't steal it for themselves or feed only Nazis. *Que passa?*"

"*Momentito*, I mean wait a minute," said Ulrich. "Let us assume the people were fed without distinction and also that the food wasn't stolen. I will say this is one of the beginnings of the ruin of Germany. You forget that my student was proud that the collection and distribution were anonymous."

"But this," said I, "is Christian charity in its very essence. I have read a Good Book lately, and in this book the scribes and the Pharisees are condemned because 'all their works they do to be seen of men.' I say unto you that anonymous giving and getting is true charity and not putting the bread in the poor man's mouth so that he will say, 'Thank you, good sir, sweet sir.'"

"I, too, have a copy of this Book," said Ulrich, "and the scribes and Pharisees are indeed condemned. But I want you to consider these same scribes and Pharisees as anonymous givers: 'Woe unto you, scribes and Pharisees, hypocrites! for ye pay the tithe of mint and anise and cummin, and have omitted the weightier matters of the law, judgment, mercy, and faith: these ought ye to have done, and not to leave the other undone.'"

"Consider," I said, "on the other hand, the widow who cast two mites into the treasury. The distribution from the treasury was anonymous, but the widow was justified, yea, exalted: she 'hath cast in more that they all.'"

"To be sure," said Ulrich, "but she was exalted, not because the distribution was anonymous, but because of her sacrifice. And so, too, I imagine, was my student, the Nazi. But this is not my point."

"Your point, I think," I said, "is that you are against public welfare, the only decent thing the Nazis ever did."

"My point," said Ulrich, "is that 'these ought ye to have done, and not to leave the other undone.' May I continue?"

"*Continuez*," I said.

"*Setzen Sie sich*," said Ulrich, pulling up a chair for me, "and forgive my English."

"*Omni peccavimus*," I said.

"Have you some time while I try to say what I mean?"

"*Ohne Hast, aber ohne Rast.* Shoot, Luke," I said.

"Perhaps you will let me begin by referring once more to the scribes and Pharisees, of whom Jesus said, 'Ye fools and blind: for whether is greater, the gift, or the altar that sanctifieth the gift?' "

"They ask for bread," I said witheringly, "and you give them an altar."

"And you give them bread?"

"I give them bread," I said.

"Do they live by this?"

I saw the trap. "Not by this alone," I said.

"*Sei'sd'rum,*" said Ulrich. "So the question is not which is needed and which is not needed. The question is which is *greater.* The question is not whether the tithe is paid, or whether the Omaha streetcar token placed in the collection plate in Pittsburgh on Sunday is a bona fide streetcar token. The question is, even when all this is done, Is there something *weightier* that must also be done?"

"Such as?"

"Such as *caritas.*"

"Hey, wait a minute," I said.

"You mean *momentito*?"

"I mean," I said, "that you say that when you have fed the poor you haven't done charity."

"I did not say charity," said Ulrich. "I said *caritas.*"

"Say it in English, like a man."

"If I say it in English," said Ulrich, "you will say I am not a man. By *caritas*, I mean love."

"Would you say there is no relationship between love and giving bread to the poor?"

"No *necessary* relationship," said Ulrich. "I think the *Volkswohlfahrt* was primarily intended to strengthen the Nazi regime. I would not call the Nazi regime a regime of love."

"But the people who gave bread?"

"They didn't give it to the poor. They gave it to the *Volkswohlfahrt*, and the *Volkswohlfahrt* gave it to the poor."

"Why did they give?"

"Why do you give to the Community Fund?"

"Why, why — for lots of reasons."

"That's why the Germans gave to the *Volkswohlfahrt*," said Ulrich. "Some gave for love, and some for other reasons. The *Volkswohlfahrt* permitted them to give for other reasons."

"For instance?"

"Fear, laziness, conformity, bad conscience — for lots of reasons. Do your great corporations give to the Community Fund?"

"They are the greatest givers," I said.

"I know nothing about America," Ulrich said, "but in Nazi Germany the great corporations were the greatest givers to the *Volkswohlfahrt*. And corporations are what we call *seelenlos*, or sometimes *leblos*. I think in English this means soulless, or lifeless. Lifeless things do not love."

"True, true," I said, "But what of the need for bread? The need is great, and the poor must be fed."

"You will think me heartless if I say, Why?" said Ulrich. "The need for bread was great in Germany and the Nazis fed the poor, but they fed them without love, and in taking over the feeding they relieved the Germans of the necessity to love one another."

"But hate comes from the want of bread."

"And love," said Ulrich, "does not come from bread. You will pardon me if I say that you sound like those simple people who thought Hitler was a magician. You seem to say that love comes from bread. But the magician made hate come from it."

"I don't understand about love," I said.

"Oh, but you do," said Ulrich. "You are full of love, but you are like us Germans. You do not resist the beginnings because you don't recognize them, and you don't recognize them because you don't know the end."

"Do you mean I should resist the welfare state?"

"I don't know what is meant by the welfare state," said Ulrich. "I don't know about America. These words seem to be a political slogan just now. I think I would say, not that you should resist the welfare state, but that you should build the welfare community."

"Oh, so you don't trust the state?"

"I come from a country where, if I may say so, we had a very bad experience with it."

"But you think the needs of society can be met by love?"

"I would rather you spoke of the needs of man. I think the needs of man can be met by love and that they cannot be met without love. There must, of course, be organized social work, but consider the professional social worker."

"Oh, so you're against the professional social worker?"

"I am for the professional social worker. I am against your hiring the professional social worker to do your loving for you. When you give to the social work agency, you are relieved of the responsibility of love. But this is not the worst, I think."

"And what is the worst?" I was getting annoyed.

"The worst is that you deprive yourself of suffering. No suffering, no love."

"William Penn," I said, "said, 'No cross, no crown.'"

"That is a very nice saying," said Ulrich, "but I thought you would say, '*Ad astra per aspera.*'"

"I always say that," I said. "It means, 'You can't get to heaven on roller skates.'"

"I think that must be true," said Ulrich. "Heaven is steep."

"I work for my money," I said, "and then I give it to the Community Fund. What more do you want?"

"The question is, What more do *you* want? If you want to love, you must suffer. Work is not suffering, and neither is giving money."

I was getting annoyed again. "Do you know what you are?" I said.

"Not a Nazi, I hope."

"Second cousin to one," I said. "You're an apologist for capitalism."

"I hope not," said Ulrich. "Capitalism is a way of making and distributing money. Money cannot love. What difference does it make if you transfer your responsibilities for loving to your public state or your private bank? A capitalist state without love is evil, and a socialist state without love is evil. The differences are interesting but small."

"Why should I suffer?" I said. "Isn't there enough suffering in the world?"

"It seems not," said Ulrich. "I think there is enough pain in the world, but too much pain comes from too little suffering."

"See here," I said, "I was eating a steak at a window table in a restaurant in the winter of 1931–32, and I saw a man standing outside looking in. He had on a ragged topcoat, and he was holding a little child in his arms. I couldn't give him half my steak, but I could vote for Roosevelt, and the WPA got them off the street."

"So you didn't see them in the street any more?"

"No. Would it be better for me if I did? Would I suffer more?"

"If you suffered at all."

"Would I suffer at all?"

"If you loved."

There was silence.

"Did you suffer when you saw that man?" said Ulrich.

"No," I said, "I didn't suffer because I did something about it. I voted for an administration that loved that man enough to give him a job. And if I hadn't loved that man, I wouldn't have voted for that administration. So I can say honestly that I gave him the job and I paid his wages in taxes. That is the scientific way, I don't care what you say."

There was silence. I was still annoyed.

"Why," I said, "should I suffer?"

"It says in this Book," said Ulrich, "that we are perfected through suffering. And it says also that though we bestow all our goods to feed the poor, and though we give our bodies to be burned, and have not *caritas*, it profiteth us nothing. So I think we must suffer to be perfect."

There was silence.

"Do you think," I said, "that I suffered enough the night I saw the man in the restaurant window?"

"Only God has suffered enough."

"Do you think I suffered at all?"

"I think you are suffering now," said Ulrich. "I think you still see the man at the restaurant window, and this is Christmas Eve seventeen years later. I think that with God's help you might become that man. But maybe the night you first saw him you were only pained."

I began to feel, not perfect, but better.

"Why, all you mean," I said, "is that before we can change the world we must change our own hearts."

"That's all I mean."

"That's what I always say," I said.

"I'm sure you do," said Ulrich.

We were walking in the woods outside a Polish town, just the two of us. I was asking the usual questions. But my companion, a Protestant pastor, was giving unusual answers:

No, no, it is not the dictatorship; that we always had. It's the mistrust. We do not tell the truth; the whole truth, that is. Why not? Well . . . One of our Church leaders was meeting with some of us old colleagues and we were chiding him for criticizing the West but not the East, and he said, "Would you like me to give up my post?" We all said oh, no, we needed him precisely where he was because the authorities trust him. "And they are right to trust me," he said, "and you, my friends, must let me decide how to speak — *if you want me where I am*. It is always a hard decision, and you must pray for me."

The most persistent impression that an American brings back from a visit to the churches of Eastern Europe is that of Christians who live in a world much more like Christ's than his own; a world where a Christian has to make hard decisions and knows it. "It is an interesting time to be alive," my Polish friend went on, "a very dangerous time, but very interesting." I remember his words and ask myself: How would an American Christian live dangerously in our time? He would have to go out of his way and "look for trouble." The Christian under communism doesn't have to go out of his way. Not that he's any holier than thou. He doesn't make his hard decisions any more eagerly — or any better — than he would here. But when he makes them badly, he has a harder time not knowing it. There are timeservers, of course; men who entered the church without vocation and study the bishop instead of the Bible. And trimmers, there as everywhere. There was an old the-

From *Harper's Magazine*, August, 1960.

ologian who insisted on telling me how free the press is and a young church official who party-lined me on the Summit Conference; but on both occasions their colleagues sat through their monologues in granite silence.

My opportunity to do something more than stare at the Communist world arose a year or so ago from a series of intimate little meetings of Eastern and Western ecclesiastics in Europe. My credentials were scandalous — a non-Christian fellow traveler of the Quakers — but nobody bothered to throw me out of the meetings. Whatever Brother Mayer wasn't, he was a real, live American who understood a little German; a curio in such circles. When I was invited to bring my wife and children to one Communist country after another, to live with the brethren and preach among them, I protested the inadequacy of my status, but in vain. So we went.

What we saw were Christians living lives unimaginable to the American churchgoer who lives (or thinks he lives) as he pleases and bestirs himself about the flooring for the Sunday school gym. Their world — which never was like ours — began breaking up in 1914. Now they live in a new one. This new world requires the Christian church to collaborate in building an order professing both atheist materialism *and* the reform of the social conditions that the church supported for centuries.

The Marxists have brought home to the Christians of Eastern Europe the reality of their condition. They are beginning to find out what they can — and must — do in the world and what they can't do. In Czechoslovakia I talked to a man who had just been discharged as the principal of a school for handicapped children; in the fall he would have to go back to the classroom as an ordinary teacher again. Had this happened, I asked, solely because of his religion? "Oh, yes," he said. "Our school authorities thought an outspoken Christian should not have the general direction of a school in a Marxist state. I said I agreed. And I do agree. I feel that the authorities are acknowledging my own view that Marxist communism and the social gospel are the two real competitors in the world. Would a Communist be allowed to be a school principal in a Christian country like America?" In an East German town there was an old pastor whose daughter, just because she was his, was not admitted to the field of university study for which she had prepared herself. He said: "We are fewer now, but at last we know who we are and what we are here for. We begin to see what is meant by *the living Christ*. Now we are invincible."

"Food grows dearer. Do our brothers grow dearer too? No — they freeze and starve beneath our heaven-bent feet." Thus Thomas Cranmer, "my good and gracious Canterbury," four hundred years ago. Four hundred years later a priest in Spain watched a shrine burning and said, "The Church forgot the poor — and now the poor have forgotten the Church." In the intervening centuries the Reformation of the church was accomplished, and in the process, some millions of our brothers, already freezing and starving, were burned and butchered in Christ's name. Now comes Marxist communism, burning and butchering just like Protestantism and Catholicism. *But not in Christ's name.* This much is new. And our freezing and starving brothers? The American State Department (a conservative authority on this point) says in its bulletins that the living standard in the Communist countries "is rising slowly," "has risen slightly," "has improved a little."

Could this — this professing Antichrist — be the profane reformation, bent so terribly upon accomplishing the alteration of society as the sacred reformation accomplished the alteration of the church? The Old Testament prophets abound in the possibility: *"Behold the Assyrian, the rod of mine anger, and the staff in his hand is mine indignation."* Could it be? There are Christians in Europe who are asking themselves if perhaps it is, and if it wasn't necessary that it come; and if it isn't here to stay and to spread wherever our brothers freeze and starve; and if the world will ever be (as perhaps it shouldn't be) the same again.

East of Pest, in Hungary, there still stands a large area of wretched barracks where the capital's unemployed lived, bred, and died. Directly across the street a large area of handsome apartment blocks is occupied by the people who once lived across the street, and they are all employed. "Between 1918 and 1938," the Communist Mayor of Banská Bystrica, in Slovakia, told us, "one hundred forty thousand out of three millon Slovaks emigrated to look for work. Today we need twenty thousand more workers in this one county alone than we can find." What did the church say to the unemployed in Banská or Pest between 1918 and 1938?

"Our brothers freeze and starve." "I am not a Communist, I am a Christian," says Josef Hromadka. "But I know that it is we, we Christians alone, who are responsible for communism. We had a burden to discharge in the world, and Jesus Christ left us no room to wonder what it was. We failed. We 'said, and did not.' And now another power has arisen to take up this burden. Remember that the Communists once were Christians. If they do not believe in a just God, whose fault is it?" Hromadka is talking not in Princeton, where he once served so comfortably, but in Prague, where he serves, perhaps less comfortably, as dean of the Comenius Theological Faculty. All over Eastern Europe one hears the same agonized words from churchmen: "The atheists had to come to teach us the social gospel."

Now humility becomes a Christian — does him proud, you might say. But humiliation is something else. The humiliated church in Eastern Europe is alien alike to the Christianity of Success and the Communism of Success. Christianity under communism is the Christianity of Failure. It is un-American. "We reject the Crucifixion," Hitler's high priest once said. So, of course, do the Communists. The Christians of Eastern Europe are learning to accept it. It is hard for Western Christians, proud of their innocence, to understand the abjection of their brethren in the East. "So-and-so," says a prominent American theologian of a new bishop in the East, "is a man with whom I would not shake hands" — the luxury of the guiltless. "What I want to know," says an American Christian who is fighting communism over here, "is what they are doing over there to fight communism. Nothing?" Nothing.

I should like to have had that guiltless American with me at a county conference of small-town pastors in a village in Hungary. After we had broken goulash together and discussed this and that, one of the pastors, who had been silent, spoke: "Isn't it true that in America you have many great social problems of crime, and of cultural vulgarity, and of juvenile delinquency?"

The room was very quiet. "Yes," I said.

"What I want to ask, then, is this: Do Americans who think and pray about these problems see any actual solution to them that might be made within your social system — any way to attack them fundamentally without changing the structure of your society? You understand what I mean?"

I nodded, and sat still and thought a bit. I thought of many things — of our private property rights that maintain slums, of the legal dodges of discrimination, of the moral tone of our unassailably free press and TV, of the cost of our unsocialized medicine and drugs. Then I said: "I think not."

"Well," he said, "that is my impression, too, but one does not know so very much about faraway places. You are the first American I have ever talked to." He went on: "And now I must say something very hard for me to say. Our social structure here has been changed fundamentally, as you know. And all these problems have been attacked with the full force of our society. As *insoluble* problems they no longer exist. I don't mean," and he smiled, "that the Communist party has found out how to eliminate original sin. These things exist, of course, but they have been checked with great success. But —" he paused, and went on: "— we pay a price for this."

"I know," I said.

"Let me speak of our children. We see them being taken away from their Christian faith. The pressure on them is great, in the schools, in the press, over the radio, over television now; in the Pioneers and the after-school recreation programs and summer camps. We see we are losing them, many of them, and in the end, without Christ —" He paused again, and went on: "At the same time we see them growing up clean and enthusiastic. Their lives are crowded with constructive activities. They are wholesome children — excuse me, I don't say more wholesome than yours in America — but more wholesome than we were in Hungary a generation ago. You must understand that as parents and pastors we are very happy about this. But — in the center of their being —"

I nodded, and he said, in the quiet room:

"You see the dilemma, Brother Mayer?"

Does this kind of talk mean that the churches have "made peace" with the Communist regimes? Of course it does. And if this sounds sordid, or even sacrilegious, to us in our free-and-easy situation, in which war with the regime is unthinkable, we may remind ourselves that nearly all great churches have nearly always made peace with all regimes. The question of political liberty is relatively modern in Christian casuistry anyway. Is the cure of souls to exclude the unfree? Historically the church has been preoccupied with liberty only when it meant the religious liberty of the preoccupied denomination; it is hard to lay a finger on the anathematization of tyranny as such. The Catholic excommunication of Communists rests on atheism, not on tyranny. But last August the presiding Lutheran bishop of West Germany delivered an exegesis on Romans 13: Christians are not subject to *godless* powers that be. In effect he called upon Eastern European believers to choose between treason and damnation. It is a call which is not likely to be answered "over there" or anywhere.

It is a call addressed by those who need not choose to those who must. One day I sat with an American official in a Communist city and listened to him talk to a local pastor. The American wanted to know what the pastor was doing to fight communism. The pastor replied that he was not fighting anything — he was preaching the Gospel of Christ. Why did he stay in such a God-forsaken country? "Well, you see, it is my country, and who knows which country God has forsaken?" But wouldn't he rather be free? "But I am as free as I deserve to be. And besides, I am ordained as a pastor and a pastor is a shepherd. Would a shepherd be a good shepherd if he ran away from his flock?" If the American official had been a religious man — he said he wasn't — he might have put the question differently. He might have asked why the churches in Europe fought fascism so much more wholeheartedly than they fight communism. The answer one hears — in both Europes — is not an easy one.

The church as such did not fight fascism, and of those minorities in it that did, Catholicism (in Protestant Germany) fought it sooner and better. In 1933 some of the highest heroes of the subsequent Protestant resistance in Germany sent Hitler their formal assurance of "loyal and prayerful support." They say now that they did not see then, at the beginning, that fascism was an aberration in human history. But these same men, men like Niemöller, who discovered that a Christian could not live with fascism, seem now to be convinced that a Christian can live with communism. They seem to be convinced that communism is not aberrant in human history, and that its aberrative elements are not at its center. They may be wrong.

It may be theologically shaky to suppose that communism is compatible with the Christian social order, but the Western church has not yet pronounced Acts 4:34–35 theologically shaky: ". . . and distribution was made unto every man according as he had need." And if voluntary communism is not at all the same thing as the present coercion, why, the coercers have no objection to voluntary communism. But Leo XII's *Rerum novarum* cried out for social justice seventy years ago, and wherever social justice came, and in whatever degree it came, it came without much benefit of clergy. The German Confessional Church, in its first synod after Hitler's fall, took upon itself the blame for his rise: "We erred in overlooking the fact that the economic doctrines of Marxism should have reminded us of our duties toward our flock in regard to their social needs in this world. We have failed to make the cause of the poor and the outcasts the concern of Christians according to the coming Kingdom of God." That was 1946.

"They freeze and starve beneath our heaven-bent feet." That was 1556.

"Does the state control the church?" is a strictly American question. In the rest of the world it has usually controlled the church and has often been the church. But what is control? We Americans are incredulous to hear that in all the Communist countries — excepting the U.S.S.R. — religious instruction is given in the public schools at public expense by a pastor of the child's own faith. But it always was. Until the end of the First World War, it was compulsory. Now the state does what little it can — here is the totalitarian dictatorship doing what little it can — to discourage it. Written application by both parents is required, so that the father has, in effect, to declare himself a Christian.

In two areas, finance and elementary education, the Communist state exercises direct control. No parochial or other private school is permitted as a substitute for public education. (Sunday school is unaffected, and the denominations still have their seminaries, radically reduced in number.) Non-church property of the church is of course socialized; the Prince Primate Mindszenty of Hungary represents the largest pre-Communist landowner in that land-starved country, the Roman Catholic church. So the church — national Protestantism more than international Catholicism — is poor now. And since Marxism has a worse opinion of faith than of reason, a pastor is worse paid than a teacher. But churches are repaired and restored, and even improved and enlarged, with financial assistance from the atheist regime. And the pastor is paid and pensioned by the atheist regime. This is nothing new, but the church as a kind of public property and the pastor as a kind of civil servant are more clearly identified now. Our own church-goers may assume that as such they have no direct connection with the state; but our courts have held uniformly that tax exemption is a *quid pro quo* for special service to the general welfare. So, too, in pre-Communist, non-Communist, and Communist Europe.

In practice, there is, of course, an immense difference between the two worlds. When the State of California required an anti-Communist oath of its 12,000 churches on pain of taxation, 11,988 of them took the oath in spite of the fact that all of the leading national governing bodies of Protestantism denounced it. If a Communist government required an anticapitalist oath of its churches on pain of worse than taxation, it is possible that twelve more out of every 12,000 would take it there than took it here. And the central denominational authorities would not denounce it. (Nor would there be an independent Supreme Court to strike it down.)

By contrast the Eastern (and most of the Western) European denominations are rigidly centralized in authority, despite the long struggle of the liberals to "build on the parish." The bishops rule the church, and they are appointed (as they always were) with government approval — and sometimes retired under government pressure. An actual Marxist is no more likely to be in church office there than here. But there, as here, the bishops are loyal citizens; an American hierarch who gave aid and comfort to the national enemy would not long remain a hierarch, nor would a Polish, Czech, or Hungarian. A bold bishop is rare in Communist countries, rarer than here (in the North); and a bold pastor rarer still. But so it always was. And boldness takes different forms in different worlds. To invite a non-Communist American to preach from the bishop's pulpit is probably bold in Budapest, and I've seen it happen. The church temporal, there as here, is not very bold, but it is the one institution to which the totalitarian dictatorship is unable to dictate totally. Unable — and peculiarly unwilling. Unwilling, because the Nazis tried, first covertly, then openly, to control the church in Germany; and the dirtiest word by far in the Communist lexicon is "Nazi." This generally unobserved fact tends to mollify the Communist government's relations with the church and, indeed, with all of its citizens and institutions.

By 1921 there was not a single church left in the Soviet Union. Religion had been exterminated, with the League of the Militant Godless as the Party's spearhead. Today the League is dead and the exterminated church is alive. Its destruction failed as nothing else the Communists have ever undertaken. The hard fact of coexistence has been forced on the Party — whose hope, I suppose, like that of all coexisters, is to coexist the enemy to death. The lesson of the mother country is not lost on the daughters: there are too many people in these anciently religious lands whom the church can reach in a way that the state can not, so there is no hot war against the church anywhere now. Shrines and cemeteries are undesecrated (although hoodlumism, including anti-Semitic hoodlumism, can still be found, there as here, by looking for it). Whoever wants badly enough to be a Christian is a Christian and survives.

"Who are they?" I said to the pastor of a crowded congregation on a Sunday morning. "Some," he said, "come because they have always come. Some because their wives or sweethearts come, but fewer of these now. Some only because — this is always strange, isn't it? — they want their children to come. All these you know in your own country — nominal Christians. But their proportion falls. Certainly more than half who come in the larger towns now know exactly what they want, and they know the price. There are very few actual opportunists left, except," with a smile, "among us pork-choppers, as you call us. Nobody can come to church any more because it is a good place to make social or business contacts. Not even a funeral director, much less a dentist or an insurance salesman, and," with another smile, "not a candidate for public office, oh, no."

The East European churches lost so many members during and after the war that they were bound to grow again in numbers. But the growth persists. And Protestant church attendance is over 20 per cent of the membership in the Communist countries and 5 per cent in Christian Democratic West Germany. More important, the age level in the Eastern churches is falling — "fast," the elders of the Prague-Nusle Presbyterian Church told me. Maybe young people — they study the Sociology of Religion in the upper schools — are induced by dialectical curiosity to have a whiff of the old opium. Or maybe man does not live by spiraling production figures alone.

The heaviest loss in the Catholic-majority countries is sustained by the Catholic church. Early Communism, like early Christianity, is addressed to what Adam Smith, in the concisest of all social characterizations, called "the laboring poor," and the laboring poor in these poor countries are preponderantly Catholic (Orthodox in Russia, Rumania, and Bulgaria). No Communist regime makes a formal distinction among the confessions, but in practice Protestantism has a much easier time than the majority church. The minority churches are natural repositories of political liberalism anyway — not that Admiralissimo Horthy of Hungary wasn't a Calvinist — and the Protestant addiction to worldly progress is a natural ally of social change. (The Czech Communists, too, claim Huss.) And there is one political evil with which Catholicism will make no concordat: political atheism.

Protestant East Germany is singular. Its advanced economy and its church were once one with the West. It is a conquered and occupied country. And it is German; where common cause has submerged confessional differences elsewhere, even between Lutheran and Reformed. "Teutonic" inflexibility still bedevils the East German Church and its relations with the regime — and with the Russians behind the regime. There are Russians who believe that the only good German is a German Communist with a Russian soldier on each arm.

What communism says and does about the church, and how Communists feel about the church are not necessarily the same thing. We were received, in the company of some pastors, by a Slovak Communist official. "In the 1944 uprising against the Nazis," he said, "many of our Christian brethren here," and he motioned around the room, "were with us. We wish they were with us now." "He said 'brethren,'" I said to one of the brethren afterward. "Yes," said the brother, "he is not against us and he is not with us. He is genuinely sorry about this. Many of the Communist leaders are more tolerant than Lenin would have thought possible." And the *New York Times* quotes a Communist party central committee member in Poland as saying, "What kind of party is it when half our members sneak off to church every Sunday?" In the "tougher" countries it isn't a half, or a fourth, but there might be a few who do and a few more who might if only —.

Total defeat in the Soviet Union, tolerance in the ideological ranks, the dread of looking like Nazis — no wonder Communist control of the church is restrained. Steady pressure — the drop that wears away the stone — is the contemporary substitute. But what say the political geologists when there are millions who believe that the stone in this case is the Rock which will not wear away? The Party newspapers have titles like "Do You Want Your Child To Lose His Soul?" He will lose it, it turns out, in the church; — another drop on the stone. In backward areas the pressures are more persistent because of what Trotsky called "the anticollective skull" of the peasantry; so year after year permission to build a rural church may be delayed;—another drop on the stone. Last summer the drops suddenly fell at shorter intervals in one distinctly unbackward country: more difficulty in obtaining temporary exit permits here; reduced publication facilities there (because, of course, of material shortages); an outburst in the Party press somewhere else. Old issues were reopened and church leaders tied up in interminable negotiations. Was it a pattern? No one was sure. If it was, did it mean that the Party was turning to the "church problem" in earnest? No one was sure. The only thing known for sure is that international tension is immediately reflected in domestic pressure.

The situation of the Christian under communism (the Marxists would say the "objective situation") is of course always subjective. And it is never the same from day to day, or from country to country, or even from town to town. We Americans may mesmerize ourselves with the image of the monstrous monolith which moves only to crush. But there seems to be just as much improvisation in the "slave" world as there is in the "free." I have met some doctrinaire Communists — but never in the bureaucracy of a Communist country. The pressures ebb and flow. Where it all will end — to use Wolcott Gibbs's expression in the right place — knows God!

The conditions of Christian survival under communism are not ideal. What is marvelous is that they exist at all. They exist because the church has proved to be indestructible — at least by communism. But the indestructible institution is only tolerated. It has got to prove, not merely that it is harmless but that it is *worthy* to exist. Its God-given right does not signify among the godless. It has got to purge itself of its history in so far as its history ranges it alongside exploitation or private profit. (The Marxists don't distinguish them.) But abjuration is not enough. It has got to prove its utility to the new order, and to do so weekdays, not just say so Sundays. This means that so long as the cold war lasts the church under communism must demonstrate its independence of those institutions, sacred and secular, which represent or even accept the Western political position. This is why those seamlessly international organizations whose power centers are in the West have special difficulty — Roman Catholicism, Judaism, and, for that matter, Rotary and the Red Cross. This is why the adherence of the East European churches to the World Council of Churches — which was cheering John Foster Dulles a decade ago — is beset with intricacies.

By identifying religion with capitalism, Marxism has driven its two enemies closer together in the West than they were a half-century ago when industrial democracy and the awakening social gospel were beginning to drive a wedge between the two. The church is guilty by association. And the Marxists point to Adenauer Germany — not to Franco Spain, which is an old story — as the full-blown reality of the association. Bedfellows make strange politics; the Christian Democratic government of the German Federal Republic is surrounded by Nazis because it works within the system of the Krupps and has to take what it finds there.

The church in Eastern Europe must not be supposed to have chosen its situation. As communism spread after the war, the historical doctrine of "withdrawal" asserted itself with great force in Eastern Christendom: the relegation of spiritual life to another world and the surrender of this world's concerns to the state. But this Erastianism — which had served the old order so wonderfully well — was precisely what the new would not tolerate. Like all other institutions, whatever their pretensions, the church, whatever its, would have to serve the reconstruction of society. "If ye refuse and rebel," the Lord God Jehovah once told the Church, "ye shall be devoured with the sword." Now the Ministry of Culture was saying it.

In this country the National Council of Churches in Christ is currently under attack because it maintains that the churches should "study and comment upon issues, whether political, economic, or social, which affect human relations." The attack is supported by economic — and in some areas military and racial — rightists who hold, in the words of J. Howard Pew, former president of the Sun Oil Company, that "the churches should stick to ecclesiastical subjects." The head of one of the attacking groups, the Circuit Riders, says that "the National Council and its program addresses itself in the main to the grievances and the animal appetites of man. The program goes under the fancy title of 'Social Gospel.' We are for a minister speaking out on any issues except the promotion of Socialism, Communism, or pro-Communist activities."

The issue, then, here as in Eastern Europe, is not in the least between "fundamentalist" and "modernist" interpretation of Scripture, as is sometimes said. It is between Christians who want the social gospel preached and those who want it unpreached. Marxism, addressing itself to "the grievances and the animal appetites of man," willy-nilly bolstered that very small element in the East European churches which maintained that man lives by bread, not by bread alone, but by bread. After ten years of Communist rule, this element is clearly dominant in East European Christendom. The "quietists" — they still exist, and no doubt in a numerical majority — are disappearing from church office.

If the church in Eastern Europe can demonstrate that it accepts the Christian — the Communists would call it the Communist — mission in the social order, there is no insuperable reason to suppose that it will not be allowed to have its Christ, too. Marxism does not oppose toy balloons per se, and second-generation communism does not have to attack on every front at once. But let the church make a move on behalf of the old order — or even hanker to out loud — and the attack will be on again. There may be westerners who want to see just this happen. It won't.

What can a Western Christian do to strengthen the hand of the church within — not against — the Communist society? Not much. "Only to imagine us and our world — as it was and as it is — is all we ask of our Western brethren," an Orthodox Rumanian said to me. "And if imagination fails them, then they must love us in our common faith and not consign us to outer darkness."

"To the people here we Christians are capitalist stooges" — I am translating very freely now from a Czech Brethren pastor — "and to the people in the West we are Communist stooges. And we *are* stooges. We try to understand what Christ absolutely requires of us in our situation. But beyond that — well, if you say we are being 'used,' we can say yes to that. We know we were sent here to be used. We know that we are not pure." I was instantly reminded of an American I had heard about who was selling quantities of forbidden PX food to Germans, at cost, after the war. He wasn't sure he should, and he took his moral problem to Eva Hermann, the German Quaker heroine. Her only response was, "Oh, to be able to afford an American conscience."

What can a Western Christian do? Nothing if, à la cold war, he requires a political declaration as a condition of religious association. His brethren in the East will not join his anti-Communist crusade or concede that the Christian witness is adequately represented by

American foreign policy. Western insistence upon a political bill of health can only mean a complete division of Christendom in the end. Those Western churchmen who view the prospect equably should remember that More and Erasmus wanted reform and found Reformation thrust upon them.

The Western Christian may simply cross to the other side of the street. And that, in the main, is what he has done. In 1958 the first Christian Peace Conference was held in Prague. There were four Westerners present, all German Lutherans. A year later there was a strong delegation from West Germany and a good scattering from the rest of Western Europe — and two Americans, a young Mennonite and a representative of the American Friends Service Committee.

"These people are still in the World Council," says one prominent American, explaining his absence from Prague. "If they really mean their irenics, let them work inside the Council. The fact is that the Communists won't let them. If the Eastern churches want to have a conference they have to have it in the East, where the Communists can control it." The agenda of last year's Prague conference called for a day of world penitence and prayer on the anniversary of Hiroshima. Some of the Western delegates expressed concern lest such a call, coming out of Prague, be badly received in the West and especially in the United States. Their concern was ventilated in a general session, and Professor Hans Joachim Iwand of Bonn was named chairman of the drafting commission. As the call was adopted — with two dissenting votes, of West Germans who felt that the guilt of Hiroshima was theirs alone — it read as follows:

. . . The atom bomb of Hiroshima . . . lit up in a flash the road of Christendom. . . . All of us share the guilt. . . . We have not loved Him Whom God loved so much. Being of little faith we have thought that weapons and human power were our help. . . . The bomb . . . has become a summons. . . .

When, therefore, we come together with our congregation and churches on the day of Hiroshima this year to hold a service of penitence and prayer, we ask all of you, both in East and in West, and all over the world, not to withhold your communion from us. Let us stand together before God as His children and make a new beginning through His forgiveness. . . .

Thus the peace conference in Prague, "where the Communists can control it."

The Hiroshima day of repentance and prayer was very widely observed in Europe last summer, East and West. It was very widely unobserved in America, and the Prague conference itself was very widely ignored in the American press, secular *and* religious. An American Christian might have noted, had he had the chance, that the conference message to the heads of state was addressed, in Khrushchev's case, "in profound Christian responsibility," and in Eisenhower's, "in the unity of our Christian faith."

Blow the winds hot, blow the winds cold, the rock-bottom irreconcilability of the Communist and Christian faiths remains. Accommodation on the economic order is not impossible; Bible communism is older than anti-Bible communism and no less fanatical, as witness the fate of Ananias and his wife, the first Christians who tried to practice a little capitalism on the side. Nor can the two parties quarrel *very* bitterly on the question of violence. What stands between them is not practice but belief as to the genesis, nature, and destiny of man.

Here we have Christianity's helplessness and communism's do-it-yourself, Christianity's dependence and communism's tumescent pride in the unaided power of the featherless biped. Communism, says William Hordern, is hateful to us because it has dragged the skeleton from the closet of Western culture: the Christian peoples worship the works of their hands as wholeheartedly as the Marxists. An eminent American scientist complains that "two years after the first Sputnik, Western peoples and institutions remain subservient to ancient elements of deflated divine revelation." The Communists have been deflating divine revelation for forty-two years, but there are Eastern peoples who still believe in God.

Faith paralyzed by faithlessness seems to be galvanized by opposing faith. In Communist Europe the Party militant and triumphant and the church stripped and humiliated stand face to face. They are alone in the arena. "Everything else" — it wasn't a Christian who said this but a Communist — "is finished." I did not meet a Communist *or* a Christian who wasn't alive to the fact, earnestly, rather than joyously, alive in that northern world whose hallmark is earnestness anyway. It is a long-term struggle; both sides see it that way now, even in the U.S.S.R. But one side always saw it that way, and there lies its advantage. The Communists are no less adept at the arts of attrition than the capitalists. But the battlefield here is crepuscular, and you can't get a man with a gun. We shall see if the profane reformation can be informed by a church which has either its faith or nothing. We shall see what Christianity can do without Cadillacs.

A Lutheran archbishop in the East (there are some) said: "Like Marxism, Christianity believes in the New Man, though we differ as to the manner of his coming to be. Like the Marxist, too, the Christian lives for the future and is willing to sacrifice, so to say, consumer goods for producer goods. To say, as some of our Western friends say, 'If I had nothing, I'd live for the future, too,' is one way to say it. But another way to say it is that people who live for the future have something to live for."

Before I left Eastern Europe, I asked an elder, and a very old elder, what the church in the West can contribute to our time. "I do not know the west," he said, "but I know that there, as here, all Christians sing the hymn, 'In Christ There Is No East or West.' So I shall simply say what I think the church, West and East can contribute. If the trouble of the world is too deep and too desperate for self-interested negotiation, then there is something left which neither capitalism nor communism offers, but only the church: brotherhood. But the church must learn before it can teach."

A MAN
WITH A
COUNTRY

Mrs. Mayer and I stood fidgeting in the plenipotentiary presence of Mr. Robert C. Ode, the American consul in Berne. The date was January 18, 1963, and the weather was the reason we fidgeted (though Mr. Ode may have thought we had other reasons). We had half an hour to get the last train to connect, via Meiringen and Brünig, with the postbus back to our mountain; and Switzerland, including Berne, was disappearing under the heaviest snow in a hundred years.

We had each slipped Mr. Ode ten dollars for a new passport. Ours would expire while we were making a quick trip home in March, and we figured we'd get the new ones now and have it over with. We had completed the application forms and handed them to Mr. Ode, who bade us swear solemnly that we would support and defend the Constitution of the United States. We said that we swore neither solemnly nor jocosely nor, indeed, at all, but we would affirm, in the fashion permitted people who follow the biblical injunction against swearing; and affirm we did. Whereupon Mr. Ode should have handed us our shiny new passports.

Whereupon, instead, he handed us a sheet and said, "Now, if you'll just sign this. . . ." The sheet contained the following mimeographed words, and no others:

WARNING

Section 6 of the Internal Security Act of 1950 (50 U.S.C. 786) prohibits application for or use of a passport by and issuance or renewal of a passport to a member of an organization registered or required to register as a Communist organization under Section 7 of the Act. The following organizations are registered under Section 7:

The Communist Party of the United States of America.

From *Harper's Magazine*, March, 1964.

61

I am not and have not been at any time during the period of 12 full calendar months preceding the date of this application (and no other person to be included in the passport is or has been at any time during the said period) a member of any organization registered or required to register under Section 7 of the Subversive Activities Control Act of 1950, as amended. (50 U.S.C. 786).

_____

Signature

"Who issues this?" I said.

"The Department of State," said Mr. Ode plenipotentiarily.

"Since when?"

"Oh, quite recently."

"And it has to be signed?"

"If you want a new passport."

"But not sworn to?"

"Apparently not."

"And what organizations besides the Communist party are _required_ to register?"

"I'm afraid I don't know."

"But how am I to know that I am not a member of any such organization when I don't know what the organizations are? Aren't you asking me to sign a blank check?"

"Well," said Mr. Ode, "I'll go upstairs and get the regulations. Nobody has raised any objection before"; with which he gathered up all the papers on his desk, put them in the safe, locked the safe, and went, I suppose, upstairs.

He returned with a sheaf and went through it. "I can't read you all of this," he said finally, "because some of it is classified. But it says here that any person who objects to signing the statement may submit his reasons to the Department for its further determination. Do you object to signing the statement?" I said I did.

"And you, Mrs. Mayer?"

All of our papers and most of our books, clothes, and furnishings, our car, and two of our children were in Switzerland; somebody would _have_ to have a passport to return from the Free World to get them. And time was wasting and the snow getting heavier. Mrs.

Mayer signed and got her passport. I got nine of my ten dollars back (the house taking its usual commission), and we went out into the glittering dusk and got back to Brünig in the frozen-fingered dawn.

I warmed my fingers and submitted to the State Department my reasons for refusing to sign the statement, sending a copy to Attorney Francis Heisler of Carmel, California, who specializes in supporting and defending the Constitution of the United States against attack by anybody (including the United States government). I explained that I had assignments in Europe for two religious organizations (the American Friends Service Committee and the Fellowship of Reconciliation, to attend the Christian Peace Conference in Prague) and four publishers (the *Christian Century*, to report on the conference; *Harper's*, to report on life in Prague; the *Progressive*, to report on Eastern Europe; and the Encyclopaedia Britannica, to report on the Americanization of Europe). Thus my freedom of press and worship was involved. My freedom of assembly, too, in that the requirement would penalize me (if I *were* a Communist) for association. And of course there was Article 13, Section 2 — but who cares? a member nation? — of the United Nations Declaration of Human Rights: "Everyone has the right to leave any country, including his own."

I forgot to invoke the Old Fifth, but I remembered to say that it looked like cruel and unusual punishment to me to deprive a man of a passport who had never been charged with or convicted of an offense against the United States or any State, Territory, or Insular Possession thereof. In conclusion I shot my cuffs at posterity: "I am willing, indeed eager, to witness openly to all of my personal and organizational beliefs and associations past and present; but I am unable to do so under duress. The test oath — and the Warning sheet in question is tantamount to such oath — requires a man to deny a crime with which he has not been charged. It is the historic instrument of tyrannies for the reduction of free men to servility. It is unworthy of my country and my government, and I hope that my protest will weigh against it. . . ."

Sincerely yours, and *Ruat caelum.*

A few weeks later, on my arrival in the United States, I sidled into the San Francisco passport office to see if my new passport was waiting there for me. It wasn't, but "Washington" had instructed "San Francisco" to ask me to fill out a new application form. The new form included the non-Communist disclaimer as a part of the oath that has always appeared on the application. I complied, inking out the disclaimer. I knew that the San Francisco application was meaningless because the Berne application was (1) prior, (2) pending, and (3) complete (the *Warning* sheet having been wholly separate from it). Nevertheless the State Department latched on to the San Francisco form so that it could claim that my application, with the disclaimer inked out, was incomplete. The Department was thereby estopped (I can see it rolling words like "estopped" around) from processing (more rolling) the application. It had to make that claim or admit that it was denying me a passport. And such admission would at once entitle me to a hearing under *Kent* v. *Dulles*, which in 1958 established travel as an inherent right of citizenship which may not be denied without due process of law.

The Kent case required (for the first time in the melancholy history of McCarthyism) that the about-to-be-injured party be confronted with the evidence against him. The Passport Office opposes confrontation, which would disclose the sources of its information. Mr. Abba P. Schwartz, the State Department's administrator of security affairs, favors confrontation (and Mr. Abram Chayes, counsel to the Department, supports Mr. Schwartz); in the midst of which slow swordplay I came clattering along in my dusty sandals and nailed my dusty theses to the door of the State Department. I do not doubt that I am a pawn (on whosever side). But what "these Bernards" — as Dostoevsky would say — always forget is that this is a game in which even a pawn can play and, in the end game, play a mortal role.

But the end game was a long time developing. My lawyers — whose name was now Phalanx — decided that every possible administrative remedy should be exhausted before I sued, so that the case would be solidly bottomed (more rolling). All spring they roamed the State Department corridors in the ingenuous hope that somebody would step out of an office and say yes or no. Came June and Miss Frances Knight, director of the Passport Office, finally told me in writing that she was estopped, etc., and I buckled on the whole armor of the law which, in its impartial majesty, alike forbids the government to oppress the citizen and the citizen to oppress the government.

The issue inside the Department (so my overcover agents informed me) had gone all the way up to an assistant secretary, who overruled Mr. Chayes on "policy grounds." Mr. Chayes had advised the Department to give me the passport and get shut of me; its legal grounds for refusal were, he thought, untenable. But Miss Knight told the San Francisco *Chronicle* that she understood that this was to be a test case of the Department's passport policy.

So *Mayer* v. *Rusk* went to court. The lawsuit (in which I disappear now except for the title of the pleadings) goes on apace, and the pace would pleasure a senior snail. We — for I am now multitudinized by *amici curiae* — were granted a statutory three-judge court to hear the matter in the first instance and were thus assured a direct appeal to the Supreme Court. But one of the three judges was just moving to Washington, so the hearing went over from July to October. We pleaded the urgency of my situation and offered, as friends of the court, to carry the judge's piano for him. No go. October it was. On December 3, 1963, the decision was given against us, the buck being expected, in such cases, to pass to the nine-judge court above. It is now passing, sedately.

I was aware that it might be months or years before I came out the other end of the juridical process. With my new passport (if I got one) I would just about make it from the house to the old people's home. The prospect didn't please, so I thought I would try to intimidate the State Department into a quick carriage of justice. I put in a person-to-person call to Miss Knight's mouthpiece, Mr. Robert D. Johnson, deputy director of the Passport Office in Washington, and when he answered, I said, "Johnson, old boy —" "This is not Mr. Johnson," said the man in Washington, "this is Mr. Whacker [or maybe it was Tibble, or Veepings] in Mr. Johnson's office." Nothing undaunted, I tried to tell Veepings just how it was. He replied, "Mr. Mayer, the Department takes the view that it is the citizen's duty to help his government enforce the law."

I say that these words of Veepings lay the foundation for the devil's very own polity. They mean perpetual martial law and the perpetual alienation of a man's natural right (especially a small man's) to pass by on the other side of the street when one policeman is arresting a dozen thugs with blazing guns. If we do not pin back these Veepings' ears, we shall find our own amputated because we did not interpose to give the man from the municipal animal shelter a pants-leg up on a rabid dog. If we do not strike down the Veepings Doctrine, there is no limit to government, and we may as well confess that we are no better off than the Russians.

But there is no arguing doctrine with a Veepings, and I thought I would try a more primitive gambit. I wrote Miss Knight a Dear Sir letter, calling her attention to Section 6 (a) (2) (b), which forbids her to issue a passport "knowing or having reason to believe" that the applicant is a Communist. I asserted (without saying I was or I wasn't) that she did not have such knowledge or belief. Unless, therefore, she informed me that she did, I respectfully demanded that she issue me a passport at once. She did neither.

I concluded that I might fare better with a man of my own sex, namely, my adversary in *Mayer* v. *Rusk*. I directed Mr. Rusk's attention to Section 6 (a) (1), which makes it a felony for a Communist to apply for a passport. Pointing out that I had applied for a passport in Berne, not to mention San Francisco, I respectfully demanded that he either give me a passport or charge me with a felony. He did neither.

But these Rusks, Knights, and Veepings' are only accomplices, after the fact, of the United States Congress in a fraud perpetrated, like all frauds, for gain; the gain being the defeat, in the next election, of the opposing candidate's furious anticommunism by one's own furiouser anticommunism. This is the actual "intent of the Congress" — which the courts are always trying to determine — but even its putative intent does not authorize the State Department to make me swear that I am not a Communist. The Department thought that one up itself. The accomplices are fraudulent in their own right.

Their fraud is not even impalpable.

Say that I'm a Communist agent, using my American passport to further my infamous interests. How best do I disguise myself? Best, I submit, by posing as an independent (if not wholly obscure) journalist who is able to rig up assignments taking him almost anywhere on a moment's notice, and by affecting, on the side, to be a religious man with an ecumenical outlook and an affiliation of some amorphous sort with a cheerful institution like Quakerism. And that is just what I am.

Why, then, do I blame the State Department for requiring me to purge myself of suspicion? Because where I come from (which is Justinian Rome, via Missouri), the burden of proof is on the accuser and my answer to him is, "Show me." I am paying J. Edgar Hoover a handsome wage to find out whether I'm a Communist. Why should I do his work for him at my own expense? Mr. Hoover is the head of what Attorney-General Kennedy calls the greatest investigative body in the world. If the greatest investigative body in the world cannot find out whether I'm a Communist without my help, it is not the greatest investigative body in the world.

Say that I'm a Communist agent, bent upon disguise. Would I be a member of the Communist party? I would not be, not only because I would not be so silly as to bait the trap for myself, but also (and much more crucially) because the State Department will give me a passport if I'm a Communist agent *provided I am not a member of the Communist party*. Just listen to this, from page A-19 of Mr. Rusk's answer to my complaint: "To obtain a passport a present member need only sever his *organizational* connection with the Communist organization; he is not required to alter his beliefs or convictions" (emphasis added).

Say, then, that I'm a Communist agent. I am asked to swear (solemnly) that I am not a member of the Communist party. I do so. I wouldn't boggle at perjury — not if I were a traitor to begin with — but the fact is that I have told the truth. But say that I'm neither a Communist agent *nor* a party member. In that case I must answer the question the same way the Communist agent answers it.

Is this — as Milt Gross used to say — a system?

It is not a system but a fraud, perpetrated, like all frauds, under a false pretense: the pretense of keeping Communist agents from going abroad. As any fairly mature infant knows, there is no way to prevent the flow of information between the two worlds anyway. All I have to do in, say, Prague, to tell the CIA that the Russians are using aspirin, and not bicarb, to trigger their new device is to put three twenty- and two sixty-heller stamps in a prearranged order on my picture postcard to Aunt Kate. Everybody knows that that's how the Russians got the bomb in the first place.

So palpable is the pretense that the State Department only pretends to enforce it. On April 19, 1963, Miss Knight wrote me that the oath I declined to take "is required of all applicants." But several weeks later applicants of my acquaintance were still being handed the old forms without the oath; and this, mind you, was at least fifteen months after the State Department announced the new regulation in January, 1962 (after the Supreme Court upheld the order requiring the Communist party to register) and at least twelve months after its new forms were issued in May, 1962. In all that time the Department had not got around to getting its new forms to its passport application offices, and in all that time it had issued, I suppose, a half-million passports, most of them, doubtless, to Communist agents who sped to Tiflis and sent Aunt Kate a picture postcard with an interesting arrangement of stamps. Either I should get my passport or the half-million Communist agents who got theirs should have them revoked, I don't care which; I want the equal protection of the laws guaranteed by the Fourteenth Amendment.

The last refuge of a Department is the stall, in the hope that something will turn up. In *Mayer* v. *Rusk* the Department's hope, in its succession of stalls, appeared to be the Flynn case. Elizabeth Gurley Flynn, who *claims* to be a Communist, had her passport revoked and was suing. If the Department could get the Flynn case up to the Supreme Court before mine, the Court might hand down a careless enough opinion in her case to bolster the Department in mine — an opinion, for instance, that the national security puts travel within the sole competence of the executive power. The executive power was vastly extended by Mr. Roosevelt's emergency a quarter-century ago. The emergency is still on. Nowadays it is, of course, communism.

The defendant in *Mayer* v. *Rusk*, having no other stick to beat me with, has to use the Red Menace — the same Red Menace that the *Chicago Tribune* was using fifteen years ago to prove the disloyalty of the Rockefeller Foundation (of which Mr. Rusk is expresident). Mr. Rusk ought to know better. He ought to know that I am not arguing that the Reds are or aren't a Menace. He ought to know that I am not arguing that the Internal Security Act is a good or bad thing. (It is as bad as it was when Mr. Truman vetoed it and said we were throwing our liberties away). I am arguing that Miss Knight is not empowered to ask me whether I'm a Communist. My political affiliation is none of a free government's business, and a government makes itself unfree when its Congress and its courts decide that communism is only a criminal conspiracy and not also a theory of man and of history to which an honest (if mistaken) man might repair. The reason that communism is outlawed in Amercia and Germany — and only in America and Germany among republican countries — is that only Americans and Germans will let it be defined for them as a criminal conspiracy and nothing more. I reject godless communism — along with godless capitalism — but that is *my* business.

The Catholic Council on Civil Liberties condemns the loyalty (or rather, the non-disloyalty) oath in general as "un-American, coercive, discriminatory, prejudicial, and ineffective." The standard oath of allegiance required of every officeholder (and of every soldier, and of every passport applicant) may be ineffective, but it is none of the rest of the things that the Catholic Council complains of. And it is the rest of the things that stick in my craw. I can take (or affirm, in my peculiar way) the oath of allegiance without its sticking. As St. Thomas said of the lady's belief that the names of the blessed were inscribed on a golden scroll in heaven — if it does no good, it probably does no harm either.

But this is the first time that I myself have had to face the loyalty oath in all its fatuous panoply and its design to make wall-to-wall people out of us. My rejection of it in the past has cost me a couple of jobs I could do without, and I sympathize with my thirty-four million countrymen who have had to take it or be blacklisted. In a high school in my neighborhood all seventy-one of the teachers protested the oath — and all seventy-one of them took it. They do not love their country the more for having taken it, and Mr. Rusk is smart enough to know that the only loyalty is love.

My real objection has no merit in a three-judge, a nine-judge, or a twenty-seven judge court: This oath is repugnant to me as an American. If my Republican father had been told he had to take it, he would have said, "What do you think this is — Russia?" Every Sunday afternoon in Chicago he used to take me to a bosky dell called Bughouse Corner in Washington Park and listen to a succession of rabid revolutionaries, each more rabid than the last. A solitary copper named Big Tom shook his club at the kids to keep them quiet so their fathers could hear the Bolsheviks. Big Tom was the FBI, the CIA, the Internal Security Act, and the Subversive Activities Control Board all in one, and between him and the ruin of the Republic stood nothing but my father's attachment to the Republican party. Had my father come to believe that the Bolsheviks were right, not Big Tom or the FBI or the CIA could have saved the country from him. No police power has ever saved a country from subversion or ever will.

Ruat caelum. Though the heavens fall, I do not intend to take that un-American, coercive, discriminatory, prejudicial, and ineffective oath. But what will I do if, some months or years from now, the Supreme Court holds against me? I don't know what I will do. But I think I know how I will feel. I will still feel like resisting.

It would be much more useful if a senator or a congressman — or a President who vetoes it — would resist a bad law like the Internal Security Act or a bad regulation like the State Department's; but they will not. They say, "It's the law. We may not like it, but it's the law." But we hanged the Nazi leaders at Nürnberg for saying that, and properly; a man who will obey the law, whatever the law, wants a form of government in which man exists for the state and not the state for man.

The great rights of man are compendent, and the vitiation of one of them, mobility, for instance, is the vitiation of them all. My sophisticated neighbor says it's a small matter, this anti-Communist jag, but a simple-minded Nazi told me, when I spoke of the persecutions in Germany, that "that was much later. At first it was only the Communists." And so, when my neighbor says, "If you're not a Communist, why not say so?" I have got to say what we say where I come from (which is where we say *Ruat caelum*). I have got to say, *Principiis obsta* and *Finem respice*.

Resist the beginnings. Envisage the end. Maybe these aren't the beginnings. Maybe they won't proceed to the end. And maybe a stand should be made somewhere further along the road. But I didn't intend to make a stand; not I. I was tending to my business when I was confronted by Leviathan commanding me to do something un-American. It is not as if I were, say, a teetotaler confronted by the Volstead Act.

Something like this happened to me five years ago, when I was invited to Hungary by the Reformed church of that country. Informing President Eisenhower (by registered mail from Switzerland) that I was going to go, I noted that my passport was inscribed, "Not valid for travel in Hungary," and I assured him that I would not use it for that purpose (and I didn't; the Hungarians gave me a separate visa). I added that the inscription, if it meant that my government *forbade* me to travel in Hungary, would not deter me from the free exercise of my religion. Like so many of us, Mr. Eisenhower is not much of a letter writer. But when I returned from Hungary, and was safely inside the American landmass, the State Department wrote me that my continued entitlement to a passport was under review because of my "violation of the restrictions contained in your passport and in contravention of existing United States foreign policy." I was given thirty days to assure the Department under oath that I would not again violate its present *or future* regulations. I replied that my religion forbade me to take an oath and that my Americanism forbade me to agree to obey any regulation whatever in advance of its promulgation. The Department replied that it would not take any further action "at this time," since my violation had not been of such a nature as to interfere with the conduct of existing United States foreign policy.

I had not been able to discover what the existing United States foreign policy was, nor am I yet. In the interval Communist Hungary has been put on limits and Communist Cuba off, and the students who went to Cuba last summer (as I went to Hungary five years ago) have been indicted by a federal grand jury (as I was not). The State Department has never told us that we cannot go to Communist East Germany (which, according to existing United States foreign policy, does not even exist). And if we are *very* good, the Department will send us to Communist Russia at its expense but under no conditions let us see for ourselves how bad conditions are (the Department assures us that they are very bad) in Communist China.

On the occasion of my going to Hungary I suppose I disobeyed a bad law. Just how I would do so, in the instant case, if the Supreme Court holds against me, I do not know. I should certainly notify the government of my intentions (since they are honorable) in advance; I am none of your hole-and-corner men. And I suppose that the government would then use force and violence and other lawful means to keep me locked up in its great big continental jail. I should then have to renounce my citizenship and abandon the ashes of my fathers and the temples of my gods and go for good. Where?

I blush to say it in these supranational days, but I love my country, and I could not more leave it lightly than I can remain and stand by while it is being pulled to pieces. This is my own, my native land. I am an American. But I am a man before I am an American; not a good man, and getting no better, but a man, and a man has the overriding duty, in jail or out, to be free.

But when did expatriation ever mean freedom? Suppose that another republic accepted me. (I say "suppose" because, though they all despise the American demonology, they may hesitate to offend the American government). What would become of me if I resisted a bad law, in, say, England? I should then depart thence for some place like Russia, where, as a non-Communist, my right to travel would be exactly what it is here as a non-anti-Communist. And I'd be short more than a few other rights besides. If I were not imprisoned (in a small jail) when I outraged a government that was not my own, I suppose I should be deported. And go where at the last? At least my own government is not threatening to deport me — just the opposite — and that is something among many things I have to be thankful for. What I want are the things to be thankful for that we have lost in this country between my father's time and mine.

PART TWO

CONSCIENCE
AND THE
COMMONWEALTH

In 1949 a man named Veepings came to see me and stayed for a week. He was a nice man, from the Bureau of Internal Revenue, and he had come, he said, to audit my 1948 income tax return. When he got through auditing, my home, my work, and I were a homogeneous shambles, and I owed the government one dollar. I thought of paying Veepings only 65.4 cents, but then I decided to pay him the whole dollar. The reason for the 65.4 was that I had undertaken, in my 1948 return, to refuse to pay 34.6 per cent of my income tax, that being the percentage of the United States Budget which was going directly into guns in that happy-go-lucky year. I had not, however, succeeded in refusing to pay, because, being, like most peaceable persons, an optimist, I had overestimated my income and paid-as-I-went 65.4 per cent of the overestimate, and at the end of the year, the government owed me money anyway. The government did not, naturally, refund me everything above 65.4 per cent of the tax due; it refunded me everything above 100 per cent of the tax due. Since I could not very well sue the government, in its own courts, for the 34.6 per cent that, under its own laws, it had taken, my refusal looked as if it would remain an empty gesture until such time as I would stop being either optimistic or peaceable.

In 1950 my telephone rang and a man said: "I am Veepings. You wouldn't remember me."

"I wouldn't," I said bitterly, "but I do."

"I have been ordered," he said, "to audit your 1949 income tax return."

"You already did," I said, "and I gave you a dollar."

From the *Progressive*, March, 1953.

"That," he said, "was your 1948 return. This is your 1949 return."

"Do you mean," I asked, "that you are going to move in for a week again, gouge my eyeballs, pull my fingernails, and all for another dollar? I'll give you *two* dollars to stay away."

I'm afraid, Mr. Mayer," said Veepings, in his double-breasted blue-serge voice, "that you do not understand me. I am *ordered* to audit your return. I am only obeying orders."

"That," I snapped, "was General Keitel's defense at Nürnberg. "You know, of course," I added, "what happened to General Keitel."

"I never meddle in politics," said Veepings. "When may I see you?"

"Any time," I said, affecting lightheartedness, "I have nothing to conceal and, incidentally, nothing to show you, either. You remember last time. I had no records for 1948, and we had to start from scratch. I have none for 1949, either. I'm the type that always assumes that the bank knows how to add."

"Then," said Veepings, evenly, "we'll have to start from scratch."

"Now see here, Veepings," I said, unevenly, "I'm a busy man. And besides, I'm a proletarian. Do you know what a proletarian is, you cad?"

"I told you," said Veepings, ignoring the epithet, "that I never meddle in politics."

"Proletarianism isn't politics; it's economics," I said, my voice like a knife. "A proletarian is a man who has nothing to sell but his labor. I have nothing to sell but my labor, and you want another week of my labor and a dollar on top of it. *You* ought to be paying *me*."

"Mr. Mayer," he said, "you don't understand my position."

"You don't understand *mine*," I said. "Last year you found that in 1948 I cheated the government by mistake. You also found that I paid five quarterly installments that year by mistake. The whole thing came to a dollar. Was it worth it? What good is a dollar to you? Eggs were 89 cents a dozen today. That's a dozen eggs and 11 cents. What can you do with 11 cents? You can make a telephone call and throw the penny away. You're throwing my money away," I concluded, fighting mad. "I won't stand for it."

"Mr. Mayer," he said, "you have what we here at the Bureau call an unmathematical mind. You have no head for figures, and you are, for that reason, a lovable fellow and you know it. You are also honest, at least as far as your income tax is concerned. You are painfully honest. You make so much noise about being honest that, if I hadn't audited your 1948 return, I'd be suspicious of you."

"Flattery will get you nowhere," I said, "I want to be let alone. I'm a busy man. I'm a proletarian. My labor is —."

"Mr. Mayer," said Veepings, "may I speak to you unofficially?"

"Sit down," I said, gesturing with the telephone receiver. "Sit down and tell me your troubles. Maybe I can help you or send you to someone who can."

"Unofficially, Mr. Mayer," said Veepings, "I think you bring this all on yourself."

"Bring what?"

"This auditing. It's extremely unusual — unofficially, Mr. Mayer — for an ordinary citizen like you — "

"An ordi—"

"I mean, for a man of modest income to have his return audited two years in a row. Extremely unusual. Especially when the first audit failed to disclose any —"

"Any what?"

"Any — substantial discrepancy, shall we say?"

"We shall," I said, icily, "unless we want to be sued for slander. Veepings," I said, "why don't you let me alone?"

"I have no choice, Mr. Mayer. I am under orders, and I don't want to hear about Keitel, or Sheitel, or whoever it is. But I wouldn't be surprised — unofficially, Mr. Mayer — if this extremely unusual procedure wasn't the consequence of your writing those long letters to the collector of internal revenue."

" 'Those long letters,' Veepings," I said, "are my reasons for refusing, or trying to refuse, to pay 34.6 per cent of my income tax. That's politics, and you told me yourself that you never meddle in politics."

"*I* don't, myself," said Veepings, "but —"

"But what?"

"Nothing," he said, "nothing at all. But I wouldn't be surprised — strictly unofficially, Mr. Mayer — if you weren't bringing all this on yourself."

So I was being harassed — unofficially — by the government of the United States — the biggest, busiest government on earth. I was not being put in prison, like Thoreau. I was not being shot, like Nathan Hale. I was not being hanged, like John Brown. I was being harassed. There is no money and no martyrdom in being harassed. There is only harassment.

In 1951 and 1952, Veepings couldn't find me; I was moving too fast around Europe. Besides, I was being paid in German money, on which I had to pay German taxes, and having no head for figures *or* German, I let the thing ride. But this is 1953, and I am back home, and the 34.6 per cent that the government was buying guns with a few years ago has risen to 60 per cent or 80 per cent or 110 per cent. I am settling for 50 per cent. (My grandfather used to say that the Mayers were early settlers — fifty cents on the dollar). I am paying 50 per cent of my 1952 income tax and sending the balance to people who will buy something fit for human consumption with it.

I cannot see why I should not persist in my folly. Like every other horror-stricken American I keep asking myself, "What can a man do? What weight does a man have, besides petition and prayer, that he isn't using to save his country's soul and his own?" The frustration of the horror-stricken American as he sees his country going over the falls without a barrel is more than I can bear just now. He tries to do constructive work, but all the while he is buying guns. I have thought as hard as I can think. I have thought about, for example, anarchy. Not only am I not an anarchist, but I believe in taxes, in very high taxes, and especially in a very high graduated income tax. I realize that a man who believes in taxes cannot pick and choose among them and say he will not spend 50 per cent of them on guns just because he doesn't need guns. I realize that anarchy is unworkable and that that is why the state came into being. And I realize, too, that the state cannot be maintained without its authority's being reposed in its members' representatives. I realize all that. But in this state — and a very good state it is, or was, as states go, or went — I cannot get anybody to represent me. My senators will not represent me. My congressman will not represent me. I am opposed to taxation without representation.

Don't tell me that I am represented by my vote. I voted against the national policy. Having done so, I am constrained in conscience to uphold my vote and not betray it. If my offense is anarchy — which I dislike — I can't help it. If the preservation of society compels me to commit worse evils than anarchy, then the cost of preserving society is too high. Society is not sacred; I am. My first responsibility is not to preserve the state — that is Hitlerism and Stalinism — but to preserve my soul. If you tell me that there is no other way to preserve the state than by the implicit totalitarianism of Rousseau's "general will," I will reply that that is the state's misfortune and men must not accept it. I have surrendered my sovereignty to another Master than the general will — I do not mean to be sanctimonious here — and if the general will does not serve Him it does not serve me or any other man.

In so far as there is any worldly sovereign in the United States, it is not the general will, or the Congress, or the President. It is I. I am sovereign here. I hold the highest office of the land, the office of citizen, with responsibilities to my country heavier, by virtue of my office, than those of any other officer, including the President. And I do not hold my office by election but by inalienable right. I cannot abdicate my right, because it is inalienable. If I try to abdicate it, to the general will, or to my representatives or my ministers, I am guilty of betraying not only democracy but my nature as a man endowed with certain inalienable rights.

I have thought about all this, in the large and in the little. I have thought about my wife and children and my responsibility to them. War will not even save them their lives, not even victorious war this time. And it will lose them their most precious possession, their souls, if they call a man husband and father who has lightly sold his own. I have thought of the fact that better men than I, much better men, disagree with me. That grieves me. But I am not, in this instance, trying to emulate better men.

I have thought about my effectiveness. A man who "makes trouble for himself," as the saying is, is thought to reduce his effectiveness, partly because of the diversion of his energies and partly because some few, at least, of his neighbors will call him a crank, a crook, or a traitor. But I am not very effective anyway, and neither, so far as I can see, is anyone else. If anything is effective in matters of this sort, it is example. I go up and down the land denying the decree of Caesar that all able-bodied men between eighteen and twenty-five go into the killing business and urging such men as are moved in conscience to decline to do so. If a millon young men would decline, in conscience, to kill their fellow men, the government would be as helpless as its citizens are now. Its helplessness then would, I think, be at least as contagious abroad as its violence is now. Other governments would become helpless, including the Russian, and thus would we be able to save democracy at home *and* abroad. Victorious war has failed to do it anywhere.

But how can a million old men who themselves will not decline to hire the killing expect a million young men to do it? How can I urge others to do what I do not care to do myself? Of course the government doesn't want me for military service. I am overage, spavined, humpbacked, bald, and blind. The government doesn't want me. Men are a dime a dozen. What the government wants is my dime to buy a dozen men with. If I decline to buy men and give them guns, the government will, I suppose, force me to. I offer to pay all of my taxes for peaceable purposes, the only purposes which history suggests will defend democracy; the government has, I believe, no way, under the general revenue system, to accept my offer. I like the out-of-doors and I do not want to go to jail. I could put my property in my wife's name and bury my money in a hole or a foreign bank account. But I am not Al Capone. I am, as Veepings himself said of me, an honest man. And I am not mathematically minded; if I did try deceit, I'd be caught.

There is only one other alternative, and that is no alternative either. That is to earn less than $500 a year and be tax-free. I'd be paying taxes anyway on what I bought with $500, but that doesn't bother me, because the issue is not, as long as I am only human, separation from war or any other evil-doing but only as much separation as a being who is only human can achieve within his power. No, the trouble with earning less than $500 a year is that it doesn't support a family. Not a big family like mine. If I were a subsistence farmer I might get by, but I'm a city boy.

I would be hard put to answer if you asked me whether a man should own property in the first place, for a government to tax. If I said, "No, he should not," I should stand self-condemned as a Christian Communist. It is illegal, under the McCarran Act, to be either a Christian *or* a Communist, and I don't want to tangle with both the Internal Revenue Act and the McCarran Act at the same time, especially on the delicate claim to being a Christian. Still, the Christian Gospels are, it seems to me, passing clear on the point of taxes. When the apostle says *both* that "we should obey the magistrates" *and* that "we should obey God rather than man," I take it that he means that we should be law-abiding persons unless the law moves us against the Lord.

The problem goes to the very essence of the relationship of God, man, and the state. It isn't easy. It never was. History, however, is on the side of us angels. The primitive Christians, who were pacifists, refused to pay taxes for heathen temples. They were, of course, outlaws anyway. The early Quakers, who were pacifists, refused to pay tithes to the established church and went to prison. But the war tax problem seems not to have arisen until 1755, when a considerable number of Quakers refused to pay a tax levied in Pennsylvania for the war against the red Indians.

The Boston (and New York and Baltimore and Charleston) "tea parties" of the 1770's were, of course, a vivid and violent form of tax refusal endorsed, to this day, by the Daughters of the American Revolution. Seventy-five years after the Revolution, Henry David Thoreau refused to pay his poll tax because the government was waging both slavery against the Negroes and war against the Mexicans. Thoreau was put in jail overnight, and the next day

The Tribute Money   83

Emerson went over to Concord and looked at him through the bars and said, "What in the devil do you think you're doing, Henry?" "I," said Thoreau, "am being free." So Emerson paid Thoreau's poll tax, and Thoreau, deprived of his freedom by being put out of jail, wrote his essay on civil disobedience. Seventy-five years later, Gandhi read Thoreau's essay and worked it into a revolution. It could happen here, but it won't. The place was propitious for Gandhi, a slave colony whose starving people had no money or status to lose, just as the time was propitious for Thoreau, a time of confidence and liberality arising from confidence. Totalitarianism was unthinkable and parliamentary capitalism was not in danger. The appeal to the rights of man was taken seriously, and McCarthyism, McCarranism, and MacArthurism were all as yet unborn.

I doubt that anybody will be able to bring me more light in this matter than I now have. The light I need will come to me from within or it won't come at all. When George Fox visited William Penn, Penn wanted to know if he should go on wearing his sword. "Wear it," said Fox, "as long as thou canst." I hasten to say that I feel like Penn, not like Fox. I know I can't say that you ought to do what I can't do or that I'll do it if you do it. But I don't know if I can say that you ought to do what I do or even if I ought to do it. I am fully aware of the anomaly of refusing to pay 50 per cent of my taxes when 50 per cent of the 50 per cent I do pay is used for war. I am even fuller aware of the converse anomaly of refusing to pay 50 per cent of my taxes when 50 per cent of the 50 per cent I won't pay would be used for peaceable purposes. In addition, if the government comes and gets it, and fines me, as I suppose it might, it will collect more for war than it would have in the first place.

Worst of all, I am not a good enough man to be doing this sort of thing. I am not an early Christian; I am the type that, if Nero threw me naked into the amphitheatre, would work out a way to harass the lions. But somebody over twenty-five has got to perform the incongruous affirmation of saying, "No," and saying it regretfully rather than disdainfully. Why shouldn't it be I? I have sailed through life, up to now, as a first-class passenger on a ship that is nearly all steerage. By comparison with the rest of mankind, I have always had too much money, too many good jobs, too good a reputation, too many friends, and too much fun. Who, if not I, is full of unearned blessings? When, if not now, will I start to earn them? Somebody will take care of me. Somebody always has. The only thing I don't know is who it is that does it. I know who feeds the young ravens, but I know, too, that the Devil takes care of his own.

I am able to muster two cheers, at the very most, for the government's recent seizure of fifty-four hundred Giant Economy Size jars of Maxwell House Coffee. Or for the government's seizure of anything. I am scared to death, these days, of government. I am so scared of it that, rather than be at its mercy, I would abide the mercilessness of Maxwell House.

I shall be told that I sound like Senator Goldwater, and I shall reply that if I sound like Senator Goldwater, Thomas Jefferson, H. D. Thoreau, and Hugo Black, so much the worse for all of them to be seen in each other's company and mine. Men may be scared to death of government for different reasons, and the issue is not the man but the issue.

The issue here is, on its face, so slight as to have escaped the attention of most of the press, which has a soft spot in its advertising department for Maxwell House anyway. The offending coffee was being sold by the National Tea Company (which apparently sells coffee) at $1.44 for a ten-ounce jar. Right next to it—here lay the offense—was the little old ordinary six-ounce jar at $.75. The government programmed all these complexities into its Giant Economy Size Computer and discovered that the Economy jar was costing the American housewife $.019 per ounce more than the little old ordinary. The government thereupon reached for its gun.

Like the man who held no brief for the buffalo, I do not care whether the House of Maxwell stands or falls. The plight of the helpless little widows and still littler orphans who own its stock,

From the *Progressive*, September, 1962.

preferred and common, leaves me frigid. Let them stew in their own brew. What unravels me — and convulses the gods — is the brand new blessing of government come upon us in the Maxwell House matter. We are now to be saved the trouble of having to divide by ten and six.

Mind you, the hapless housewife, bellowing for help from Washington, was not being sold a ten-ounce jar containing nine ounces, or powdered barnyard for powdered coffee. There was no false bottom, no chemical impurity (at least none charged), no artery-hardening ingredient, in the giant jar that wasn't present in the dwarf. So let there be no moaning at the coffee bar that the housewife can not protect herself without carrying a portable laboratory in her shopping bag. The offense consisted entirely in her being offered an uneconomical article labeled "economical."

The point is what the lawyers call a nice one. Let the defendant take the stand and plead that time is money and the giant jar saves the housewife a trip or two to the store. Or that (as Einstein demonstrates) an erg of energy is worth an ohm of money and toting one ten-ounce jar is more economical of energy than toting one-and-two-thirds six-ounce jars. Or that at current garbage-disposal rates it is cheaper to throw away three big jars than five little ones. I turn aside to dab my eyes and then put it to you, gentlemen *and ladies* of the jury.

Is the buyer no longer to beware — that is, to be aware — of anything? Is government to spare him the rigors of elementary arithmetic? Say it not in Gath. If the consumer is too imbecile to figure out the price of coffee, how much more needful is he of having his hand held by government as he shops for politics and confronts such involved phenomena as radiation fallout, military needs, and civil liberties?

The Maxwell House seizure is "the first such action ever undertaken by the Food and Drug Administration." The FDA was established, you will remember, by the Pure Food and Drug Act of Congress in 1906. Now where is the impurity here? The answer is inescapable: The impurity is the *moral* impurity of calling the uneconomical economical.

The Communists, too, undertake to protect their people from moral impurity. The Communists believe that grown men and women cannot think for themselves in great matters of state. The Food and Drug Administration does not believe that people can think for themselves even in matters of common commercial hokum. The public interest, which government undertakes to protect there and here, is taken to be the interest of fools.

The unending drudgery of the American housewife is beguiled by bargain-hunting. Wherever she turns there are pitfalls awaiting her along the primrose path of free enterprise — and the hot possibility of gulling the gulls herself. The way is beset by con men, sharpies, and sleight-of-hand artists displaying the gadgets — by, in a word, *adulterers*. And it is high adventure.

This was America, where a judicious amalgamation of furniture polish and licorice root was sold the yokels for what ailed them, from falling hair to fallen arches. This was America, where the court held for the defendants in the celebrated prohibition case of the two laddies who ran through the Elks convention train at a quick stop selling "cold tea" at five dollars a pint. (After the train was in motion again the Elks discovered that what they had bought was cold tea.) This was a wicked, wicked America, but the housewife who picked up the cutest little bolero for next to nothing was a girl again.

True, people who couldn't afford a doctor died of quackery. (Now they just die.) But once in a while the sucker got his own back in the big bazaar. And when the plausible stranger in the non-stop collar passed off a fifth ace on him, he smacked his thigh and said, "It does beat the devil," and once in a while it did; or "Live and learn," unless the sugarwater he took for his cancer killed him. It was an America that needed social legislation in those areas where the mature individual could not possibly protect himself without a Doctorate of Biochemistry, or of Fine-Type Reading of Insurance Policies. Outside those areas the individual needed to be smart and was smartened up by progressive exposure to the evils of this melancholy life, Freedom was — and is — risky business. At some point the toddler is released from his father's hand to cross the street on his own; if he isn't, he will toddle to an old, old age.

Democracy is first of all the experience of the individual — and not of his grandfather, who has taken his experience with him. Without this experiential maturation the form of democracy, as we see in the new "democracies," is unsupportable. Government here already deprives us of the political experience of military and foreign policy decisions; a unanimous Congress rubber-stamps the first and the CIA takes care of the second (which we ultimately hear about from Khrushchev). Now, in this small incident of the coffee jars, government proposes to take us back to the most undemocratic institution of them all, the company store, where the slave and the immigrant were deprived of the economic experience of buying for themselves.

Is it really too much to ask the American housewife, who has time to kill, to calculate the price of a household staple? Does she need the colossus of modern government to see her to the store, with a stop-and-go light over every item on the shelves? Is her intelligence too tiny for the big, buzzing confusion of the market place? "Economy size" (when the net weight is specified) is a matter of one's doing just a little commonplace thinking for himself. Let the Food and Drug Administration persuade us that we haven't the intelligence to cope even with Madison Avenue and the FBI will swarm into Greenwich Village.

As John Milton observed a while back, the Government we call upon to fend every evil from us will end by fending every virtue from us, too: "If it comes to prohibiting, there is aught more likely to be prohibited than truth itself." Would we be cribb'd, cabin'd, and confined by regulations put forward (as all regulations always are) under the "general welfare" clause, which, in every country's constitution that has fallen under totalitarianism, is so solemnly invoked to swaddle grown men? If we would be spared the trial of judgment in coffee, we will yet be spared the trial of judgment in doctrine. Why should we torture ourselves with choosing men when we cannot choose among jars? We do not need to go all the way back to Rome to learn that he who wants more government, rather than take time and trouble himself, will wind up with nothing else. My assembled admirers protest with Lincoln in 1862 that it is government's business to do for people what they cannot do for themselves. We are agreed, but are we agreed that people cannot divide by ten and six? This is not 1862. This is 1962, and in 1962 I protest that government everywhere is too big for its breeches and that anything more that people cannot do for themselves is better left undone than done by government.

I know that in our country the old — and most of the young — are victimized by the inhuman conspiracy of the doctors, druggists, and hospitals. Maybe it would be possible for the consumers through co-operatives to destroy it. Maybe it would be necessary to invoke — and, to be sure, enhance — the *negative* power of government to break it open. But the alternative now presented is the subsidy of the racket by the government. Medical insurance is pre-eminently sensible, and if there is no other way to attack the private insurance racket than by the equitable device of taxation, so be it. But let us be careful what we call it, and consider its instrumental character rather than cry it up for political democracy. I am writing these words in Czeckoslovakia, where every last citizen is fully insured against every first and last illness. It is a fine scheme, nonetheless fine because the Communists are for it. But it is not a concomitant of democracy exclusively.

If there is anything that we can do by some other means than government, let's get cracking. Let's finish off Jim Crow, *if we want to*. But as for government's doing anything more for us — at the price it now charges — I bespeak your attention to the belated discovery of Baron von Weizsäcker. Weizsäcker had gone along with the Nazi government as it got bigger and bigger and worse and worse. He hated it, but he could not see how men could get anything good done in any other way. At the end of 1944 he saw the light, and then it was too late: "The only possibility now," he said, "is to resist, resist, resist." Why wait until 1944?

My admirers let out a howl here: Am I comparing our government with the hideous autocracy of Hitler? Don't I know that there are different kinds of government? Indeed I do, and I know that

Germany's was once another kind than it became. Let us leave off, at once and for all, pointing to somebody else's government which is so much worse than ours and, instead, consider government as such and consider whether any government gets much better as it gets much bigger. (Or, indeed, whether any man does.) It is not this government or that one but government itself that seems to get more irresponsible the more responsive it becomes to people's needs. The characteristic development of our time, as of Rome's, is simply this, that the more government "does for the people," the more independent of them and insolent toward them, the more remote from them, the less accessible to them, it becomes. Is there any doubt—forget about Russia—of this here? I think not.

In permitting the Food and Drug Administration to seize these jars of coffee in, of course, the public interest, we are beefing up Big Brother. I say rather be hooked in the supermarket like men — benighted men, I grant you — than let government wheel us through in the cart. And I know that my admirers do not agree with me; they never do; they admire my good looks. And one of them does me the courtesy of putting his anguish in writing: "Would you," he says, "want to go back to the sixty-hour week, child labor, and the sweatshops? Would you want to throw the wilderness open to rape by the timber barons and the mineral monopolies? Would you want to abandon federal subsidy of public housing, public health, education, the indigent aged, the blind, and dependent children? Would you want to fly in uninspected planes, eat in uninspected restaurants, ride in uninspected elevators, drive on privately built highways at any speed or on any side of the road you chose? Would you want to relinquish workmen's compensation, unemployment insurance, and social security because 'anything that the American people cannot do for themselves is better left undone than done by Government'?" He "can't believe" (he goes on to say) "that this is what you mean, and if it is, I think you have gone stark mad and need to be protected from yourself."

I pass over his rhetorical questions (observing, once more, only that I am reading his words in Czechoslovakia, where the government has eliminated all the evils and provided all the blessings he cites, and much more thoroughly than ours has, and that, even so, the arrangement seems to leave a little something to be desired). I advert, instead, to his view that I may need to be protected, not from the timber barons, but from myself. Here is the governmental sentiment in a nutshell. My friend is so exercised by my madness that he wonders if — in my own interest, mind you — I should not be laid away in protective custody.

I exaggerate here, as he does. But I insist that the issue is real. Nor is it one to be resolved by the book, and I should not be allowed to disguise its difficulty by discussing it in terms of a piddling fifty-four hundred jars of pulverized coffee. I should be made to say how much government is too much, how much is too little, and how much is just enough.

There is always a principle buried somewhere, and as principle is the only rational starting point of attitude or action, we ought to unearth it. No sooner do we start digging for this one than, I say, we discover that central to it is the question of when and where.

In 1933 we liberals wanted more government. We felt that the situation was so desperate that we were willing even to let the Leader have a try at the first cousin of the corporative state; he was a good fellow, and he would not do anything that wasn't good for us. And when the Court said no to his corporative state, the Leader was miffed and tried to convert the judiciary into a People's Court. And even at that point there were liberals who thought that that was all right, too — not in Germany or in Italy or in Russia, of course, but only among a truly self-governing people like ourselves. Well, the New Deal got things done in a hurry, a hundred things in a hundred days, and that was the beginning. And they were good and great things like those my admirer writes me about above. They were long overdue. In our eighteenth-century colonial prejudice, we had always had too weak a government. We needed a stronger one, and, brethren, we got it. I put it to you in 1962: How do we like our great big blue-eyed baby now? Is there no one around except me who is persuaded that we've got about all the government we can handle and maybe a little more?

It depends, I say, on when and where. Look you to the instant situation here. The most awful evils of our society just now are

Jim Crowism, know-nothingism, and militarism. They are the most awful because they are the most popular. They are the most popular because they are the most profitable, the first two emotionally, the third economically. If we could get rid of them — just these three evils — nothing serious would stand in the way of our being a successful and benevolent democracy. Why not call upon government to get rid of them? To say that not enough of us find it in our self-interest to do so is only to say that we are to that degree uncivilized. But what is asked here is why people should not invoke government if, instead of being uncivilized, they are civilized. But to the extent that people are civilized they rid themselves of their own vices without calling upon government to compel them to do it. True, the law is a teacher; the Holy Doctor Aquinas himself says so. But the same Doctor says of teaching that the pupil, to be taught, must be docile, that is, he must want to learn. A law which forces its lessons down men's throats — near-beer, for instance — is a law which must either fall or, forcing its lesson, pull freedom down and establish a tyranny. A principle, then, begins to emerge, namely, that government, which is useless (except as a clerk) when men are civilized, is dangerous when men are uncivilized and useful when they want to civilize themselves.

Consider the perfidious Albionese. A few months ago the Royal College of Surgeons urged measures to discourage cigarette-smoking, and the British government at once issued public posters inscribed with statistically graduated black coffins and the words. "The more cigarettes you smoke the greater the risk. You have been warned." Meanwhile (back at the split-level ranch house), five years have passed since the American Cancer Society reported that its study of eight hundred thousand cases "demonstrates beyond a reasonable doubt that cigarette-smoking is the major cause of lung cancer." Now it may be assumed that the British people, like the Americans, cannot stop smoking. But knowing that they are weak-willed — itself a mark of civilization — they call upon government to bully them into doing what they cannot do for themselves. Two immediate reactions (or non-reactions) are seen at once in England. First, neither the British tobacco industry nor the advertising media raise a voice against this intrusion of government upon private enterprise and the still more private right (outside of canon law) to kill one's self as one pleases. Nor, secondly, is there any indication, in or out of Parliament, that any disinterested watchdog of British liberty sees it threatened by this much more government. And yet the powers of government in England (and in Scandinavia and Holland and Switzerland) are incalculably vaster than ours. Why is liberty — civil and political — so much greater in these big government countries than in the United States? The Englishman neither cries "tyranny" where we do nor assaults liberty where we do. Weak-willed and perfidious as he is, he is that civilized that he need not be afraid to instruct government to take an inch lest it take a mile. His devotion to liberty permits him to establish a government-owned broadcasting system, knowing that its programs will be the fairest in the world. Neither is there any possibility that anyone will get a job in the government-owned railways of Switzerland because his uncle is an official of the party in power.

I submit that the more civilized men are — that is, the less government they need — the more they can safely invoke. The Englishman can do with a little more government, if he thinks he needs it. We, like the Russians, cannot, or it will gobble up everything in sight. Turn the Marines loose on Mississippi — where there is less liberty than in Czechoslovakia — and you will have turned them loose on a Marine-prone America. And where that is the case, there's a fatal joker — apart from the money it costs — in the Giant Economy Size Government.

I do not know whether it is treasonable to discourage recruitment for the United States Army in peacetime — I don't even know if this is peacetime — but one way to find out whether an act is treasonable is to commit it and see what happens; which, with your kind permission, I shall proceed to do here.

We Americans (we Americans all tell each other) are a peace-loving people. We are not fazed by the fact that we have horned into every war within reach since the republic was established. Neither are we fazed by the further fact that we have always been a nation of pistol-packin' papas with a record of private and public shooting, slugging, mayhem, assault, battery, contusions, abrasions, lynching, and vigilantism unmatched by any people who come readily to mind except, perhaps, the ancient Cossacks. We go right on teling each other that we are a peace-loving people.

But what is honored in a country, as Homer says, will be cultivated there; and, as Homer's cousin, Scott Nearing, points out, the one profession which we cultivate as a nation is war. In no other occupation in America, including schoolteaching and statesmanship, is a man guaranteed, at public expense, lifelong food, clothing, shelter, medical care, and when the long life is over, burial. Only the soldier is thus honored in America; only war is thus cultivated by us peace-loving Americans.

In order to entice young men into war, we peace-loving Americans have found it necessary, after losing two world wars in succession, to up the ante. In my Capone days, it cost two hundred

From the *Progressive*, September 22, 1947.

fifty to five hundred dollars, around Taylor and Halsted, to hire a young man to kill a party unknown to him. We peace-loving Americans now pay seventy-five dollars a month, for life, to young men merely *willing* to kill parties unknown to them. The occupational hazards are the same, whether the young men work for Uncle Scarface or Uncle Sam, but the legal hazards are different. Uncle Scarface's hired killer is subject to the Hot Seat, or Old Smoky, if he gets caught at his work, while Uncle Sam's is subject to the Congressional Medal of Honor, plus ticker tape, pension, and puttees. And the seventy-five dollars is regular, while the two hundred fifty to five hundred dollar piecework comes and goes.

The slogan at the recruiting stations is "The Army Builds Men," and since the recess in hostilities following Nagasaki, approximately one million men have been found who want to be built by the army. The slogan is a scream. It's as if the state penitentiary advertised free steak dinners without specifying that in order to be eligible you had to be scheduled to be hanged the next morning. What the army builds is one-legged men, blind men, armless men, paralyzed men, psychotic men, and dead men.

The slogan is, in this great land of slogans, even more crooked than that. The condemned convict actually gets the steak dinner, but the soldier, who is ultimately going to get his head full of holes, does not even get built into a man in the intervening period.

One way in which the army builds men is to put them into an environment where the venereal disease rate is 29.6 cases per 1,000, compared with 5.1 among civilians. (The navy builds even handsomer men, with a venereal rate of 85.8.) These, by the way, are peacetime rates. Peacetime admission of civilians to mental hospitals are 299.1 per 100,000; of soldiers, 950. Peacetime civilian suicides are 14.2 per 100,000; peacetime soldier suicides, 29.

Now we peace-loving Americans know all these things about army life, and have always known them. We know that if a soldier is not a bum, it's only because he was fortified against being a bum before he ever entered the army. But we Americans love war so much that we are willing to lie to our young men in order to persuade them to be killers.

The army builds dead men and has never built anything else — any army, anywhere in the history of the world. The proper business of every army everywhere is killing. Its proper business is not physical training, or education, or travel, or companionship, or the life of Reilly; it is killing. Killing, and nothing else, is what the army is for, and the only thing it can properly build is killers and killees.

Since the army does not build men, nobody who wants to be a man should ever join the army. Anybody who wants to be a man should keep out of the army, whatever else he may do. Since a man does not run away, he should not run away from the army. He should fight it.

The army is hard to fight because it does not fight fair. Take Secretary of War Patterson. Testifying in behalf of peacetime conscription — or, as Mr. Truman suggested it be called, "universal training" — Secretary Patterson said, "Young men from our cities and industrial centers would live together with those from farm, forest, and plain. Sectional prejudices and misunderstandings would be replaced by the spirit of tolerance and mutual respect that is the essence of our democracy." But if that is the case, then, as the National Council against Conscription points out, Hitler's army was democratic, Mussolini's army was democratic, and slavery is democratic. Secretary Patterson does not fight fair, and, since he is a graduate of an expensive university, he knows that he doesn't fight fair. The only possible inference is that he doesn't care. The army will say anything in order to get young men to kill and be killed.

Power has not saved us from our troubles, which increase with every increase of our power. We are now the most powerful nation on earth — indeed, if we still have the exclusive possession of the atomic bomb, the only powerful nation on earth — and we are not saved. Our hope now, however unrealistic it may appear, is to get rid of our power, no matter what any other nation does with its, and locate a substitute that will save us.

I suggest, and not humbly, that the substitute is Men, Men consecrated to the Manly virtues of wisdom, temperance, fortitude, and justice. Such men, if they want to join the army, may join the army of the Lord. The rations are short, and the work hard, but it is Men's work and not beasts', and the eternal reward is said to be more enjoyable than seventy-five dollars a month or two hundred fifty to five hundred dollars a murder.

It is no longer considered alarmist to assert that this is the eleventh hour; for all any of us know, the fifty-ninth minute. Our government — which was once our mere minister — will tell us nothing. By way of telling us nothing, it repeats the gigantic historical falsehood that the way to keep out of war is to be strong. But our physicists tell us that the way to be dead is to be strong. We shall go out with neither a bang nor a whimper but in a cloud of deadly dust. We shall have the satisfaction of destroying the Russians, only we shall not be here to have it.

World government has not arrived in time to save us — as if any government could save us from ourselves — and there is no sign that it will. Its advocates are doomed to live and die as servants of of the sovereignty they deplore. When the bugle blows, they are doomed to fall in line behind the sovereign flag of their sovereign state and annihilate the world government advocates of other sovereign states who have fallen in line behind their sovereign flags. This, to paraphrase the vulgar railroad joke, is a hell of a way to run a world government movement.

The pacifist does not understand the non-pacifist advocates of world government. He knows that they are men of good will. But he does not know what makes them think that there are so many of them that half of them can be spared to kill the other half. He does not understand them. He does not understand them when they say that world government depends upon world community. If world government depends upon world community, the thing to do is build the world community for the world government to depend upon. The second thing a member of a community does is codify his surrender

From *Common Cause*, May, 1950.

of his sovereignty over the lives of his fellow members; the first thing he does is surrender it. This the pacifist does. He has taken the initial step to create the world community. He believes in world government so fervently that he will not live in voluntary violation of its first requirement.

No advocate of world government is impressive waving a petition in one hand and a sovereign sword in the other other. Having put up the sword, the pacifist may be unimpressive, too, but there is no danger of his being misunderstood. He advocates world government not with one hand but with two. The non-pacifist is bound to be misunderstood by the heathen Chinese — and the infidel Russian — as he stretches out the petition to them and they ask, they of little faith, "But brother, why do you keep your other hand behind your back?"

The pacifist advocate of world government is not a better man than the non-pacifist but only a wiser. He knows that "states are not made of oak and rock, but of the human natures that are in them." He knows that as the men are, so will the state and the world state be. So he goes to work on the men, beginning with the man who is easiest to reach and hardest to work on — himself. It is uphill work, but he remembers the Talmud: he is expected neither to complete the task nor abandon it.

In the absence of the state, men must go to war when they hate. But as long as men hate more than they love, they will go to war, to the war of states or, if there is only one state, to civil war. So the pacifist tries to stop hating, knowing that hate overtakes men faster than petitions; knowing, too, that if he proves that he can overcome (or just subdue or sublimate) his hate, he will have imitators who, like him, are hungry for love, and some sunny day, centuries away, but centuries closer than petitions, the men of the world will say to one another, "With all our infirmities, we love each other more than we hate each other. We have a community. Let us give it a government." First the Mayflower, and then the Mayflower Compact.

"You can do anything with bayonets," said Talleyrand, "except sit on them." The pacifist is not satisfied with long or short truces; he does not want to measure his life by its length. And he knows that men who simply cannot give up weapons simply cannot give up war.

He has seen too many alcoholics go on the wagon carrying a flask in case of snake bite. He has seen too many agonized Augustines take leave of their mistresses "soon, soon, but not yet." He has seen too many New Year's Morning penitents. He has seen them and been them — he is no better than the non-pacifist — but he knows something the non-pacifist doesn't. He knows that men can change their condition.

The non-pacifist does not seem to believe that men can change their condition, but he wants these same men, he among them, to change their situation. He is suffering from what Freud should have called, instead of compulsive neurosis, cart-and-horse trouble. What he has got to seek first he believes will be added unto him. I do not speak here of the bogus advocate of world government, who simply wants to live and doesn't care how; who thinks that world government will save his 6 per cent gold debentures from the Russians and that, once he is saved from the Russians, somebody will find a way to save him from the worms. The bogus advocate is irrelevant here, though he may constitute a substantial proportion of the world government membership organizations. I speak here only of the genuine advocates of world government. The genuine advocates divide not on the issue of dying but of killing.

There is no time left to be utopian. Violence has failed even those who have used it most successfully. After two victorious world wars for democracy, there is less democracy in the world than there was before they started. We cannot afford even to win again. In 1918 and again in 1945 we destroyed Prussianism — whose root evil, said Woodrow Wilson, is peacetime conscription — but the Prussianism entered our soul. We tell ourselves that Stalin would overrun our country and destroy our liberties, forgetting, as the Danes under Hitler did not, that there is nothing that Stalin can do to us that we cannot do to ourselves more easily. Hitler indeed imposed Prussianism on us, but he was beaten and dead when he did it.

The pacifist is not a better man than the non-pacifist but only a wiser one. The non-pacifist thinks that men have to choose between the evils that are visited upon them. He does not seem to understand that the choice is not of evil but of evil-doing. He casts out love with fear of the greater evil and recommends the lesser evil, which always turns out, in the end, to be war, which always turns out, in the end, to be futile. The Devil is a traveling man, and his disposition does not improve with punishment. Hitler was nastier than Hohenzollern, and Stalin shows tendencies to be even nastier, if possible, than Hitler. When *they* lose, they win. When *we* win, we lose. Hitler fought for the "heartland" and proposed to pick up the "world island" in a century; five years after the destruction of Hitler, Stalin has nine-tenths of the "heartland" and half of the "world island" besides.

The pernicious doctrine of the lesser evil, justifying, as it does, every evil because there is always one greater, never meant anything more than worsening one's lot a little more slowly than otherwise. But the gap between the lesser and the greater has closed, more rapidly than the advocates of the lesser ever supposed it would. Mr. Truman's allocation of 71 per cent of the national budget to war makes a peacemonger out of Bismarck.

We are trying to keep our eye on the ball here. We do not want to chase the Devil from Berlin to Moscow, and then maybe back to Berlin, or to Washington. We do not want to gratify our indignation, however righteous. We do not want to avenge the dead; the dry bones of six million Jews did not come to life when Ribbentrop's neck broke. What we want is a world fit to live in.

"World peace requires world law," says one of the distinguished non-pacifist advocates of world government. We wait for him to tell us what world law requires, but we wait in vain. World law is to spring full-panoplied from the brow of Moloch, to be codified by men whose ace-in-the-hole is always uniformed genocide. These good men are bad logicians. "Justice versus Force, Peace embattled against War," says one of them. But Peace and War are contradictories, while Justice and Force, as they speak of Justice, are not contradictories or even contraries. When they equate Force with War, without separating Force from Justice, they embarrass themselves. The pacifist insists upon realism. The realistic alternative to force is not world government, which not only could be a tryanny but, in the present pattern of events, would be likely to be. Neither is it the advocacy of world government while the advocates are armed to the teeth with sensitive explosives. The only alternative to force, which does not convince, is love, which does. And if love faileth in ninety-nine cases out of a hundred, it is still more convincing than force, which approaches the end of its history as a total loss. In the end, the commandment to love our enemies — "If ye love them which love you, where is your reward; do not even the publicans do the same?" — turns out to be the law of temporal no less than eternal life.

One of the original distinguished non-pacifist advocates of world government used to say it would come in five hundred years. He seems to think that new bombs have expedited its advent. He ought to know better. As a psychologist and sportsman, he ought to know that antagonists of approximately the same size have never yet been bombed into brotherhood, or even durably terrified. If at the close of the third world war there are two men left in the world, they will need each other, but they will not be in a mood to know it. Bombs are irritants. If true world government was five hundred years away ten years ago, it is five thousand years away now.

The pacifist cannot wait five thousand years, or even five hundred, for his sovereign state to relieve him of the obligation to kill the people of other sovereign states for no other reason than that they are the people of other sovereign states. The only excuse for the existence of separate sovereign states is geography. Geography no longer exists. World government is not only a logical but a historical necessity. But it does not come, and it will not come, until we want it. And we will not want it until we are prepared to pay the price it requires. Of all the patented world government organizations, the only one that appears to be aware that the price is excruciatingly high is the Committee To Frame a World Constitution. It is, for that reason, the least popular of all of them.

"Associate yourselves together, O ye people, and ye shall be broken in pieces; associate yourselves together, O ye people, and ye shall be broken in pieces." Men like us cannot have a world government in a world like this or even secure the blessings of the government we have. Our hands are full of blood. We are prepared, and preparing, to stain them further. We are the haves, and we want to hang on to what we have. We cannot. What we have, and have stumbled on or stolen, is not ours. It is God's, and we withhold it from the poor. These Hitlers and Stalins are the scourges of God — woe unto them, too, O rods of His anger — and we shall be scourged until we surrender to God what we have for distribution to the poor. This is the way to be saved, and from this way we young men of many riches turn sorrowfully and cock our pistols.

We advocates of world government — except for the pacifist advocates — are prepared to shed the rest of the world's innocent blood if our movement fails, and that is why our movement will fail. We will then say that we have no choice, but when Field Marshal Keitel said the same thing, we hanged him at Nürnberg. If we insist that German and Japanese — and, I suppose, Russian — persons have choice, then we must insist that American persons have choice, too. Instead, we insist that we haven't. We want a world government of free men when we are unwilling to be free men ourselves. When we are told to kill, we kill. "What choice have we?" says one of the non-pacifist advocates of world government who dabbles in hydrogen bombs on the side. "I am only a soldier," said Keitel. We are willing slaves, and the last full measure of our devotion to freedom consists in a petition to the tyrant.

The abdication of self-government is the quintessence of communism and fascism. The slaves of communism and fascism can pass the buck to their rulers. But the American doctrine, so vigorously asserted at Nürnberg, is that men are by nature free and therefore by nature responsible for their public, no less than their private, acts. The state as an organism is denied; the tyrant as the repository of its responsibility is repudiated. Governments are representative, and whatever they do they do because their responsible constituents order or consent to it. The man who shucks his responsibility finds himself shucked of his freedom.

It is fashionable, in world government circles, to throw rocks at those non-profit merchants of death, the physicists. The physicists are not heroic. But what of the rest of us? The physicists happen to have been called up first in the brave new genocidal world. A few of them squeal and squirm, but in the end they do as they're told. But, again, what of the rest of us? Just exactly what will the non-pacifist non-physicist advocates of world government do if Russia rejects the most acceptable of their propositions? Will their answer be yea, yea, or nay, nay? Will they kill their fellow-advocates of world government in other countries, or won't they? Or can it be that they actually suppose that they will not have to cross that bridge until they come to it? Now they say, "We can't win the next war," and indeed, they use this as their recruiting slogan for world government, but then they will wage it, and they will stop saying we can't win it or be had up for interference with recruitment for the armed forces. The chips are down for the physicists now. When the chips are down for the non-pacifist non-physicist advocates of world government, they will buy the bombs that the physicists are making and go for a ride on them. Like the Germans, they will obey the law of the land, though, unlike the Germans, they have already illegitimized it.

The issue, in the end, is one which nobody but a negativist really enjoys, and none of us wants to be a negativist. The issue, in the end, is resistance. Resistance is the last of a man's acts, but it is implicit in all the rest. He needs to know the end in the beginning; he needs to know the answer to the question, "Where will I say 'No'?" so that he can remind himself of the answer when the time comes to make it. The end is not yet, but we can hardly suppose that there will be time to steel ourselves when it comes; the tragedy of the German churches under Hitler should be instructive.

Since violent resistance is demonstrably futile, the only alternative, in the end, is non-violent resistance. Resistance is hard to come by; the physicists have discovered that it was easier to break down the atom's than to make their own. Non-violent resistance is hardest of all to come by and requires the hardest preparation. Non-violence — the last great affirmation of saying "No" — has been generally attacked, in the nineteen centuries since its invention, as a spectacular simplification. We have arrived at a spectacularly simplified situation in which he who takes up the sword is at that instant defenseless.

No man can extricate himself from war, but any man can extricate himself from the intention to make it. The Holy Roman Empire, the Congress of Vienna, and the League of Nations did not disarm the world by a single man. The United Nations has not disarmed the world by a single man. But any single advocate of true world government can do more than alll these false world governments ever did. He can disarm the world by a single man and, perhaps, by his example, by one or two more.

"What good would it do?" says the non-pacifist, and so, because he cannot do good (by which he means changing the course of history), he accepts the lesser evil of enrolling one man, himself, in the world's evil-doing. He cannot make a move to extricate himself, not from war, but from making war. He wants peace, but he cannot drop his gun to go and get it. Between the greater and the lesser evils he is doing a bubble dance on a bed of deadly coals. Sooner or later, unless he asserts his responsibility to govern himself, he will be taken off his blistered feet and put to work developing a callus on his trigger finger.

At bottom the non-pacifist is sick with the slavish sickness of the world. His faith has failed him. He does not believe in God's power to heal man's wounded nature, and so he settles for the wounded nature and says, as if the wound had not been dealt in the first place, "But this is the way men are. The best we can do is organize to protect ourselves from each other," and then the war starts over the delicate question of who is to organize the protection. The non-pacifist advocate of world government is, whether he knows it or not, at the end of the humanist trail; only man and the machine he has made are left, and maybe man can pull a god out of the machine.

How can men who do not — and with reason — believe in men continue to worship the work of men's hands and suppose that still more of it is enough to save them? How, in the time of the end, can they still suppose that the City of Man will be built by men unaided? How can they suppose that they can love Stalin — whom they have so much *reason* to hate — without being lifted up by a stronger power than reason? Who do they think they are? Do they think that human life is a human achievement? Do they think they can stop the destruction of the world or start its creation? Do they think that the Voice out of the Whirlwind is the Voice of America?

The non-pacifist world government movement has been a diversion, in both popular senses of that term. It has been educational, to be sure, but the seeds of its death were within it and now they are sprouting. Its adherents were honorable, energetic, and even consecrated men, but they should have allocated their energies more shrewdly so as not to be caught unprepared when the movement fails. The twentieth century is not the nineteenth. The atomic age is running out. Fabianism, as it has been too much and too soon for a world sick with slavishness, has been too little and too late for men who must choose not what will be done to them — their choice there is illusory — what what they will do to others.

The reason there has never been a just war — though wars have been fought for just causes — is that war requires the annihilation of the innocent and justice forbids it. Modern war requires the annihilation of whole communities of innocents, and the machinery of modern war enables a surprising number of the guilty to get away, as witness Hitler, Himmler, Goebbels, and Göring. If there never was a just war, there never will be now. The pacifist advocate of world government is passionate about justice because he knows that world government must be just. He and the non-pacifist both want justice, but only the pacifist will refuse to commit the extreme injustice, namely the annihilation of the innocent, in the pursuit of their common objective. The pacifist does not see how he can bring justice to the world by bringing injustice to it. Nor does he see how he can export what he hasn't got. So he sets about trying to get what he hasn't got. What he seeks is the good which alone is within a man's own power. Knowing that he cannot avoid suffering injustice, he seeks to avoid committing it. He really believes that he is a little lower than the angels, who neither suffer nor commit injustice, and a little higher than the brutes, who do both.

The world government movement will disintegrate as the world war movement accelerates. Only the wildest utopian could have supposed that the dream would never end. But the end is in sight. War will come faster than world government — and neither in spite of nor because of the efforts of pacifists or non-pacifists — and at the end of the war there will be a bit of charcoal to constitutionalize.

The case is a hard one. It is next to impossible. But it is not impossible. Ancient Sodom was not to have been saved by a majority vote or a constitutional convention or a neatly balanced stockpile of spears, and neither is modern Sodom. We are only pretty sure that the world will be destroyed; until it is we won't know for certain, and then we certainly won't know. In the time that we have, we can build. But we will have to begin with the building blocks. We can neither talk nor shoot nor legislate ourselves en masse into the world state we seek. We shall have to come up the hard way, building the men who build the state and struggling to preserve the means we still have, at least in America, for building the men.

The non-pacifist world government movement would have disintegrated, as a mass campaign, at the beginning instead of at the end of its history if it had asserted the first principle of world or any other kind of government. The movement had to hang on to its guns in order to get the adherence of those who hang on to their guns. It sought millions; it got a few thousand. In the end, it will have hundreds, or tens, and the difference between the ten pacifists and the ten non-pacifists, in terms of political effectiveness, will be inconsequential. Both groups will be forcibly silenced if they persist in their folly. The pacifists will persist. The non-pacifists who intend to persist might well ponder the minor indignity of being hanged for goats instead of for sheep.

Our country's official behavior everywhere in the world and in every realm of activity — including the Marshall Plan, excused as a currency deal and used as an open bribe — is evidence that our official heart is hardened. Our doors are closed to the innocent victims of Hitler and Stalin. We are prepared to exterminate more innocent Russians than the Nazis did innocent Jews. The official proclamation will be the same: "They attacked us. We had to defend ourselves." The Nazis knew better, and so do we. And so do the Russians. On August 8, 1945, the hand that held the dagger plunged it into its neighbor's back. Our ally Russia attacked our enemy Japan. The crime was instigated by the United States government at Yalta. The assassin's price was the instigator's admission that a little thing like Christian morality would never stand between them. What our government needs, in order to distinguish itself from the

Russian, is Christian morality. It cannot get Christian morality on its own without being unconstitutional; it will have to get the consent of the governed first.

The problem is the same as it was in Eden and in Egypt. The problem of changing the world is the problem of changing our own hearts. The pacifist advocate of world government knows where to begin in order to reach the objective that both he and the non-pacifist seek. He is the realist and, in so far as random activity is no activity, the activist of the world government movement. The pacifist is not better than the non-pacifist; indeed, his life is a greater hypocrisy than his less ambitious neighbor's, and he knows it. The man who wants to be perfect commits the sin of Lucifer if he thinks that perfection is within a man's power. But it wasn't Lucifer who told him to be perfect even as his Father in heaven is perfect. The perfectionist does not live up to his faith — but at least he has it. Therein is his chance, and if his faith doesn't fail him, he can bear up under the small penalty of being called, and rightly, a hypocrite. He would rather grind his own teeth than other men's faces.

The revolution of redemptive love is the only one that is radical. The rest have all been tried and tried and tried and have failed. They failed because the means they used consumed the end they sought; men who will do anything to win a garden will win a desert and die there. The radical revolution of pacifism is the American way, and the only American way, if America wants to be a Christian country.

Before the Second World War — and the First — the pacifists said that our country was morally unprepared for victory. They were called Cassandras and, like Cassandra, they were unattractive at court. But like her, they were right. Their way may not work today, or tomorrow, or in ten thousand years. But we will never know until we try. The only thing we know for sure is that the non-pacifist way to peace — and to world government — is unworkable. There is no way to peace; peace itself is the way, and the man who will not make it now will find it much harder to make it when the bugle calls. The choice is as old as Socrates of Athens:

"He will gladly accept and enjoy such honors as he deems likely to make him a better man; but those, whether private or public, which are likely to disorder his life, he will avoid."

"Then, if that is his motive, he will not be a statesman."

"By the dog of Egypt, he will! In the city which is his own, he certainly will, though in the land of his birth perhaps not, unless he have a divine call."

"I understand; you mean that he will be a ruler in the city of which we are the founders, and which exists in idea only; for I do not believe that there is such a city anywhere on earth."

"In heaven," I replied, "there is laid up a pattern of it, methinks, which he who desires may behold, and beholding, may set his own house in order. But whether such a city exists, or ever will exist in fact, is no matter; for he will live after the manner of that city, having nothing to do with any other."

THE
DUTY OF
FREEDOM

I come to you today as the highest official of the United States of America. My title is Citizen, and as such, I am the American sovereign. I wish to speak to you, in my official capacity, on the rights of a sovereign Citizen and his duties.

Hitler deprived you and your fathers of the rights of Citizens, and so would Stalin. Hitler assigned you and your fathers duties unbecoming a Citizen, and so would Stalin. If you wish to be a Citizen, you must never let any ruler or any government, German, Russian, or American, act upon you in any way except as your faithful servant.

My rights and duties as a sovereign Citizen do not come from government. They come from God. The purpose, and the only purpose, of government is to secure them to me. And so I must oppose any government, even my own, if it violates those rights or degrades those duties. If I did not, I would not be a good American. I would not be a sovereign Citizen.

Your situation, not as Germans, but as children of God, is identical with mine. Your rights and duties come to you in the same way as mine. They are inalienable and non-transferable. They cannot be turned over to a representative unless he is bound to represent you. Your representatives in the Bundestag are not bound to represent you. Neither are mine in the American Congress. A sovereign Citizen, in case his representatives should ever fail to represent him, must always be prepared to represent himself. It is my right as a

A speech delivered in German, April 6, 1952, at a Hessian youth rally, sponsored by the Darmstadt Action Group, in Offenbach, a suburb of Frankfurt am Main, West Germany. It was later printed in English in *Fellowship* (published by the Fellowship of Reconciliation), April, 1953.

Citizen to speak my mind and my conscience, no matter whether my fellow Citizens are pleased with me at the moment. This right cannot be circumscribed by the national interest, by the national security, or even by the national survival, because it does not come to me from the nation.

I cannot believe that it is important that a nation survive just because it is now surviving. No nation has ever survived very long, and the first historian, Herodotus, observed that even in his time those nations which were then great had been nothing, while those which were then nothing had once been great. Nor can I believe that it is important that Germans, or Americans, or Russians survive just because they are now surviving. None of us survives very long in any case. What is important is the *way* in which we survive and the way in which we cease to survive. What is important are the rights and duties of Citizens. What is important, in one word, is God.

My duty to God compels me to love my brothers — in the East Zone, in the West Zone, in America, in Russia, whether or not they love me. My duty to love my brothers compels me not to kill them or their children, or to prepare to kill them, even if they kill me. The World Council of Churches, after reading the Ten Commandments and the Sermon on the Mount, has recently discovered that war is contrary to the will of God and to the spirit of Jesus Christ. If this is a valid discovery — and I take it to be — it follows that men who do not want to violate the will of God and the spirit of Christ must not and will not make war, or prepare to make war, even if others make war on them.

I do not know how to solve the East-West problem, though I wish I did. I do not have the power to solve it, which perhaps is just as well, since I do not have the knowledge. I do not want the Russians to remain in East Germany. I do not want the Americans to remain in West Germany. If I were a German, and I had the unpleasant choice of one or the other, I would certainly prefer to live under the American. That may be a purely local prejudice on my part, but I think that the choice is a clear one. The West Germans live pretty well under the Americans, all in all. But if they had not resisted the

American invasion in 1944 and 1945, they would have lived still better. On the same basis, it seems to me fair to predict that if the Russians invade you, they will treat you worse if you have resisted them. They have reason enough to be impatient with you already, because of your country's relations with them between 1941 and 1945. You are, of course, aware that militarily you cannot turn back either the Russians *or* the Americans; militarily you can merely complete the destruction of your country.

I do not, as I say, have either the knowledge or the power to solve the East-West problem, nor have I seen anyone who has. But as a sovereign Citizen, and a sovereign Citizen by virtue of my relation to God, I do have to try to solve the problem of living and dying as God wants me to. This problem, and this problem alone, is within my power. This power no man and no government can ever take from me. Any government can kill me — so can any streetcar — but no government can make me kill. Any government can oppress me, but no government can make an oppressor of me. Any government can treat me godlessly, but no government can make me godless. Only I can do that.

I am told that Stalin is the Antichrist. Ten years ago I was told that Hitler was the Antichrist. Though I did not like Hitler, I was skeptical then. Though I do not like Stalin, I am skeptical now. The reason that I was and am skeptical is that every time we kill the Antichrist and bomb his cities and burn up his people, he turns up somewhere else with a still bigger army. I cannot believe that Christ cannot destroy Antichrist, and that is why I cannot believe that everybody I deplore is the Antichrist.

We Americans did not come to Germany to teach the Germans how to prepare for war or prosecute it. The Germans were already expert at that. We did not come to Germany in order to enable Germany to survive. If that had been our purpose, we would have let Hitler alone. What we came to Germany to do was to bestow the blessings of freedom on the Germans. Ours was a noble purpose; we were, with our fanatical faith in freedom, well suited to be its ambassadors; and the Germans needed faith in freedom worse than any people I have ever seen. But freedom and militarism do not go well together. It was militarism, long before Hitler, that stifled freedom in Germany. And militarism has always led to war. It led the Germans to war twice within my lifetime. It has always led everybody to war. It always will. Americans are now embracing it, in a big way, and unless they relinquish it, it will lead them to war, too. I am happy to be able to report that the American Congress recently succeeded in defeating the proposal of full peacetime conscription in America. It was peacetime conscription that the late President Wilson in 1919 called "the root evil of Prussianism." In 1919 President Wilson was right.

Tyranny can afford another war, but freedom cannot. It is not that freedom cannot afford to lose another war but, rather, that freedom cannot even afford to win. After two victorious world wars to preserve freedom, freedom is somewhat less well preserved than it was before those two victorious world wars began. Even in America we are afraid of losing our freedom, if not from without, then from within. Look at the world of 1952, and look at the world of 1913, and you will ask yourselves who won, freedom or tyranny?

There has never been an occasion in human history, from the time of the Medes and the Persians, when an armaments race between two great powers, face to face and alone in the world, has not led to war. As a patriotic American I labor, even at the risk of a little unpopularity, to save my country — not from the deadly peril of defeat in war, but from the still deadlier peril of war itself. We should have learned, in our time, that war is self-defeating and victory an illusion. If you ask my fellow Americans — as I do — what they have won in two victorious world wars, you will find them hard put for an answer. In 1945 President Truman said that another war would be the end of civilization. In 1945, President Truman was right.

Freedom and war do not go well together. Every time freedom wins a war, it loses some of itself. But every time tyranny loses a war, it wins. The reason, I think, is that freedom thrives on confidence and love, while tyranny thrives on hopelessness and hate. War is the parent, as well as the offspring, of tyranny. And if you do not like communism — as I fervently hope you do not — you should observe the historical fact that the more war there is, the more communism there is, no matter who wins or loses the war.

If you want your country to be free — and I know you do — you must first be free yourselves. Countries do not make men free; men make countries free. You must free yourselves, and thus your country, from fear and hate and despair. Atlantic Charters cannot free you from these mortal evils. You must free yourselves from them, and you must not wait for official permission. If you do not dare now to be free, you will never make your country free or keep it free, and in the end, you will suffer the worst fate of all: you will come to love your chains and be satisfied with your slavery.

I beg you not to let yourselves be distracted by false dichotomies. You will be asked if you prefer to live on your knees or die on your feet. The dichotomy is false. The question should be: Do you prefer to live on your knees or kill your brother? You will be asked whether you prefer liberty or death. The dichotomy is false. The question should be: Do you prefer killing to dying? I beg you not to let yourselves be distracted by false dichotomies and by frivolous, utopian alternatives.

If you ask me what you should do if your government, or any other government, including the Russian or the American, tries to militarize you, I will reply with one question and with one warning. My question is: Do you want to be slaves or Citizens? If, like us Americans, you choose to be Citizens, no government, including the German, the Russian, or the American, can ever compel you to pick up a gun. My warning is this: The International Military Tribunal at Nürnberg hanged some of your fellow Germans because they obeyed laws which men in conscience should never obey. The United States and the Soviet Union, sitting together in the International Military Tribunal, asserted the moral responsibility of the individual citizen to maintain his individual sovereignty, even against his own government when his own government orders him to commit a crime against humanity. War is one of the crimes against humanity, and as Georges Clemenceau said, it is the cause of all the rest. As the highest official of the United States of America — in my official capacity of Citizen — I leave you with that question and that warning. As Citizen, deriving my rights and duties not from government but from God. I leave you with the lesson of Nürnberg, the Ten Commandments, and the Sermon on the Mount.

PART THREE

THE
VESTIGE
OF GOD

THE IDEA
OF THE
AMERICAN FRIENDS
SERVICE COMMITTEE

Governments, like clocks, go from the motion men give them, and as governments are made and moved by men, so by them they are ruined too. Wherefore governments rather depend upon men than men upon governments. Let men be good, and the government cannot be bad; if it be ill, they will cure it. But, if men be bad, let the government be ever so good, they will endeavor to warp and spoil it to their turn. . . . Good laws may want good men and be abolished or evaded by ill men; but good men will never want good laws or suffer ill ones. . . .

— WILLIAM PENN
Preface to *The Frame of Government*
of Pennsylvania (1862)

I have with me this morning a proverb smuggled in from the Chinese mainland. The proverb is: When you bow, bow low. I take this occasion to bow low to the American Friends Service Committee. Not to its staff; that I cannot, in pride of place, bring myself to do. After all, a man who in some way has been connected with an institution during half of its life must be reckoned among its elders. My gray hairs commend me to your respect, not you to mine.

I bow low, then, to the disembodied spirit of the Service Committee — a spirit most marvelously disembodied in its staff. As an independent entrepreneur I have had some association with the Container Corporation of America, and I can testify that its employees are, on the whole, much more selflessly dedicated to the organization's purpose than the employees of the Service Committee are; and the former achieve their purpose much more regularly than the latter. In terms of production and distribution, too, the Corporation

An address given before the staff of the American Friends Service Committee in Philadelphia, February 10, 1958.

119

seems to me to have the edge on the Committee. True, the Corporation uses the more responsive ingredient — pasteboard. The Committee uses a resistant ingredient — men. Perhaps I should add that the Corporation's purpose is the production of empty boxes; the Committee's is the worship of God.

Your admirer Robert Hutchins once said to me, when he was young and I was much younger, "A university is a wonderful place. The faculty is terrible, the students are terrible, the courses are terrible, and the graduates are terrible. But a university is a wonderful place because the idea of a university is a wonderful idea." The idea of a university is crystallized in the motto of the university in which Robert Hutchins made this statement. Its motto is: "Let knowledge grow from more to more, and so be human life enriched." And even while he was making this statement, that same university was engaged in the achievement of a controlled nuclear chain reaction. The human life of Hiroshima has not been enriched.

The idea of a university is not a wonderful idea, because the assumption beneath it is false. We should have known this when my ancestor Isaiah said of his countrymen, "They are wise to do evil, but to do good they have no knowledge." We should have known this when your ancestor Augustine said of himself, "See how these simple spirits storm the gates of heaven, while we with all our learning are stuck fast in the mud of earth." In the past six months we Americans have discovered that there is no connection between knowledge and morality, that political slaves make just as good scientists as political freemen, and that freedom does not produce technological and inventive superiority. The corollaries of this discovery are irresistible: Freedom is superfluous (if not an actual handicap) in the production of the knowledge necessary for survival. If, therefore, what the American people want is survival, they should hasten to scuttle freedom and pursue knowledge.

The idea of a university is not a wonderful idea. Knowledge without God enriches war. With God, even ignorance enriches peace. The Service Committee can, in its ignorance, be trusted with knowledge because the Service Committee worships God. The idea of the Service Committee is the wonderful idea. We are told that those who first heard it expounded marveled at it and that one who saw it practiced to the limit concluded that the practitioner was the very Son of God. The Service Committee is a wonderful place, as a university is not, because the idea of the Service Committee is a wonderful idea. It is a wonderful idea and a successful one. It is successful in two respects, upon which I should like to dilate.

In the first place, it has changed the lives of those happy few who, formally or informally, work for it and are overworked by it. I have known many such persons. I have not known one whose life has not been changed, and I confess that I have not know anything else that has changed anyone's life. By change I mean, of course, change for the better. I have seen people ouside the Service Committee change for the better and change much more than those inside it; but I have never been able to discover, in any such case, what it was that brought about the change. Seeing, then, that everyone connected with the Service Committee has changed, however little, for the better, I have long since concluded that the idea of the Service Committee was the cause. If you who have known me longest are unable to detect any improvement in me, I can only say that you have not known me long enough.

That, I think, is the greater of the Service Committee's two successes, and I say that an institution that in a few decades has changed a few thousand lives a little is a greater success than any other institution I know.

The second success is external. I suppose that if there were any way to measure the Service Committee's effectivness in terms of its purpose — the worship of God — it has been a losing proposition. An old Greek said that it is hard to love but harder still not to love, and God said, "If ye cannot love your brother, whom ye see, how can ye love me, whom ye see not?" During the last decades the world appears to have chosen ever more preponderantly the harder course of not loving (although this appearance may be deceitful). If, however, what appears to be is, then the Service Committee has, in terms of its purpose, lost. But it has shown the world how easy it is to go on losing and loving, and this is its second success. It has validated the ancient claim that it is not necessary to hope in order to undertake or to succeed in order to persevere. It has been true to its forlorn mission.

But the mission, involving means, is not exhaustively defined by the purpose or end. Just what is the mission, and what is the mission to be? The idea by itself is wonderful. The Service Committee by itself is successful. But the combination requires a mission, or program.

I remember that while I was, singlehanded, writing *Speak Truth to Power*, one of the interruptions up with which I had to put came from Clarence Pickett. His voice was ever low, but he spoke as one having authority, and he said: "The business of the Service Committee is still to put a cup of cold water in the hand of a thirsty man." Like all durable pronouncements, this one could be taken two ways. I felt I should take it literally, knowing as I do that by doing this, and only this, are all men judged. "The business of the Service Committee is still to put a cup of cold water in the hand of a thirsty man." If this is true, then any part of the program that ministers to any other need than this is, if not irrelevant, secondary. Education — by which I *hope* we mean indoctrination — is secondary. And if, by education we mean education and not indoctrination, then education is irrelevant, because the idea of a university is not a wonderful idea. Agitation is certainly secondary, if for no other reason than that it only makes people thirstier. The whole peace program is, if we take Clarence Pickett's words literally, secondary. It ministers at best indirectly; at worst it diverts personnel from the business of the Committee. The only important contribution the peace program can make to the business of the Committee is the practice of simplicity, because simplicity alone conserves water.

So the peace program is unimportant. But that is no reason to make it even less important by diluting its energies and (what is much more serious) its testimony in the bootless pursuit of effectiveness. A Service Committee friend of mine and I were discussing effectiveness recently, and after we had discussed it to death, he said, "So you place your hope in the righteous remnant rather than political action, do you?" The question was rhetorical, but, while I hadn't known that that was where I placed my hope, the word "remnant" said something to me. It said that the dichotomy between righteousness and effectiveness is an unreal dichotomy in an organization whose purpose is the Service Committee's.

The purpose of the Service Committee is the worship of God. God requires nothing of his worshippers but *their* faith and *their* works. The fruits by which they are to be known are not the fruits of victory. Faith and works constitute, and exhaust, the effectiveness required by the Lord: to do justly, to love mercy, and to walk humbly in His way. These are the full, complete, and perfect use of His freedom, to which none of us, though we bend our lives to these ends and no other, may ever attain. The event — outside of the freedom He gives us and the grace with which He fortifies it — is in His hands. Effectiveness, except in so far as faith and works are effectiveness, is wholly outside our power. It deserves our incidental interest, that we may always be watchful not to be corrupted by it and to be thankful to its Giver; it deserves our spare time effort if, as I hope no Service Committee person has, we have spare time. It deserves nothing more.

We leave the world worse than we found it. We were not required to leave it better. The plan of the world was not ours, nor is it ours to say how, if at all, we have served it. The words of Red Schaal, who does embody the spirit of the Service Committee, are preceptory here: "We do not *have* to be effective. We *have* to be right." And if we let our fear of being thought self-righteous deter us from being right, we are lost. If we let our desire to be effective deter us, we are lost too. There is no point in being a remnant; remnants go cheap; we have got to be right.

We are politically ineffective, as the world reckons effectiveness. We always have been. We always shall be. We are not God, who alone is politically effective, nor are we the majority of men, who alone enjoy the hallucination of effectiveness. Work as we will in the world, howl as we will for justice, mercy, and humility, we are always a handful with a handful of fair-weather friends. In a twinkling a Lexington or a Concord blows us and our howls all away — a Sumter, a Maine, a Lusitania, a Pearl Harbor. If, on June 25, 1950, a Truman without the legal power did not bother about Congress, why, in 1958, should an Eisenhower with the legal power bother about us? We have just seen how, in a twinkling, the Russian Sputniks wiped out the crusade for the restoration of liberal education in this country; and the crusaders for liberal education were infinitely more powerful at court than we are or ever shall be. They had the Founding Fathers on their side; we don't.

We are puny and temerarious supplicants in the world of affairs. I say no more. You all know the fate of the diluted petition against nuclear tests, diluted in the name of effectiveness to call for universal instead of unilateral action. I understand that, after many, many months, somebody has at last been found somewhere who has undertaken, after all our vain efforts, to deliver these petitions to somebody somewhere in the White House — not, of course, to the addressee himself. What did we — I was one of the organizers — think we were doing? What did we actually do? In my community our Friends Meeting was the official sponsor of the petition. It gathered a sensational number of signatures. But the editor of our local paper was against the petition, and against disarmament, and after the petition was in he told his readers that everyone knows that the Quakers who sponsored the petition are pacifists, who really want to disarm our country and lay our countrymen open to Communist slavery. Why, he asked, hadn't the Quakers come out in the open in their petition and said what they really wanted? Because, he replied, they knew that if they did, they would not get very many signatures.

What, then, had we done? We had done what the Commonwealth of Massachusetts, according to its late governor, had done with Sacco and Vanzetti: We had got the right men for the wrong reasons. We had got people to join us — or to present the appearance of having joined us — who were moved by the desire to save their skins. But we are forbidden by the purpose of the Service Committee to be moved by any such motivation. The purpose of the Service Committee is to worship God, and our brethren who think they can save their skins by petition today will think they can save them by powder tomorrow.

My point has nothing to do with our going to people where they are and taking them only as far as they want to go. I cannot see how we are unfaithful to our purpose in doing that. The brother who is willing to work on the race issue with us, but is unwilling to go any further, is nevertheless going our way. He is motivated, in his willingness, by the spirit that we hope motivates us. We can go with him, and he with us, as far as he will go, and in the course of our company he may find that he wants to go further. But the brother who wants the kingdoms of this world to save his skin, and will pay with the ink in his ball-point pen, is not going our way or, as far as we can see, going anywhere. We love him, but we must go our way, not his.

If we are to continue to justify our association, as a Committee, with the Religious Society of Friends, we have got to publish the truth. The truth is available in synopsis in the fifth, sixth, and seventh chapters of the Gospel according to Matthew. You may say that we are running a social enterprise here, and I will agree with you. You may say that we have got to get people to come into our shop who are not yet ready to buy, and I will agree with you. You may say that we have got to advertise a few loss leaders to get them to come in and look around, and I will agree with you. But I say that we must display our stock items in the window and display them prominently all the time; otherwise the shoppers who shop for loss leaders only will, as every chain-store manager knows, put us out of business.

There is nothing morally unforgiveable about political effort by the Service Committee, but there is something intellectually unforgivable about some degree of some of it. It is intellectually unforgivable on Ortega's principle of economy. The principle of economy is, roughly, that a man or an institution consider its program in terms of its purpose, eliminate the irrelevant, relegate the subordinate, and among the primary possibilities that are left, tackle only those which nobody else, for whatever reason, will tackle at all and, if it has any energy left over, tackle those that are not as massively tackled as it can tackle them with its excess energy. It seems to me that in 1958 the problem of racial equality, which the Service Committee tackled when few other people were interested, is being massively tackled by the United States Supreme Court, the United States Army, and several other agencies. It seems to me that in 1958 there are other political problems, which the Service Committee tackled when few other people were interested, that are being tackled by many other, sometimes more massive, agencies — problems such as the abolition of nuclear tests without reference to total disarmament, civil liberties, technical assistance, mental health, the narcotics traffic, Indian rights, family relations, penal reform, ex-convict rehabilitation, juvenile and adult delinquency, immigration, and refugee aid.

Please do not misunderstand me. Every one of these problems is a primary possibility to an institution with the Service Committee's purpose. Every one of these problems is colossally important. No one of them must be neglected, and many of them would have been, perhaps, if it had not been for institutions like the Service Committee. But they will not be neglected in 1958, or, at least, not as badly neglected as something else. That something else is peace.

We pacifists used to be wrong. We used to say that peace was the proposition and that there was no other of importance. To our friends who said that there could be no peace without justice, we used to say that we would have to keep the peace first or the justice would be illusory. We were wrong, because the justice of increased racial equality, for example, has not been illusory. But in the end we turn out, through no fault or wisdom of our own, to be right. The thermonuclear age is drawing to a close, and the age of the cinder is opening.

"The proposition," said that old reactionary, Edmund Burke, "is peace." In 1958 that is the only burning proposition and, unlike all the others, which enjoy some measure of active acceptance, it has no powerful friends, no spectacular witnesses, no social respectability, and no advocacy without contempt. War, including cold war, snatches the cup of water from every thirsty man's hand. War, including cold war, mocks every advance on every other front and in the end devours them all. The proposition is not a sane nuclear policy. The proposition is not school integration. The proposition is not a better United Nations or a better League of Nations. The proposition passeth understanding. The proposition is peace: international peace, if possible; national peace, if possible; but peace at any price in the human heart where war begins. If the peace program, at least, of the American Friends Service Committee, is not called to the single-minded and uncompromised witness to this proposition, what organization excepting the Fellowship of Reconciliation, the Jewish

Peace Fellowship, and a few others even less massive will be? I say to you: None; no, not one.

We have nothing, on the principle of economy, to say but peace. We have nothing, on the principle of economy, to practice but peace. In the world we shall lose — so we shall not think in terms of "crash" programs — but we should have the habit of losing by now and have it down pat. The utopians and idealists believe in politics. We must be realists. To be realistic we must be right. I have not heard it said that politics is the art of being right.

The world's peace is in God's hands; our own he has placed, in part, in ours; and, for all we know, the peace of two or three others whose hearts may be compelled by our serene example in the pursuit of our only purpose. The Service Committee is not a political organization. It is not a welfare agency. It is not a humanitarian movement. It is a religious meeting, committed to the only revolution that will ever be. It is a wonderful idea. To it — and not to you — I bow low.

During the Nazi occupation of Norway, a Norwegian schoolgirl, twelve years old, was caught smuggling food to Russian soldiers held as prisoners of war. The camp was only half a mile from the school, and the knowledge was notorious that the prisoners were being starved. The girl was brought before a Gestapo interrogator, who asked her if she knew that her activity was illegal. She said she did. Why, then, did she do it? "Because," she said, "I have been taught that I must feed hungry people." "But," said the interrogator, "these Russians are not people; they are beasts." "I was also taught," said the girl, "that I must feed hungry beasts."

In this anecdote — it happens to be true, but no matter — I sense the irresistible imperative to right action. I should like to be able to teach myself that imperative. I should like to be able to teach it to my children. I should like to believe that people generally could be taught it, even in the modest degree required for conceding its validity, as the Gestapo interrogator conceded it when he tried to flank it instead of assaulting it.

The schoolgirl said she had been taught it. How?

Socrates, before he acquired his *ad hoc* inner voice, worked out two incomplete, and contradictory, answers. Knowledge is that which can be taught; right action depends (in one dialogue) upon a form of knowledge, "the art of measurement." But in another dialogue, it depends not upon knowledge but upon "the gift of God," the gift, in him to whom it has already been given, that can only be buttressed by knowledge.

Since Socrates, we have not made any appreciable progress in the problem of right action. Natural science — the area of distinctive

From *Commonweal*, April 14, 1950.

advance in the interval — has made two tentative contrbutions that come to mind. Some of the handmaidens of psychology suggest, gaily, that the problem can be solved by the discovery that it does not exist. And some of the handmaidens of biology suggest its solution by frontal lobotomy, known to newspaper readers as "the immorality operation." The handmaidens are at present in dispute. "I think," said the director of the New York State Psychiatric Institute recently, "that lobotomy should be stopped before we dement too large a section of the population."

Meanwhile, we continue to praise, without being able to produce, intentionally and in quantity, those few schoolchildren and still fewer alumni who *must* feed the hungry. The formal educational process — the school system, from bottom to top — by definition eschews the irresistible imperative. Since it is compelled to affirm the ideal of the state, it talks about "education for democracy"; but its proper objects are knowledge, which merely tells us what is, and art, which merely perfects us in doing whatever is to be done. "What is to be done" is properly frowned upon as propaganda, indoctrination, or dogma, except where all the alternative "whats" are taught indifferently. (There are those, and their names might be said to be legion, who would forbid even the indifferent teaching of certain "whats," such as communism, on the presumptive ground that they contain an irresistible imperative.) Even those educators who subscribe to the indifferent teaching of what is to be done would reject the notion that it is either their business or their power to teach what should, much less what must, be done.

The Norwegian schoolgirl had been *taught* that she must feed the hungry. Teaching is the distinguishing act of education, but I have never been able to discover an educational answer to the question, Why must I feed the hungry? Yet this is the question that most insistently, and phrased in various forms like, Why must I be good? or, Why must I be just? demands an answer of me.

I have been taught, by no less than Rousseau, that I must feed the hungry because they and I are members of the same biological species. But I know of biological species whose members not only do not feed each other but feed on each other. I have been taught, by no less than Plato and Freud, that I must be good lest I suffer disharmony of the psyche. But I find that many of my acquaintances — not I, of course — have been able to achieve a balanced discord which, though it oppresses the righteous, is music to the ears of the damned. Some of the most unjust men I know sleep the sleep of the just. When I tell them that they sleep so soundly only in order to escape their own injustices, they say, "There is nothing like a good night's sleep." I have been taught that I must be good lest I be caught, but I have been a police reporter in my time, and I know that the proportion of bad men who are never caught is high enough to justify my taking a chance, especially if I am clever and more especially if I am both clever and under great pressure to be bad.

I have been taught that I must be good because I need my fellow men. I can see that I would be impressed by this argument if I were poor, weak, and stupid — not otherwise. I do not need the hungry man I feed, and my feeding him will not increase my chances of being fed by still a third party. I shall never be an old lady standing in a street car; why should I give up my seat? If I am strong, power- ful, and clever, I shall not need my fellow men generally (above all, the hungry); and among my own kind, who are more interesting than the generality of my fellow-men, I shall not want for close com- panions.

As a student, I have asked the question of my teachers. As a teacher, I have been asked the question by my students. And those are the only educational answers I have ever been able to get or give.

I am walking down a dark street late at night. The street lighting has failed and the street is deserted. As it happens, it is the night of the policeman's ball. I need exactly five dollars to pay my wife's hospital bill. A blind man sits at the curb. In addition to being blind, he is dumb, legless, and armless. I approach the man and ask him if he would like a cigarette. He nods and opens his mouth; I place a cigarette in it, and by the light of my match, I see that his hat has two pencils in it, some small change, and a five-dollar bill.

Why shouldn't I take the five-dollar bill?

(I'll replace it next week, next month at the latest.)

Why shouldn't I take it?

(I'll bet he doesn't even know he has it.)
Why shouldn't I take it?
(The silver alone is a good day's haul for a blind man.)
Why shouldn't I take it?
(*I need it desperately, and I'll never be caught.*)
Why shouldn't I take it?

This question, in any of its forms and under any of its circumstances, including labor relations, business relations, race relations, and international relations, is the only serious question I have. If the question is outside education, and if this is the only serious question I have, of exactly what use to me is the education I get or give, be it liberal or vocational, general or specialized, humanistic or scientific?

I can make an argument for the kind of education known as liberal, general, and humanistic, but my argument leaves something, namely the answer, to be desired. True, this kind of education, in contrast with the vocational, specialized, and scientific, will acquaint me with the question, with the methods of answering it, and with the answers that others have made. But life itself acquaints me with the question at every turn — I asked it when I was four years old — and method of mind, rather than of action, always fails me at the instant of actual answer. And the answers of Aristotle and Kant, as well as those of Rousseau and Plato and Freud, I have already found inadequate.

In despair, I leaf through the poet, any poet. This one tells me that I am not an island unto myself but a part of the main. A lofty sentiment, but I can neither teach nor learn sentiments. I am looking for an imperative. In deeper despair, I leaf on, and the poet tires of telling me what I am and passes to a form of discourse that is neither sentiment, which cannot be taught, nor science, which can be:

> That learning, thine Ambassador,
> From thine allegiance wee never tempt,
> That beauty, paradise's flower
> For physicke made, from poyson be exempt,
> That wit, borne apt high good to doe,
> By dwelling lazily

On Nature's nothing, be not nothing too,
That our affections kill us not, nor dye,
Hear us, weake eachoes, O thou ear, and cry.
                    Pater noster, qui es in caelis:
                    Sanctificetur . . .

Now I know why I shouldn't take the blind man's money. I shouldn't take the blind man's money because I love him. And I don't love him because he and I are members of the same species, or because I sleep better (or worse) for loving him, or because it won't always be the night of the policeman's ball, or because I will be a blind man myself some day — still less because mine is a loving heart (it isn't). I love the blind man because I *must* love him. I am *commanded* — but this is not within my or any man's power to enforce, and certainly not any intellect's — to *love*. Now I know how the Norwegian schoolgirl was "taught" that she must feed the hungry. I have found the imperative — "And this commandment have we from Him" — but I have not found it in education. Is it there?

Even in the nominally denominational schools of my acquaintance, God is an elective, and almost nobody takes him. The mottos of these schools are sometimes godly, but the mottos do not seem to govern the curriculum. In one of these schools, the ancient charter proclaims its purpose as "the total abolition of all forms of sin," but this purpose has not been achieved, even locally, nor is the faculty or, of course, the student body slavishly preoccupied with achieving it.

The public schools will not tolerate God even as an elective. He is excluded along with gumchewing and other childish diversions. Jefferson wanted him in the public schools [1] because "the relations existing between man and his Maker, and the duties resulting from those relations, are the most interesting and important to every human being," but Jefferson has been found unconstitutional.[2] Freedom of worship necessarily means freedom not to worship. When we do not want to worship, necessity becames the national policy.

[1] *The Writings of Thomas Jefferson, Memorial Edition* (Washington, D.C., 1904), pp. 414–17.

[2] *McCollum* vs. *Board of Education*, 333 U.S. 203 (1948).

There are left the truly denominational schools. In these we find a vestige of God. But this very vestige serves as a handicap to these schools in so far as they are schools and, as such, are established to *teach*. They offer teachable courses in stage swordplay, cosmetology, and garage-accounting as avidly as the secular schools, but they cannot compete with the secular schools as teaching institutions because their religious commitment compels them to concern themselves with the character of the teacher. The sole concern of the secular schools — and the basis of their academic freedom — is the competence of the teacher to teach. The ethics professor may be a reprobate week ends as long as he teaches ethics competently from Monday through Friday. The secular and nominally denominational schools are not handicapped by the vestige of God in their hiring policies.

I see no evidence, and so far as I know, there is none, that the compulsory devotionals and the course requirements in religion change the course of the lives of the truly denominational students. Instead of finding more godliness in a truly denominational university than I find in a nominally denominational or secular university, I find an absolutely unbeatable football team, and I find its alumni no more godly than those of its sister institution's and a little more monotonous on the subject of football.

The vestige of God turns up in the truly denominational schools of every denomination but nearly always in the same odd and embarrassed areas of the school's activity. The faithless say that God fails to change the course of the denominational students' lives, but the students encounter only the vestige of God. The vestige is better than nothing; even compulsory courses in religion, like the liberal education referred to earlier, raise the right question. But the transition from question to answer, especially when one is in the intellect (or in the memory) and the other in the will, has never been clearly demonstrated. The humanistic scholars of my acquaintance are not peculiarly humane.

To know God the way I think the Norwegian schoolgirl knew him, to know him as the master whose imperative to love is the law of life, courses in religion may not be enough. St. Thomas says that knowing God is like knowing a country; it is not enough to have maps and histories and descriptions — one must live there. But living with God is not, and cannot be, the function of the school *qua* school. The function of the school is to communicate the only knowledge to which the intellect is receptive, the natural knowledge of maps and histories and descriptions.

The vestige of God in the truly denominational institutions confuses them as to their purpose as educational institutions. It handicaps them in their hiring of professors of stage swordplay and ethics. It competes unsuccessfully with the football team for the attention of their students. And it diverts the entire civilization from bothering to try to answer the question put to the Norwegian schoolgirl by the Gestapo interrogator.

To the extent that the truly denominational institutions nourish the vestige of God, they further handicap their own hiring policy, they lose their football team, and they deny that the communication of knowledge, for which educational institutions are established, is central to answering the Gestapo question. To the extent that they nourish the vestige of God, which they alone now harbor, they will, I think, progressively lose their status as educational institutions. Since they are now handicapped, they might as well go whole hog. Cosmetology and football are clearly irrelevant to the pursuit of the irresistible imperative. It may turn out that other, perhaps all other, educational subject matters are, too. The pursuit of the imperative may involve the transformation of education into something else. But it is important, and if the denominational schools do not undertake it, it will not be undertaken.

By nourishing the vestige of God, and forgetting all about tax exemption and constitutional rights in bus rides, the denominational schools will join the issue, frontally, with the prevailing educational doctrine that what can be taught is of use in answering man's critical, and only critical question. If that doctrine, which is now accepted as axiom, is wrong, it is mortally wrong and the prevailing quarrels over content and method, based as they all are on the axiom, are less important than they seem.

Perhaps the Norwegian schoolgirl did not know what she was talking about; she was only twelve. Do we? We have constructed a two-billion-dollar educational plant, in which we constructed a two-billion-dollar bomb, without stopping to ask ourselves what education would do for us. It will be depressing to discover, when our time runs out, that we have just been whiling it away because we ignored the problem that was posed at the opening of the first recorded discussion of education: "Can you tell me, Socrates, whether virtue is acquired by teaching or by practice . . . or in what other way?"

The Jews of America are afraid that their number is up — if not today, then tomorrow or the next. They know that war breeds chauvinism and that chauvinism breeds bigotry. They know that every war since Napoleon has been followed by collapse, and they know that the postwar collapse will remind a bitter and bewildered nation that "the Jews got us into the war." The Jews of America are afraid.

And they are not fooled by the lull in anti-Semitic activity since the beginning of the war. They know that anti-Semitism reached an all-time high in this country before Pearl Harbor. They know that there is something tentative and temporary in the notion that "we are all Americans now." They know that enduring hatreds are not done away with by the addition of passing hatreds. They know all these things and they are afraid. And the Jew in the suburbs is just as fearful as the Jew in the slums.

As he sees the flood of anti-Semitism rising slowly, subterraneously, to his doorstep, as the realization dawns on him that the Wandering Jew has nowhere now to wander, the Jew finds himself wondering — wondering why this is happening to him here, in America, after he tried so hard to adjust to his environment, and after he had adjusted, as he thought, so successfully. In his unstinting effort to adjust, he had moved away from the "kikes," the noisy orthodox "kikes" who, he assured himself, had always been responsible for all his troubles. Then he had moved into nice gentile neighborhoods, which somehow became nice Jewish neighborhoods. Then he tried to move away from himself.

From *Saturday Evening Post*, March 28, 1942. © 1944 by the Curtis Publishing Company.

He changed his name in New York and his nose in Los Angeles. He had himself baptised Christian Scientist and his children Episcopalians. He "reformed" his ancient ritual and then abandoned it altogether, just like the Gentiles, for the movies, the rumba, and the night clubs.

He changed his day of rest and contemplation from Saturday to Sunday and gave up the rest for golf and the contemplation for fried chicken, just like the Gentiles. His rabbis delivered public lectures instead of sermons and lived like high priests instead of prophets. There was no upsetting of the money-changers' tables in the temples; there was nothing upsetting in the temples. And he taught his children that the Jews were not a race but a religion. But there was no religion, just like the Gentiles.

In their dream of "assimilation," these adjusting Jews tried to shake the symbols of unassimilability from their coattails, beginning, of course, with the "kikes." They denied the Jews were disproportionately radical and disowned the radicals who appeared among them. They cursed Trotsky for being a Communist and blessed Browder for being a Gentile. They regretted that Morgenthau was in the cabinet and begged Roosevelt not to put Frankfurter on the Supreme Court. One of the most prominent Jews in America told me he had voted for Wilkie for no other reason than that the anti-Semites were supporting Roosevelt.

In their dream of assimilation they were even willing to be anti-Semitic, just like the Gentiles. Some of their leaders opposed the refugee movement because "there are enough Jews here now." Many of them refused to hire Jewish employees because "it isn't good for business." Still more of them said they wouldn't mind a Hitler who would take care of the "kikes" and the radicals. A few of them, their faith undimmed in the assimilative power of money, took heart at the spectacle of Baron Eberhard von Oppenheim, whose contribution of two hundred thousand marks to the Nazis won him a special dispensation proclaiming him an Aryan.

They tried to adjust, this pitiful people who once were proud. They tried to look like, talk like, be like everyone else. They tried to lose themselves in the crowd, like men who have picked a pocket on a busy street. They resorted to every dodge known to fugitive criminals, from changing their names to changing their faces. And for all their trying, they were strangers in Egypt still.

They knew they weren't accepted, and they were willing to accept the contemptible condition of tolerance. The Jew who got into a fashionable Palm Beach club in 1932 by paying an unheard-of ten thousand dollars for a membership wanted only to be tolerated. With enough gold and enough brass they sometimes managed to ascend to the lower strata of gentile society, but even the Gentile, the tolerant Gentile, was unable to help the Jew lose himself. The tolerant Gentile would let something slip about "the Jews," and the tolerated Jew would sweat and squirm beneath his uneasy disguise as a "good" Jew.

Even if he changed his name from Schönburg to Belmont and nobody knew he was Jewish, *he* knew it. And he studied himself in the mirror, comparing his clothes, his manners, his words, and his life with those of the Gentiles, and asked himself, full of wonderment, "Why am I still a Jew?" "My friends," said the great Rabbi Hirsch to his congregation, "you can change your noses, but you cannot change your Moses."

And their consciousness of their inability to change their Moses pervaded their lives. And then Hitler came and pulled off the mask and called them all Jews, and they showed him their baptismal certificates and said, "A case of mistaken identity, your honor," and they showed him their houses and their cars and said, "You can't do this to me." But he did it.

And in England and America, as the black shadow of Hitler lengthened over Europe, the terrors that beset trapped men beset the adjusting Jews, and with the false hilarity that trapped men assume, they laughed at themselves and at their terror and at their failure:

Otto Kahn met a hunchback in front of the Episcopalian Church on Fifth Avenue and said to the hunchback, "I belong to that church."

"I know," said the hunchback.

And Otto Kahn said, "I'm very active in the church; I'm one of the vestrymen," and the hunchback said, "I know."

And Otto Kahn said, "I used to be a Jew." "I know," said the hunchback, "I used to be a hunchback."

Every "adjusted" Jew told stories like that one. The proud Negro resented mockery; the pitiful Jew mocked himself. Self-mockery had a bitter masochistic pleasure for him, as breast-beating had for his anguished ancestors. It reminded him that he was a Jew and that it mattered, amid all the pretenses that he wasn't and that it didn't. Everywhere he went, in his gentile car, in his gentile clothes, his gentile money in his hand, he found himself face to face with GENTILES ONLY or, if the Gentiles were genteel, EXCLUSIVE CLIENTELE, or just RESTRICTED. And sometimes there was no sign, but only the whisper, "They don't take Jews." He might be Einstein or Brandeis, Lasker or Rosenwald, or Cohen or Goldstein — still the pleasant city of Saugatuck, Michigan, had only this to say to him: MICHIGAN'S FINEST GENTILE COMMUNITY.

This was, and had to be, the inescapable lot of the Jew in the modern world. The historic wisecrack that if the Jew hadn't been born he would have had to be invented is confirmed by the story a Nazi official told me in Germany: When Doctor Goebbels proclaimed his first "cold pogrom" in the form of a national boycott of the Jews, he received a telegram from the mayor of a small town on the North Sea: "Send us a Jew for our boycott."

And why did the world need a whipping boy? Hitler, I am sorry to say, suggests the answer: "Greek civilization will be remembered for its philosophy, medieval civilization for its cathedrals. Ours will be remembered for its department stores." The modern world had as its ideals money, fame, and power. The pursuit of money, fame, and power as the ends of life was bound to be frustrating, because there is no such thing as enough money, fame, and power. The rich were no nearer respite than the poor; success left them somehow unsuccessful. Having none but insatiable desires held up before them, the creatures of the modern world tried to find respite in perversions, the oldest of which is the persecution of the Jew. Anti-Semitism is *ersatz* religion.

The practices of the modern world were certainly no better than those of Athens or the Middle Ages, and its ideals were worse.

Stemming from the denial of the fatherhood of God and the supremacy of the spirit, the modern world's ideals flowed inevitably into a consuming materialism which denied the brotherhood of man and asserted the supremacy of the goods of the body. How could it have been otherwise? The men who established this nation spent three hours every Sunday listening to prophets like Jonathan Edwards preach on goodness and then went home and thought about it. They were interested in being good because they thought they would someday be judged. But their descendants, having denied the existence of goodness and the coming of judgment, were not interested in being good but in getting by. Their preoccupation with "getting something out of life" converted the world into a continuous bank run. The bank is now closing.

This was the world to which the Jew tried to adjust — a world, incidentally, which itself proclaimed "adjustment to the environment" as its compelling principle. Rulers and revolutionaries alike agreed on the principle of adaptation, differing only on the delicate question of who should adapt whom. Businessmen affirmed the principle with the slogan, "Nothing succeeds like success." Al Capone's defense was, "Everybody's doing it." Psychiatrists prospered by adjusting the maladjusted. And fashionable preachers, their theology thoroughly biologized and sociologized, sanctified the doctrine that the customer is always right. It was a world which had the freedom to worship God, but had no God to worship. It put "In God We Trust" on its pennies, but it put its trust in the pennies. It was a gentile world, to be sure, but it was not a Christian world. It was a pagan world, and the Jews were second-class pagans. There were Jews who lived like Jews, just as there were Christians who lived like Christians, but they were neither popular nor prosperous.

He who would crawl must stoop. The Jew, if he wanted to crawl into the modern world, had to stoop even lower than the Gentile. The gentile world could compel him to do its ditry work, could compel him to practice the speculative and the shady professions, as the price of admission. And the Jew who wanted badly enough to be admitted had to pay the price. Thus the "cunning" Jew, debased and dishonored by a world which honored cunning in its heart.

There was nothing that a Gentile would stoop to that a Jew wouldn't if he could. Shamelessly callous to their own "best interests," Jews in the South exploited Negroes as callously as Gentiles did. In New York's Harlem and Chicago's Bronzeville tremendous anti-Semitism has developed in the past decade because of the Jew's tenement profiteering. The trade unions know that there are few employers as conscienceless as the Jewish sweatshop operator employing Jews. The Gentile called the tune, and the Jew, if he wanted to dance at all, had to dance on his hands and knees.

If the Gentiles were Fascists, the Jews would be Fascists too. Three of America's foremost Jewish industrialists who employed a notorious labor spy to save them from the horrors of unionism, were amazed when they learned that their savior was peddling *The Protocols of the Elders of Zion* on the side; and in 1933 a committee of forty-three Jewish editors cited Mussolini as "one of the greatest champions of the Jewish people" because he had "demonstrated that Italian fascism does not tolerate social and religious persecution." "I wouldn't mind fascism," a Jewish movie producer told the Reverend L. M. Birkhead a few years ago, "if it weren't for the anti-Semitism."

There is a Jewish organization whose sole purpose is to fight anti-Semitism. There are members and large contributors to this organization who have so operated their own businesses as to run afoul of the law, fighting anti-Semitism with one hand, feeding it with the other. Now they wondered why it was happening here. Had they not done in Rome as the Roman did? Had they not exploited and extorted, preached and pretended, just like the Gentiles? Why was it happening here?

And now, even now, that the Jews of America have failed and know they have failed, they place their last chip on adjustment — adjustment, this time, to a world of force. At a dinner party recently, an almost assimilated Jew — a distinguished scholar, by the way — said he wanted America to get into the war so that he could "bash in a few Nazi heads before I die." "My friend," said another Jew, a philosopher with an accent thick enough to skate on, "bashing in heads is for the ninety-six per cent, not for the four per cent."

If the four per cent can't win playing the game of the ninety-six per cent, what is there left for them to do? I will tell them what there is left for them. I will tell them the game they must play. I will tell them what Isaiah told their forefathers who whored after false gods twenty-six centuries ago. I will tell them in the six thundering words of Isaiah: "In righteousness shalt thou be established." And I will tell them exactly what I mean.

I have a Jewish friend, a well-known newspaperman who has had his children baptized in another faith and who plans to make a get-away "somewhere" if anti-Semitism engulfs America. "Why should I suffer as a Jew?" he asks. "I have never really been a Jew. I haven't practiced Judaism. I don't feel like a Jew." One night recently, my friend, a little to the windward of the weather, broke down and told me that he was haunted, haunted by the recollection of a day in Warsaw during the Nazi invasion. The mobs were going through the streets tracking down the Jews. My friend, in Warsaw as a foreign correspondent, was riding on a tram. Across from him sat an old, bearded Jew — a "kike," my friend called him — wearing a robe and a skullcap. He was reading his prayer book, plainly oblivious of all the turmoil and terror around him. A half-dozen Nazi *Schutzstaffeln* got aboard the tram, and as they passed the old Jew, one of them spat upon him.

"He didn't wince, or move, or even look up," my friend said.

"Well," I said, when I realized that that was the end of the story, "why does it haunt you?"

"I don't know," said my friend, who "doesn't feel like a Jew," "but somehow that old Jew makes me feel like a heel."

That old Jew was "established," as my friend and all the almost assimilated Jews are not. He was prepared for suffering because he had something worth suffering for. The old Jew in Warsaw was being crucified for something he was; the new Jew in America is being crucified for something he isn't. The Judaism of the Jew in Warsaw was his banner; the Judaism of the Jew in America is his brand.

It is said that when the Jews were still Jews, they sustained themselves with the knowledge that though they had lost everything else they still had their God. How will the pagan Jew, the "adjusted" Jew, sustain himself when he has lost everything else? He crowds into his lavish temples and cries out to the One God to save him, as his forefathers did twenty-six centuries ago. "For they have turned their back unto Me, and not their face; but in the time of their trouble they will say: Arise, and save us. But where are thy gods that thou hast made thee? Let *them* arise, if they can save thee."

Like most tragic heroes, the Jew is confronted at last with this alternative — righteousness or death. If he chooses righteousness, he may still lose his life. As long as Egypt is Egypt, the Jew will be a stranger in Egypt and his life will be in jeopardy. His life will be safe when his righteousness, his radical righteousness, has, by the persistent power its example, created a righteous world. But if his life is lost in the world that is Egypt — and it seems likely that it will be — his righteousness will still establish him in the same strange sense in which the old Jew was established in Warsaw. I do not care whether he grows a beard and wears a skullcap. I do not care whether he goes to temple on Sunday or Saturday, or whether he goes at all. And I do not think that God cares either. Neither the dirty robe nor the tailored morning coat — no, nor even the yellow badge — will make him a Jew. The only thing that will make him a Jew is the radical righteousness of Isaiah.

If he wants to know what righteousness is, I can tell him where to find out. The Jew keeps a book on the closet shelf; he keeps it there because he is afraid either to read it or to throw it away. If he will take down that book and open it to Micah and Isaiah, to Amos and Jeremiah, he will learn that righteousness consists in knowing what man is and what, in the light of man's nature, the ends of human life should be. He will learn that the righteous man is the man whose bodily goods serve the goods of the spirit, and that the unrighteous man is the man whose bodily goods begin by being ends in themselves and end by devouring the spirit.

If he wants to practice righteousness, I can tell him how. He can practice righteousness by doing justly, by loving mercy, and by walking humbly with his God. Nobody can tell him how to walk humbly with his God, and nobody needs to tell him what it is to love mercy. But he needs to know how to do justly, and I think I can tell him.

Every man is an end in himself; no man is a means to be used by another. The man who, in Lincoln's simple words, wrings his bread from the sweat of other men's faces is unjust. He may turn philanthropist and repay a nickel on the stolen quarter, or a dime, or the entire quarter; he is still unjust. He may endow a university or support a cathedral or build a string of orphan asylums; he is still unjust. He is unjust because he has used men as means.

That is why righteousness is radical, so radical that the modern Communists would shudder at it. It is worse than radical; it is impractical. Of the three most perfectly righteous men who come to mind, one was crucified in Jerusalem, one was forced to drink the hemlock in Athens, and one was shot from behind in Washington. The fate of the millions of righteous men who do not come to mind — some of them Jews, some of them Christians, and some of them idolators — may not have been as dramatic. If they escaped the slaughter of the innocents in Pharaoh's time, in Herod's, or in ours, they probably wandered the streets half-starved and went into unmarked graves. For the road to good intentions, today as in Ancient Athens, is paved with hell.

The nice thing about righteousness, as Socrates told the Greeks, is that it is free. Unlike money, fame, and power, every man can have as much of it as he wants. Now the Jew is, above all things, insecure in his possessions, in the possession of his goods, his freedom, and his life. It is possible, it seems to me, that the psychosis which prevents the Jew from adjusting would fall away if he possessed in abundance the one thing not all the armies of the Caesars can take from him who has it.

The Jews refused to be God's chosen people, and now, in the end, they are Hitler's. They adopted adjustment as their principle, and they practiced it to the limit. It is hard to see how they could be any worse off if they had practiced righteousness. "They have forsaken Me, the fountain of living waters, and hewed them out cisterns, broken cisterns, that can hold no water." And their failure, it seems to me, is a sign to all men, a sign that men cannot survive by saving their skins. Their tragedy, it seems to me, is a demonstration of the falsity of the driving principle of our time, the principle of adjustment to the environment.

The platitude that "the Jewish problem is really the Christian problem" is a pleasant platitude. But it is still a platitude. It is equally true, and equally platitudinous, that the Christian problem is really the Jewish problem. But platitudes will not save the Jew. The Jew who wants to be saved cannot pass the buck for his salvation. The Jew who wants to be saved cannot wait for the Gentiles to turn Christian. The Jew who wants to be saved will have to save himself. Running away hasn't saved him. Resettlement hasn't saved him. Changing his name, his face, his clothes, and his faith haven't saved him. The Jew has not been saved. And the suddenly crowded temples won't save him. Denouncing Father Coughlin won't save him. The destruction of Hitler won't save him. All these fallacious faiths are based on the grand fallacy of adjustment. The Jew will be saved when he saves his own soul.

COMMENCEMENT
ADDRESS

As you are now, so I once was; as I am now, so you will be. You will be tempted to smile when I tell you that I am middle-aged and corrupt. You should resist the temptation. Twenty-five years from now you will be ineluctably middle-aged and, unless you hear and heed what I say today, just as ineluctably corrupt. You will not believe me, and you should not, because what I say at my age should be unbelievable at yours. But you should hear me out because I know more than you do in one respect: you know only what it is to be young, while I know what it is to be both young and old. In any case, I will not lie to you in order to make you feel good. You will be old much longer than you are young, and I would rather that you believed me the longer time than the shorter.

I tell you today that instantly is not a moment too soon if you are going to escape the fate I predict for you and embody myself. For what was said long ago is still true, that corruption runs faster than death and the faster runner overtakes the slower. It may indeed be too late already, unless you mend your ways this least of all likely moments. I once heard Robert Hutchins tell a graduating class that they were closer to the truth that day than they would ever be again. I did not believe him. But I have seen most of the members of that class since, and I regret to inform you that Hutchins was right. Mind you, he did not say that they were close to the truth; he only said that they would never be so close again. They had been taught what right and wrong were and had not yet had a chance to do what e. e. cummings calls "up grow and down forget." If my own history and the history of the race is instructive,

Reprinted by permission from *Christian Century*, May 14, 1958. © 1958 by the Christian Century Foundation.

this commencement is for nearly every last one of you the commencement of disintegration. A cynic once said that he would not give a hang for a man who wasn't a socialist before he was twenty or who was one after that. I do not know if socialism is a good ideal, but I know that it is an ideal and I know that the cynic was confident that you would lose your ideals. You may even have trifled, in your springtime, with such radical aberrations as pacifism. But you will soon stop trifling; and when, at thirty, you have already begun to molder, your friends will tell you that you have mellowed.

All societies are deplorable, and history indicates that they always will be. You have lived twenty years in a deplorable society. You have lived sheltered lives, but you have had no one to shelter you from your parents and teachers. Your parents have done what they could to adjust you to the deplorable society to which they, as their advanced age testifies, have successfully adjusted themselves. When they said you were improving, they meant that you were getting to be like them. When they said they hoped you would keep out of trouble, they meant that you should not do anything that they wouldn't do. But some of the things that they wouldn't do should have been done. The condition of the society to which they have accommodated their lives is the proof of their criminal negligence. Your teachers have been no better, and no better an influence on you, than your parents. They may have had higher ideals; it takes higher ideals to teach children than to have them. But your teachers' survival (like your parents') testifies to their adjustability. They have done as they were told, and in a deplorable society there are some things that men are told to do that no man should do. A high-school teacher in California told me that not one of his colleagues wanted to take the anti-Communist oath required of teachers in that state, and neither did he; but every one of them took it in order to hold his job and escape the national black list. As they are now, so you will be.

Like your teachers and your parents before you, you will be told to do bad things in order to hold your job. In college you may have quit the campus daily or defied the old fraternity on principle. It will be harder to quit the metropolitan daily or defy the old country on principle; it will be easier to forget the principle. And if, in addition to holding your job, you want to be promoted, you will think of bad things to do on your own. And you will have good reasons for doing them. You will have wives (at least one apiece) and children to maintain. You will have a home and mortgage to enlarge. And life insurance, purchased against the certainty of death, dread of which in turn adds preciousness to staying alive at any price. And neighbors who are having their children's teeth straightened. Your dentists' bills alone will corrupt you. You will have doctors' bills to pay, and they will increase as you grow older, becoming extremely heavy when you are moribund and powerless to earn money. You will have lusts, as you have now, to gratify, but the lusts you have now are relatively inexpensive and they will give way to more expensive if less gratifying lusts. You will have worthy philanthropies to support and the respect of people whose respect depends on your supporting those philanthropies. You will have an automobile (if you are so wretched as to be a one-car family), and you might as well turn it in every year because the new model will be so revolutionary that it will depreciate the old one to the point where there's no point in keeping it.

Some of the things you will be expected to do (or will expect yourself to do) for the sake of your wife and children, your community, your health, or your burial are bad things. You will have to have good reasons for doing them; and, thanks to your education, you will have them. The trouble with education is that it teaches you rhetoric while you are young. When, for rhetorical purposes, you embrace the doctrine of the lesser evil, you ignore its fatal flaw of present certainty and future contingency; being young, you think you will live forever, so that you may do bad things today in order to do good things tomorrow. But today is certain, tomorrow contingent; and this night an old man's soul may be required of him. When you are old, and too tired to embrace doctrines for rhetorical purposes, you will find that the doctrine of the lesser evil has embraced you and destroyed you. You protest my melancholy prediction, but the Great Actuarial Table is against you. Twenty-five years from now nine out of ten of you (or all ten) will tolerate an existence which, if you could foresee it now, you would call intolerable. If such an existence has any virtue at all, it has only one: it will give you a wistful old age. You will look back to your springtime, fifty years gone, and say, "Those were the days." And you will be right.

The only thing that will save you from wistfulness is the one talent whose lack now redeems you — the talent for self-deception. You won't even know that you are corrupt. You will be no worse than your neighbors, and you will be sure to have some that you won't be as bad as. You will have friends who praise in you the characteristics you have in common with them. They will persuade you that there is nothing wrong with either hoarding or squandering as much money as you can get legally. And if, some sudden night, you go berserk and bawl out that life is a sell, they will put you to bed with the assurance that you will be all right in the morning. And you will be. Worse than being corrupt, you will be contented in your corruption.

Twenty-five years from now you will celebrate your twentieth wedding anniversary. Because you love your wife — still more if you don't — you will want to celebrate it in style. You will reserve a window table for two at the choicest restaurant in town, and the champagne bucket will be at the table when you arrive. You will not be the cynosure of all eyes, but you will think you are. The head waiter (or maître de, as he is known here) will address you by name. As your eye travels down the menu it will be distracted by something outside the window, which will prove to be a hungry man. What will you do? Do you know what you will do then, twenty-five years from now? You will call the maître de and tell him to have the drapes pulled, and he will tell the waiter, and he will tell the bus boy, who will do it.

Your table, even before you have ordered, will be laden with rolls and crackers (of several sorts) and butter pats on butter plates. Hungry, and a little nervous, as you should be, you will break up a roll and butter it and eat it as you wait for your wife to make up her confounded mind. The waiter will ask you if you want the champagne poured, and you will say yes; and he will open it with a pop which, beneath the dinner din, will be unheard by the rest of the diners (but you won't know that). Thirsty, and a little nervous still, you will sip your glass, forgetting to toast your wife, and resume your study of the menu. And then, for the first time, you will see, in fine italic print at the bottom, the words "The Management reserves the right to refuse service to anyone." And then you will know (for you will be an educated man) that you are sitting in a Jim Crow restaurant — that being the meaning of the words "The Management, etc."

Now the country in which you were raised calls itself a Christian country, and the parents who raised you up called themselves Christian people, and the church whose vestry has just elected you calls itself a Christian church, and you call yourself a Christian. Jim Crowism is un-Christian. It is also un-American, and you call yourself an American. What will you do? What will you do then, twenty-five years from now?

The champagne is open and sipped. The roll is buttered, half-eaten. Will you get up from the table and tell your wife to get up and tell her why, and tell the waiter and the maître de, and maybe the management, that you are leaving the restaurant and why, and pay for the champagne and the rolls and the butter pats and, if necessary, for the dinner, but refuse to eat there? Or will you pretend, as the management (by printing the notice in fine italic type) intended you to pretend, that you did not see the notice. You will stay at the table and order your dinner and eat it.

You will have been measured for corruption and found to fit. You may be the man who raised the flag on Iwo Jima — a hero abroad but not at home, where it's harder to be a hero. At Iwo Jima you had either to raise the flag or drop it. It was publicly shameful to drop it. But the night of your anniversary dinner it would have been publicly shameful to *raise* the flag by leaving the restaurant. And public shame was what you could not bear, either at Iwo Jima or in the restaurant.

There are a lot of involuntary, non-voluntary or reflexive heroes. I am one myself. I do not doubt that I would have raised the flag at Iwo Jima rather than let it drop in public. But I was the man who took his wife to dinner at the Jim Crow restaurant. Believe me, there is no contradiction between the corruption which will consume you, day by day, in the face of unpopularity or public shame and the heroism of the moment accompanied by public praise. And when you have been measured often enough and long enough for corruption, you will like what you see in the mirror. I don't mean that you won't continue to have good impulses. You will. But you will have persuasive reasons for suppressing them. From time to time, as the vestige of your springtime idealism stirs you, you will want to do the right thing. But you will have to put off doing it until you have buried your father, and then your mother, your brother, your children, and your grandchildren. You may live to be very old, but you will not outlive the last descendant for whose sake you will suppress your good impulses.

What life did to me, because there was no one to tell me what I am telling you now, it will do to you if you do not at once adopt *Principiis obsta* as your motto and spurn every other. "Resist the beginnings." At twenty I was what you are; I had had all the middle-class care that a middle-class society and a middle-class home could provide. My parents wanted me to have what they took to be advantages, and I had them. But my advantages were of no use to me at all when life came down on me, as it will upon you, like a ton of bricks. I had studied morality, just as you have, but it was the easy morality designed to sustain my character in an easy world. I would not steal another man's watch unless my children were starving, and my children would never be starving. Nor will yours if, with what your parents call your advantages, you do as you are told and get to the top. The reason your children will not be starving is that you will have been corrupted. Your corruption will save you from having to decide whether to steal another man's watch. I was prepared, like you, to be a hero the instant heroism was required of me. I saw myself at Iwo Jima, at Gettysburg, at Concord. But I did not see myself at home, so weakened by the corrosive years ahead that I would not be able to stand up on my hind legs and say no when I had to do it alone. Never knowing — as you do not know — that my needs would be limitless, I never imagined that my surrender would be complete.

My education prepared me to say no to my enemies. It did not prepare me to say no to my friends, still less to myself, to my own limitless need for a little more status, a little more security, and a little more of the immediate pleasure that status and security provide. Corruption is accompanied by immediate pleasure. When you feel good, you are probably, if not necessarily, doing bad. But happiness is activity in accordance with virtue, and the practice of virtue is painful. The pursuit of happiness requires a man to undertake suffering. Your intelligence, or your psychiatrist's, will tell you whether you are suffering for the right reason. But it will not move you to undertake the suffering.

God is said to come to us in little things. The Devil is no fool: he comes that way too. The Devil has only one objective, and if he can persuade you to justify your derelictions by saying "I'm only human," he has achieved it. He will have got you to deny the Christ within you, and that is all he wants. If you are only human you are his. The Devil will keep you quiet when you ought to talk by reminding you that nobody asked you to say anything. He will keep you in your chair when you ought to get up and out by reminding you that you love your wife and it's your twentieth anniversary. He will give you the oath to take and say, "As long as you're loyal, why not say so?" He will tell you that the beggar outside the restaurant would only spend the money on whiskey. The Devil has come to me in little things for twenty-five years — and now I say and do the things in which, when he first began coming, he had to instruct me.

I tell you that you are in mortal jeopardy today, and anyone who tells you differently is selling you to the Devil. It is written on Plato's ring that it is easier to form good habits than to break bad ones. Your habits are not yet fully formed. You are, in some measure still, only potentially corrupt. Life will actualize and habitualize every bit of your corruptibility. If you do not begin to cultivate the habit of heroism today — and habits are formed by acts — you never will. You may delude yourselves, as I did, by setting about to change the world. But for all that you do or do not do, you will leave the world, as I do, no better than you found it and yourselves considerably worse. For the world will change you faster, more easily, and more durably than you will change it. If you undertake only to keep the world from changing you — not to lick 'em but to avoid j'ining 'em — you will have your hands full.

Other, more agreeable commencement orators have warned you of life's pitfalls. I tell you that you are marked for them. I believe you will not escape them because I see nothing in your environment that has prepared you even to recognize them. Your elders tell you to compare yourselfs with the Russians and see how much worse the Russians are; this is not the way to prepare you to recognize pitfalls. Your elders tell you to be technologists because the Russians are technologists and your country is technologically backward; this is no way to prepare you to recognize pitfalls. You are marked for the pit. The Great Actuarial Table is against you.

What you need (and the Russians with you) is neither pharisaism nor technology. What you need is what the psalmist knew he needed — a heart, not a head, of wisdom. What you need is what Bismarck said was the only thing the Germans needed — civilian courage. I do not know where you will get it. If I did, I would get it myself. You were divinely endowed to know right and to do right, and you have before you, in the tradition of your country and of human history, the vision to help you if you will turn to it. But no one will compel you to turn to it, and no one can. The dictates of your society, of any society, will not serve you. They are the dictates that corrupted your parents and your teachers. If Socrates did not know where virtue came from — and he didn't — neither do I. He pursued it earlier and harder than anyone else and concluded that it was the gift of God. In despair of your parents and your society, of your teachers and your studies, of your neighbors and your friends, and above all of your fallen nature and the Old Adam in you, I bespeak for you the gift of God.

PLEDGE
IN
POMONA

Like 16,811 other American cities of less than 50,000 pop., Pomona, California, is known as The City of Churches. And no wonder; it has fifty-two of them, or one for every 730.77 Pomonans. It is also the Site of the New $50,000,000 Home of the Convair Guided Missile Division of the Consolidated Vultee Aircraft Corporation. Everything holy and profane that man can do to protect Pomona has been done. And yet there is fear in Pomona.

One evening recently I was scheduled to speak at Pomona's Junior High School on "The Struggle for Europe." On the platform with me, as panel discussants, were Professor Albert Britt of Scripps College; Professor Philip Merlan of Claremont Graduate School, and Mr. Herbert Tay, the Junior High School history teacher. There was also, as chairman of the meeting, Ferner Nuhn, distinguished authority on American culture. On the platform, also, was an American flag. Admission to the meeting was free. An offering would be taken for the work of the American Friends Service Committee, whose work, in small part, consists of sponsoring such meetings in the interest of peace.

A goodly crowd, around three hundred, was there. But the auditorium seats eight hundred, and the crowd was too thinly scattered for that pleasant packed-in sense that goes, on both sides of the apron, with a full house. But the brightly lighted auditorium disclosed a few people at the far sides, both front and back. Mr. Nuhn opened the meeting. Or tried to.

No sooner had Mr. Nuhn said, "It is my pleasure, this evening, to welcome — " when a man at the right side, in the front row, called out, "Let's all take the pledge to the American flag."

From the *Progressive*, January, 1953.

Mr. Nuhn said, "I beg your pardon, sir, but you are out of —" and a man at the left side, in the back row, called out, "Come on, everybody, take the pledge of allegiance."

And then, when Mr. Nuhn said, "I beg your —" a man at the left side, in front, called out, "Everybody who isn't a Communist get up and take the pledge to the flag," and then a man at the right side, in back, called out, "Don't be afraid of the Commies, folks — get up."

"I'm sorry," said Mr. Nuhn, the distinguished authority on American culture, "but —"

"Come on, everybody," an elderly man in the middle called out, "we're not Commies in Pomona."

"Please —" said Mr. Nuhn, in his cultured American manner.

"Ah, come on," one of the earlier callers in front called out, and at the same time, another of the earlier callers in back called out, "Let's go, Americans — the pledge to the flag," and then still another of the earlier callers, with an overseas cap tucked into the shoulder strap of his army shirt, went to the front, faced the audience, and started reciting the pledge of allegiance to the flag, with his right hand over his heart.

Mr. Nuhn sat down. The other four of us on the platform were already sitting.

When the man with the overseas cap began reciting the pledge, perhaps twenty persons, of the three hundred in the auditorium, stood up to recite it with him. As the recitation proceeded, others got to their feet, slowly, in ones and twos and threes, and joined in. A few, at first, and then more and more, but ever more slowly, all over the auditorium. By the time the recitation ended, there were not more than twenty persons, of the three hundred in the hall, who were still in their seats. The five men on the platform, including me, were still in their seats at the end, too.

I don't know about the other four — and I haven't seen them since — but my heart failed me for fear. I doubt that I could have got to my feet if I'd wanted to, I was that afraid. I knew that the people who had got up were afraid; that was clear, not only from the way they stood up, but also from the way they sat down, just as slowly, at the end. But I hadn't suspected how afraid — how unprepared — I would be to do what was right the first time in my life I ever had to do what was right in the presence of fear all around me.

I was the reason for the outbreak and its prime object. At a meeting in Syracuse, New York, in 1947 I had said that some of the people who oppose world government believed that the advocates of world government wanted to defile the American flag. A local newspaper reported that it was *I* who advocated defiling the flag. Although the newspaper subsequently published the finding by the district attorney that I had been misquoted, the canard kept appearing in (and only in, as far as I know) Southern California.

The evening preceding Pomona, at a similar meeting in a Pasadena church, people outside the church distributed handbills reading, "Milton Mayer said: 'HAUL DOWN THE AMERICAN FLAG . . . HAUL IT DOWN, STAMP ON IT, AND SPIT ON IT!' This man is a subversive sponsored by a subversive organization, the American Friends Service Committee. WHY is he allowed to speak in a Christian Church or Public School?" The cards were signed, "KEEP AMERICA COMMITTEE, Box 3094, Los Angeles 54, Calif., H. W. Courtois, Sec'y." Outside the Pasadena meeting sample ballots also were distributed for the MacArthur-Tenney presidential ticket of Gerald L. K. Smith's Christian Nationalist party, along with copies of Smith's pamphlet entitled *Is Communism Jewish?*

The church in Pasadena had been filled. A lady in front — H. W. Courtois turned out also to be a lady, who was afraid if General Eisenhower were elected, Rabbi Silver of Cleveland would run the country — succeeded in diverting the discussion from the struggle for Europe to the honor of the American flag, but nothing serious had happened. I had been rattled a bit; the man on the platform is supposed to handle this sort of thing with an iron hand, and I am not the iron-handed type. But the Pasadena meeting was never in danger of disruption. After all — Pasadena.

But Pomona, away out in the citrus groves, is a good bit spookier, by night at least, than Pasadena. Or so it seemed, while I sat in my seat, along with the other four men on the platform, and two hundred eighty of the three hundred people in that great big big brightly lighted auditorium took the pledge of allegiance to the American flag.

I didn't know, as I say, how the other four felt or whether, indeed, they would stay in their seats to the end. I was afraid to look at them. I was afraid not to look straight ahead at all those people in the auditorium with their right arms stretched out toward the flag on the platform. Ferner Nuhn, the chairman, was a Quaker; maybe he was prepared for what was happening, because Quakers are supposed to be prepared (according to an old engraving) to go on with their worship even when Indians with tomahawks break into the Meeting House. Professor Britt of Scripps, a small, spare, elderly man, had been president of Knox College, in Galesburg, Illinois; I didn't know about him. Professor Merlan of Claremont had a strong foreign accent; I didn't know about him, but I suspected that he might be a refugee and, like so many refugees, afraid of ever having to be a refugee again. Teacher Tay hadn't said much at dinner before the meeting, and the meeting was taking place in the very school where he was employed. Certainly the other four — except maybe Ferner Nuhn — hadn't bargained for trouble. But here trouble was.

What was the trouble?

What were the people in the auditorium — including those who had called for the pledge to the flag — afraid of? Why did a few, so widely scattered, call out so wildly, like people in a burning theatre, and why did the rest get up so submissively when these few called out, "Get up"? What was the matter? What was the matter in sunny Pomona, The City of Churches, Site of the New $50,000,000 Home of the Convair Guided Missile Division of the Consolidated Vultee Aircraft Corporation? What was the matter — for that matter — in me?

The few who had called for the pledge appeared to be afraid of Communists; afraid of Communists in a land flowing with grapefruit juice and guided missiles. The many who had got up, reluctantly, appeared to be afraid of the few who were themselves afraid. If the many had remained in their seats, wouldn't fear have melted away in sunny Pomona, the fear that had seized both the few and the many, and from Pomona wouldn't fearlessness have spread through the land? Why were people afraid in, of all places, Pomona?

Why was I? Was I afraid of being hurt? I don't think so. I've been hurt before; it doesn't hurt much. Of being shamed in Pomona? I don't think so; I hadn't been shameful, and the world is wide. Of being thrown out into the street? What's that, when a man has, as I have, a clothesbrush? Of a general disturbance, with the police coming in? Why, they would protect me; "Pomona," says the Chamber of Commerce, "is virtually crime-free. Led by FBI-trained Chief Ralph E. Parker, one of the youngest and ablest police chiefs in the State, the Pomona Police Department has been recognized by the Federal Bureau of Investigation as. . . ."

What was it I was afraid of? Was it only because the man on the platform is naked, unhidden? I wondered — even in my fear — if Ferner Nuhn was afraid of American culture. *I* was. This was *my* country, *my* people, *my* home, rich and strong and not, like old Germany, stripped and impoverished. I was just back from Germany, where, when it happened there, beginning with the way it was happening here in Pomona, people said, "Oh, well — Germans." I was afraid of American culture.

But that was secondary, and I can't say I really thought of it while we five sat in our seats on the platform and the people below, their arms stretched out, palm upward, recited in unison the pledge to the flag. Primarily I was afraid because I felt fully, for the first time in my life, the power of fright over people of my own kind, of my own country and condition. In their capacity for fright, for being carried away from their reason and their training, I felt fully, for the first time in my life, my own. The bright lights of the auditorium didn't help; on the contrary, it seemed all the harder to hide. Congregation didn't help, either; all seemed to be adding their fright to the fright of each.

When the recitation of the pledge to the flag was finished, everybody sat slowly down. There was a quiet in the auditorium. Nobody, including those who had called for the pledge, knew what to do next — or rather, what was going to be done. But nameless anticipation was not the only ingredient of the quiet; there was catharsis, too. The fear had called out — to a flag, to be sure — and was quieted. Why? Weren't the five men on the platform, and the twenty below them on the auditorium, as dangerous now as before? They had refused to take the pledge, hadn't they? But they appeared — paradoxically enough — to be less dangerous, for the time. At least the meeting was allowed to proceed.

I wanted to address myself to "The Struggle for America," but I had been billed to discuss "The Struggle for Europe" and I discussed it. When I finished (to uncertain and mild applause), I was scheduled to call upon each of the panel discussants to discuss the discussion, and I did so.

Mr. Tay, the history teacher, discussed free enterprise, favorably, as the basis of American strength in the world. I didn't think I had discussed free enterprise, but Mr. Tay, who had not taken the pledge of allegiance, was a public school teacher in Pomona, in the very school where he had not taken the pledge. Mr. Tay was in a tight spot. I admired him.

Professor Britt of Scripps, the retired president of Knox College, did not discuss the struggle for Europe any more than Mr. Tay did. He discussed freedom of discussion, and the respect of every American for the freedom of every other, as the basis of America's strength. Very briefly, very sharply. Professor Britt seemed to surprise the audience; to me he simply revealed himself as one of those ordinary great Americans to whom the Americanism of the founding fathers is simply the natural state of human society.

Then Professor Merlan of Claremont rose to discuss the discussion. Now up to that point no one (at least, not I) had considered anti-Semitism as an element in the meeting. We should have, I suppose. And we most assuredly should have assumed anti-foreignism. When Professor Merlan stood up — uncertainly, I thought — I saw suddenly that this was the deadly moment. Professor Merlan was clearly a foreigner, and, I was sure, a Jew. Professor Merlan's spot was tight in the extreme.

"You must excuse me," said Professor Merlan, in an accent which frightened me all over again, "if I do not discuss Professor Mayer's analysis of the European situation except to say that, in general, I agree with it. I must discuss something else. I must discuss loyalty to America." He paused — again, I thought, uncertainly. The quiet in the hall was dreadful anticipation now, unmixed with relief. "Yes," he said, "I must discuss loyalty to America."

I heard him breathe a deep, uneven breath — he was almost next to me — and then say in his foreign accent: "I try to be loyal to America. I think I owe more to America and also to the people of America even than most of you do. I owe not only my happiness and my good position, but I owe also my life. If it had not been for America, I would have been killed in Europe long ago. And so you see, it is natural that I try to be loyal."

Professor Merlan looked around, through his thick glasses. "If I try to be loyal," he said, "I must do all that I can to keep harm from coming to America. Terrible harm came to Europe. Part of this harm, perhaps much of it, came because people became afraid to be thought disloyal. In the end, everyone was afraid. Everyone wished to be sure to do what every other one was doing, and especially to say how loyal they were, and to take pledges like the one I could not take this evening."

He paused again, and took another long, uneven breath. "These pledges do not prove that one is loyal. Loyalty is in one's acts and in one's life, and also in great ideals, and not even in the symbol of great ideals. And when these pledges are taken under compulsion, because someone, anyone, says, 'You must take them,' then they prove that everyone is afraid only. An America which would be afraid, afraid of freedom, would not be an America to which I would wish — to which I would wish to be loyal with my life. As long as America is good, and as long as we have the wish to be free with ourselves, here in Pomona, in Claremont, in every city, America need not be afraid."

The applause did not start at once. Then it started slowly — much the way the people had got up out of their seats to take the pledge — and then more and more people joined in. And it went on, and the earth shook in Pomona. Professor Merlan looked around, still, I thought, uncertainly, as if to say, "What do you think of what I have said? Would you say it was correct? Would you agree?" Then he sat down, and in the presence of one who had been prepared to be crucified, the fear of all fell away.

There wasn't anything more to say, but, as the speaker of the evening. I had to discuss the discussion of the discussion. I didn't. I said thank-you to Professor Merlan — I didn't say what for — and then I said that most of us in the auditorium had been brought up to take the pledge of allegiance to the flag, and that I had never before supposed that it might do any harm. I did not think it made men loyal or illuminated treason, but neither did I find it objectionable. But, I said, those of us who did not mind taking the pledge of allegiance could not, as good Americans, believing in freedom of worship, compel others to take it who believe literally in Christ's injunction against taking oaths to human beings or to human institutions. The freedom of conscience of our Christian countrymen, I said, was more important for the safety of our country even than the pledge of allegiance to the flag.

That was very good, but there was not much applause.

Then Ferner Nuhn added an anticlimax of his own. He called — doubtless in the interest of American culture — upon an elderly man in the middle of the auditorium who had been demanding all evening, and always out of order, to be heard. Mr. Nuhn asked him if he would like to come to the platform and speak, though it was late, for five minutes.

He was Joe Higgins, candidate of the Liberty party for President of the United States. His ancestors, he said, came over here in 1532 — really early, when you think of it — and he and his ancestors had been fighting ever since against the world conspiracy of the Rothschild international bankers. His ancestors had fought, he said, in every American war and on both sides of the Civil War. Then Joe Higgins poured it on, on the mess in Washington, the perfidy of the UN, Mrs. Roosevelt, the English.

People in the auditorium were laughing, more and more. Ferner Nuhn, as chairman, rose frowning to his feet and the laughter subsided. But it began again. Some people left. More and more who remained were laughing. Ferner Nuhn stood up again, frowning. "All right, Joe," called one of the men who had earlier called for the pledge of allegiance. "that's enough." Nobody was afraid now. Everybody was having fun with Joe Higgins. And when Joe Higgins finished, Ferner Nuhn thanked him for his contribution to the discussion, and the meeting ended.

There are just four footnotes.

Before we left the hall, a pastor from nearby Claremont came up to the platform and said to me, "I needed to have this experience tonight. I needed to realize that what can happen anywhere can happen anywhere else. I hadn't believed it."

A Republican advertising man from Los Angeles, one C. Richard Creamer, got hold of the man who had led the pledge of allegiance to the flag, shook hands with him, and thanked him for letting the meeting go on after the pledge was taken. "I think," said Republican Creamer, "that it's a darned good idea to let everyone talk, don't you?" "I guess so," said the leader of the pledge, "but I was wounded in Korea and I don't like these fellows. But I guess you're right, I'm glad they had a chance to talk." "Me, too," said Republican Creamer, "I'm a veteran myself, but I'd a lot rather talk than fight." "You bet," said the leader, and shook Republican Creamer's hand.

Outside the school — I was one of the last to leave because some college youngsters had come up to talk to me — two very little thin ladies broke away from a conversation they were having with Joe Higgins and came up to me. "You're not a Christian," one of them said, "you're a Jew." "That's right ma'am," I said. "What right have *you* got to talk about Christianity?" asked the other one. "Why," I said, "Jesus said He came to fulfill the Jewish Law, and Paul said there would be neither Greek nor Jew — don't you believe that?" "You get away from me, you Jew," said the first very little thin lady, and they both rejoined Joe Higgins, leaving me standing there.

A little later, while we were having a council of peace at the home of Dr. Joseph Griggs in Claremont, another lady came in, with her young daughter. "My daughter stood up in the meeting when I did," said the lady. "I did wrong, and she did it because I did it. But I wasn't expecting anything like that. I had never given a second thought to taking the pledge of allegiance to the flag. Now I think I'm better prepared when it happens again, so I'm glad I had the experience. And I think that most of the people who were at the meeting won't be afraid the next time."

"Be ye unafraid, for I am with you always," said somebody in the room.

"With a foreign accent," said somebody else.

The next best thing to eternal salvation is temporal salvation, and you can't blame a man in the prime of life, or a little past, for wondering what he might do for himself in case of nuclear war. I'd spent some time wondering lately, until I saw a headline in the local paper: "County Man Builds A-Bomb Shelter." The second paragraph of the story went like this:

Eager to share his experience in building a shelter for protection from nuclear blast and fallout, yet reluctant to pinpoint the location of the shelter, its owner declined to be named. In event of nuclear attack, or even panic due to rumor, he does not wish his family shelter mobbed by persons less well prepared.

Within an hour and a half — never mind how — I had the name and address of the man with the shelter. It was Henry T. Babcock, and he lived about two miles away from me. Professor Edward Teller, the "Father of the H-Bomb," says that there should be a shelter for everybody within ten minutes' walk. (I used to be a miler, took a third for Englewood High in the City Meet in 1925, and there's nothing to keep a man of my age from getting back into trim.) I tossed little Dicken into the car, got in myself, fastened the safety belt, and drove over to Babcock's without ceremony. Babcock and I were acquaintances, as people are in small towns, but just acquaintances. I knew he was scientifically trained and a successful, respected practitioner of his profession. Nice fellow. We didn't meet at the same parties, but, then, I don't get out much any more.

He was working in the garden, and he said he was glad to see me, and I said I was interested in his bomb shelter. "Everybody is," he said. "There doesn't seem to be any way to keep it quiet."

"I guess it's the only one in the County," I said.

"I guess so," said Babcock. "I've asked Civil Defense, but they

From the *Progressive*, September, 1961.

don't know. They don't know anything. I've been trying to get a Geiger counter from them for the past three years. I've got a ten-year-old counter, and I don't know if it's any good. Now that I think of it, I'd better put it down in the shelter. That's where you're supposed to keep it."

"You'd think other people would build shelters," I said.

"You would," said Babcock, "but you know how people are. They just don't want to think about it. But it stands to reason that there will be war. There always has been."

"I suppose the cost is a problem," I said.

"I suppose so," said Babcock. "It cost me four-thousand-some dollars just for a hole in the ground."

"You could have a nice swimming pool for that," I said.

"You can say that again," said Babcock, but I didn't. I was beginning to think that Babcock wasn't completely happy about the whole thing, though I couldn't see why. Here was his family — nice fellow, nice wife, three nice children — nicely sheltered from nuclear attack. But it's as Babcock himself said: "It's like insurance. If you have it, you don't need it. If you need it, you don't have it."

"Well, you've got it," I said.

"Well, I guess so," said Babcock. "But there are problems, lots of problems."

"You bet there are," I said.

Babcock excused himself to get the old Geiger counter and a pick, which he said he thought he might as well put down there because he had no use for it in the house and you're supposed to have some tools in the shelter. Dicken and I were left in the living room. The house was one of those new ranch-style affairs with merging "areas" instead of rooms. There were no bookshelves visible, but the coffee table had a book on it, dealing with Babcock's profession, and several copies of *Life*, *Time*, and *Reader's Digest*. Our host returned with the pick and the Geiger counter and said, "Well, let's go." We followed him out of the house and across the yard in the rear.

"I should have built it under the house," said Babcock thoughtfully, as we crossed the yard.

"Did you build it yourself?" I said.

"No," said Babock, "it was built by a contractor."

"But you designed it," I said.

"No," said Babcock, "we had the architect of the house design it." The shelter was about forty feet from the house (which was made of wood) and ten feet from the wooden two-car garage. There were three protrusions from the ground, an air-intake pipe (capped with a filter), an air-exhaust pipe, and a tilted entrance hatch. The intake was about five feet from the wooden fence surrounding the house and garage, and the exhaust was surrounded by a large pile of kindling.

"Well," said Babcock, "this is what it looks like from the outside. Here," pointing to the capped intake, "is where the air goes in. We draw it in with a blower in the shelter."

"What if the fence was on fire?" I said.

"What if what?"

"What if the fence was on fire, or the garage, or the kindling?"

"'Oh," said Babcock. "Yes. That would be bad. We'd be drawing the smoke right down into the shelter. That would be bad."

"What's the kindling around the vent for?" I said.

"That's just our kindling pile," said Babcock. Then he said, "I suppose I ought to move it away, but there's so darned much to do all the time."

"Of course," I said, "if you had a real fire storm above ground, with everything burning, I suppose the fire would suck the oxygen right out of the shelter. That's what happened in the ten-night raid on Hamburg." "Is it?" said Babcock. "Yes," I said. "The people in the shelters were asphyxiated." "That would be bad, all right," said Babcock.

We went over to the iron hatch-lid set in concrete. It took a lot of lifting. "Pretty sturdy," I said. "Yes," said Babcock, "pretty sturdy." The lid had a heavy hasp for a padlock on the outside, but there was no padlock. I asked if the hatch could be locked from the inside, and Babcock said it couldn't be. I thought about this and said, "Then the whole town could follow you into the shelter, couldn't it?"

"Well," said Babcock, "that's a problem, all right. Of course, there's an inside lock on the door at the bottom of the stairs. Once we got into the shelter itself, we could lock ourselves in."

"Then somebody might snap a lock on the hatch from the outside," I said, adding, "but nobody would do that."

"I hope not," said Babcock.

"Of course," I said, "you couldn't let *everyone* in."

"No," said Babcock, "there's just room for Nettie and me and the kids. It's not much more than a five-man shelter, really."

"I suppose you might have to stand off some of the people who wanted in," I said. "You know how people are," I added.

"Well, that's a problem," said Babcock. "Everybody would want to get in. I don't know what we'd do about that. One fellow said I'd need a gun."

"It might take a lot of shooting," I said. Babcock didn't say anything for a bit, and then he said, "The trouble is, you can't figure out everything."

"You can say that again," I said.

The inside of the hatch-lid was lined with sponge, and I asked Babcock why. "Well," he said, frowning, "theoretically it's to keep the lid from sweating. He emphasized the "theoretically." The wooden stairs to the floor of the shelter were steep but the stairway had an iron handrail. I was surprised to learn that the roof of the shelter was covered by only three feet of earth, but Babcock explained that the deeper you dig the more it costs. With its seven-foot ceiling, and its foot-thick floor, the bottom of the hole was eleven feet nine inches deep. (The roof was nine inches thick.) The construction was all steel-reinforced concrete except for the hatch-lid, the stairs, and the door at the bottom of the stairs. At the foot of the stairs was a 180-degree turn to the shelter door. Babcock said that that was the only idea he had ever been able to get from Civil Defense, and that every time he ever tried to find out anything from Civil Defense he ran into a stone wall of red tape. Whatever else made him unhappy, there was no doubt about Civil Defense. But there seemed to be something more than Civil Defense weighing on him. The local paper had described him as eager to share his experience; I found him willing rather than eager. His manner was that of a real estate agent showing a property he'd just as soon the client didn't buy.

"What was Civil Defense's idea about the 180-degree turn?" I said. "Well," he said, "the radioactivity is supposed to travel in straight lines, so it can't turn the corner. I suppose that's so," he added. I thought that was interesting and said so. Babcock said nothing.

The door of the shelter itself was made of wood, with steel trim. I opened and closed it a few times and asked if it was airtight. "I don't know," said Babcock. "It's snug, but I guess you wouldn't call it airtight." "I was just wondering," I said. I was just wondering about poison gas, and whether bacteria, once you took them off the leash, would turn 180-degree corners.

I don't know why, but I had thought that the shelter would consist of two or three rooms, at least. It consisted of one clammy concrete bunker eight by ten feet. Very clammy. My host began mopping up the dew with small bags scattered around the floor. "They're filled with chemicals," he said. "They're supposed to absorb the moisture, and then you bake them out in the oven." I said they didn't seem to work too well, and he said No, they didn't. He'd heard there was some cans of stuff that worked better, but he didn't know what it was called or where you got it.

The decor of the shelter was simplicity itself. There was one naked light, shelves of tinned and packaged food, a bunk spring (without legs) leaning upright against the wall, a plastic garbage can, a slender cylinder of oxygen about two feet tall and six inches in diameter, and one metal cleat in the ceiling. And, of course, the Geiger counter and the pick. Nothing else. No furniture of any kind, no hooks or hangers (or clothes to put on them), no copies of *Life* or *Time* or the *Reader's Digest*.

I asked Babcock how long he figured they might be down there. "You mean," he said, "in case of — ?" "Yes," I said, "in case of —." "There doesn't seem to be any way to find out. Some people say weeks, and some say months, so you don't really know. It's a problem." I agreed that it was and asked him how the family planned to occupy itself in the shelter in case of —. Babcock said they hadn't really thought about that. I asked him how he'd know when to come out. "You mean — afterward?" he said. "Yes — afterward," I said. "Well," said Babcock, "we've got a plug-in here for a portable radio, if we remember to bring it down when we come, and an antenna up through the vent." "So, then," I said, "you'd find out over the radio." "If we remember to bring it down," he said again, and then, "I guess we'd find out that way, unless —" "Unless —?" I said. "Well," he said, "unless the station is knocked out, or the current goes off. Of course," he added, "we've got this old Geiger counter, if it works, but we'd have to go outside to use it, so I don't know what we'd do about that. I guess it isn't much use, when you come to think of it."

"And where," I said, "is the Gents' Room?" "There," said Babcock, indicating the plastic garbage can, which was four feet tall. "And the garbage can?" I said. "There," said Babcock, indicating the plastic garbage can. I thought that the place ought to be pretty spicy after a week or so, and Babcock said, "The CD literature says to have a chemical toilet, but I can't find out where to buy one or how to build one. And I'm afraid to use chlorine, in case the fumes are poisonous. So we got this plastic garbage can. But we haven't been able to figure out —"

By way of changing the subject, I asked him what the single cleat in the ceiling was for. He said, "We thought we could get those cleats into the walls, to hang the bunks on, but for some reason we couldn't," and he pointed to the pockmarks in the concrete. "This is the only one we could get to stay in, so we haven't been able to put up the bunks." I said that the concrete must be pretty hard, and he said that I could say that again.

I asked him about the food, and he said that that was a problem. "The trouble is," he said, "that it spoils. Rust. I guess it's the damp, or something. I opened a can of tomato juice a while back, and it was spoiled. Somebody said you should rotate the food every two years." "Every year," said his little boy, who was with us. "Every year," said Babcock. "Here," he said to his little boy, handing him a can, "take this spaghetti up to the house, and we'll have it for lunch." "Every year," said the little boy, going out with the spaghetti.

Besides the canned and packaged foods, there were twenty-four beer-sized cans of water for a family of five. I asked Babcock if he thought it was enough. "I guess not," he said. "I ought to get some more. Of course it depends on how long —" "But," he went on, "we have some other stuff to drink," and he pointed to maybe a dozen cans in all of ginger ale, root beer, and juices, and two bottles each of king-size Coca-Cola and Seven-up. He said they had instant coffee, too, and he thought they had a hot plate somewhere. "I guess we'd have to drink it cold, if the current went off," he said.

I asked him what they would do for light if the current went off. "Well," he said, "I don't know, exactly. If the current goes off, we've got this flashlight, of course." He showed me the flashlight, of the sort that burns out in a night. I asked him about candles. "I don't think they'd do," he said, "they'd use up the oxygen." "But you'd be getting fresh air through the blower," I said, "so you'd be all right." "Well," said Babcock, "that's the biggest problem, I guess you might say. As long as the current is on, the blower works fine." He turned it on. It worked fine, but it roared. "It's a little noisy," said Babcock, "on account of the concrete, I suppose. But you can see for yourself, it works fine. The trouble is, it might be drawing the radioactive particles right in through the filter from outside. I haven't been able to find out if the filter would keep them out. Another thing is that you're supposed to change the filter, but you'd have to go outside to do that." At this point, he seemed to become thoughtful, and so did I.

"And if the current goes off?" I asked. "Oh," said Babcock, brightening "you can operate the blower with the hand crank. Here, try it." I tried it, for twenty to thirty seconds, and it nearly broke my arm. "It goes a little hard," said Babcock. "I guess we'd have to do it in shifts if we were going to do it all the time. Of course it depends on how long——" "And," I said, "on whether the filter was drawing radioactive particles in, or napalm, or gas. They"—I meant the Russians—"might use napalm, or gas."

"Gas," said Babcock, without any tone or emphasis. "If they use gas and we use the air pump, I guess we've had it." Neither of us said anything, and then Babcock said, "You know, I guess the pump isn't really much use, except the blower part, to circulate the air you've already got." Neither of us said anything again, and then Babcock said, "We might be better off to depend entirely on the oxygen tank," and we walked over to the tank, which was as I've said, a cylinder about six inches in circumference and two feet tall. "How much oxygen is there in it?" I said, thinking of his scientific training. He looked at the tag on the cylinder. "I don't really know," he said.

"They give you a formula to calculate — by the cubic feet and number of persons and so on — but I haven't had a chance to calculate the formula, there's so darned much to do. The darned thing's on my desk in the house. It's pretty complicated." I asked him what it said on the tag. "It says two thousand pounds pressure," he said, "but I don't know what that means. If I knew the *weight*," and he turned the tag over. It was blank. I asked him if he had any idea how long it would last in case —. He shook his head and said, "Several days, maybe. I don't really know. I ought to calculate that formula." He shook his head slowly and said, "My wife's a chain smoker. I guess that affects it, too."

It wasn't getting any warmer in the shelter, and I asked Babcock what they'd do for heat in case —. Babcock said that would be a problem, he guessed, but an old Navy man told him that with enough bodies down there it would be warm enough. I said, "Of course, there's such a thing as too much heat in a shelter. The people in those deep shelters in Hamburg died of asphyxiation, but their bodies were charred from the heat above the ground."

Babcock was frowning, and there didn't seem to be anything more to say or to see, and we went on up and out into the summer day. "It's nice outside," said Babcock. "It will be nice to come out after —" I said. "I don't know," said Babcock, "I just don't know. It's a problem." "*It's* a problem?" I said. Babcock nodded. "Food and water," he said, "what if they're contaminated?" "And air," I said. "Air," said Babcock. "And people," I said. "I suppose," I went on, "that you'll have to keep away from contaminated people." Babcock nodded and said, "But maybe they won't keep away from you." "Well," I said, in a tone with which I might have slapped another man on the back, "keeping away from contaminated people has always been a problem, socially." He was still frowning.

If I had to put an adjective to Babcock, I suppose it would be "apathetic." He had certainly lost interest in the shelter. (Had he ever had any?) But there was something more than apathy there. I seemed to be making him actually miserable by asking him the questions that anyone would ask about it. He had done his duty by showing me the shelter; he had done his duty by building it; but doing his duty appeared to have touched him with a deep melancholy. Even when he said, "It's nice outside," he said it without much zest.

We stood there in the summer day and said good-bye, and he said, "If there's anything else you'd like to —" and I was still trying to figure out how he felt. Babcock's trouble is that he doesn't want to die and he knows he's going to die and where he's going to die and where he's going to be buried.

I put Dicken into the car and got in myself and fastened my safety belt, and we started home. Now Dicken may not think a lot — it's hard to tell — but he doesn't say much. He didn't say much on the way home. He didn't say anything until I asked him what he thought about it, and then he said, "It's a tomb, if you ask me." "You can say that again," I said, and Dicken said, "It's a tomb, if you ask me."

It looks as if the United States Supreme Court will have to decide whether Roger the Terrible Touhy really kidnaped Jake the Barber Factor on the night of June 30, 1933. If the Court says yes, he really did, he will have to remain in the Illinois State Penitentiary until, counting time off for good behavior, he is one-hundred thirty-four years old. If the Court says no, he really didn't, he will go free after more than twenty-two years in the pokey.

That will be a great day for me because I covered the case as a cub reporter in Chicago and I was sure, as only a cub reporter can be, that Jake the Barber had kidnaped himself. And for twenty-two years I have had to listen to people saying, "So maybe he didn't kidnap Jake the Barber. What difference does it make as long as they got a gangster like him locked up? Who cares about Terrible Touhy?" Nobody. But some people, including some lawyers, cared about justice. Seventeen times a succession of such lawyers went into the courts for justice. Seventeen times — including four times in the Supreme Court — they heard the words "Petition denied." The petitions were all denied on points of law. Not once, in all those seventeen lawsuits, were the lawyers able to get a court to review the case on its merits — on the question, that is, of whether Terrible Touhy really kidnaped Jake the Barber.

And then, one day, seven years ago, *United States of America* ex rel. *Roger Touhy* came up again, this time in the United States District Court in Chicago, and it landed by chance on the docket of the Honorable John P. Barnes.

From the *Reporter*, November 17, 1955. © 1955 by The Reporter Magazine Company.

Judge Barnes was, according to his own admission, "born Republican in Pennsylvania at a time when only Republicans were being born there." He came up the hard way, beginning as a $7.50-a-week law clerk and rising to a profitable partnership with former Republican Senator Otis F. Glenn of Illinois. In 1931 Glenn asked him for his recommendation for a federal judgeship. Barnes suggested the best man he knew, and Glenn went to President Hoover with two recommendations — Barnes and the man Barnes suggested, in that order. And for twenty-four years he has served on the federal bench and watched Democrats go past him up the judicial ladder. The New Dealers didn't like him because he held the National Recovery Act unconstitutional (and the Supreme Court sustained him). The Old Dealers didn't like him any better.

When it comes to dealing, one of Barnes's infrequent statements off the bench reveals his attitude: "I don't think the government is any different from any other litigant." Barnes has the reputation of being the toughest judge on the federal bench, single-minded and implacable, even unmerciful, in his servitude to the law. When the Supreme Court, on a rare occasion, reversed one of his decisions, he said placidly, "Confronted with the same set of facts again, I would make the same decision."

In 1943 the United States District Court in Chicago, sitting *en banc*, dismissed Touhy's petition for a writ of habeas corpus on the ground that he had not exhausted his remedies in the state courts. But on November 16, 1948, over the protest of the State of Illinois — which didn't want the case reopened — Judge Barnes ruled that he would hear Roger Touhy's case on its merits. For six years he heard it. Back went the wonderful record into a wonderful past, the Chicago of a quarter-century ago. Some of the past, Barnes found, was curiously mislaid, some of it buried alive.

Ghosts, some of whom wouldn't walk without a subpoena, walked into his courtroom and gave him ghastly glares when he said "Objection overruled. The witness will answer the question." In the course of that six-year hearing he sentenced the head of the FBI in Chicago to jail for contempt of court because he wouldn't produce his records and told him that if his boss, the Attorney General of the United States, took his place, he'd send *him* to jail, too. Ancient coppers and still more ancient convicts were called to the stand. Jake the Barber was called. Clara Touhy, still married to Roger, was called. Even I was called. And the courtroom buzzed when No. 8711-E — the "E" is not for Excellence; it's for Escapee — was called to the stand. "That's him. That's Terrible Touhy."

And then on August 9, 1954, the tough little mug who had somehow managed not to go stir-crazy yet, his lips half-curled, his hair now gray, watched Judge Barnes ascend the bench in the business suit he wears because he won't wear a robe. He had before him his opinion. J. Edgar Hoover had once said that Touhy's claim of innocence was "too funny to talk about." Judge Barnes's opinion talked about it for 774 typewritten pages. When he read the words "The Court is of the opinion . . . that the Relator Roger Touhy should forthwith be discharged from custody," Roger the Terrible Touhy broke down and bawled.

In between pages 1 and 774 was Barnes's finding that Jake the Barber had faked his own kidnaping in order to avoid extradition to England for an eight-million-dollar swindle there and that Police Captain Dapper Dan Gilbert, chief investigator for the state's attorney of Cook County, had framed Roger Touhy in conspiracy with the Capone gang with whom the Touhy gang had been having difficulties. Furthermore, said the court, the frame-up was made with the knowledge of the then state's attorney, Honest Tom Courtney.

After twenty-one years and twenty-one days in prison, Roger Touhy was free. He remained free for forty-nine hours. Then he was back again, on an order obtained by the State of Illinois from the United States Court of Appeals. Last July — almost a year after Touhy went back to prison — the Court of Appeals reversed Judge Barnes's decision on a jurisdictional technicality that had nothing to do with guilt or innocence. Now the case has gone to the United States Supreme Court — for the fifth time. The outcome involves a labyrinth of law and is anyone's guess. But John P. Barnes has the habit of being sustained in Washington.

Let me tell you — because I was there — how a swindler like Jake the Barber Factor could pretend to be kidnaped and get the

State of Illinois to hang the rap on an innocent gangster like Roger the Terrible Touhy. Let me tell you how the whole thing could have happened, right smack in the middle of the twentieth century. But let me begin by saying that it didn't happen in the twentieth century: It happened in Chicago, which in 1933 was prehistoric.

Chicago grew faster than any other city in history. When Chicago was growing and you wanted to cross the country, you crossed it at Chicago. If you couldn't make it across, you stayed there. The town grew so fast that it never got organized. Of course it had a mayor and fifty aldermen and a chief of police, but they were just for receiving distinguished visitors or arresting undistinguished bums caught sleeping under bridges or begging bread in the streets.

Now don't misunderstand me. If you behaved yourself in Chicago, you lived like people anywhere else. If your name wasn't Bugs Moran or Greasy Thumb Guzik, you could live peaceably and die in your bed and be buried in Cicero and never be bothered. But the state of nature — in which every man has to protect himself as best he can — prevailed in certain trades. Spirituous liquors, for instance. Everybody except Congressman Volstead wanted to drink, and there was a sort of civil disobedience movement on — Gandhi with an elbow bent. Even in the state of nature there's a law of supply and demand. Since supplying was illegal — and this went for gambling, women, and dope as well as for booze and beer — the law could intervene. The mayor and the chief of police and the sheriff and the state's attorney had to be persuaded, if possible, not to intervene.

The men who ruled the streets of Chicago in 1933 were roughnecks who had fought their way up on the streets. Their parents were illiterate immigrants, they themselves half-literate. Take the three central characters in the drama called *United States of America ex rel. Roger Touhy*. Touhy himself and Police Captain Dapper Dan Gilbert got no further than grammar school and spoke very bad English. The third, Jake the Barber, had come to America at ten or eleven and had only a hazy recollection of "several months" of schooling in Poland. Roger, Dan, and Jake got their educations in a place called the Valley. Originally the Valley was a row of shacks at the bottom of the B. & O. embankment, just outside Chicago's central business district. It spread until it occupied the whole of the "near" southwest side of the city. Its political headquarters was the Democratic Club at Madison and Paulina, where Dapper Dan Gilbert, teamster boss, policeman, and ultimately police captain, could always be reached. Hoyne and Madison — a saloon four-corners — was where the young teen-agers, including Dan and Roger's big brother Tommy, hung out. But the Valley's Supreme High Command was Paddy the Bear — I don't remember his last name, and maybe he had none — and its G.H.Q. was the back room of Paddy the Bear's saloon at Fourteenth and Halsted, a few blocks from the ghetto where Jake Factor lived when he came from Poland as a kid. The specialty of Paddy the Bear (he weighed three hundred pounds and couldn't get through the front door of his own saloon) was a process for making ink disappear from police blotters. He was, in a word, a "clout," that is, a cover for criminals, and his saloon was their nest. Tommy Touhy, Roger's big brother, was hatched there. Paddy the Bear was killed by Shrimp Quinlan in 1920, and the Shrimp was killed by Paddy's son, Paddy the Cub in 1926.

In the 1920's — long after Tommy Touhy was hatched — the Valley's most eminent sons were Frankie Lake, Terry Druggan, and Samuel Nails Morton. Frankie and Terry were partners, and after they hit it rich in rotgut, they took to playing golf. Federal Judge James H. Wilkerson tossed them into the Cook County jail for a year on a prohibition charge. One day a reporter on the old Chicago *Journal* called up the jail and asked for Mr. Druggan, just for the ducks of it. "Mr. Druggan is out," said the operator. So the reporter asked for Mr. Lake. "Mr. Lake is out, too. They'll be back for dinner; they're only playing golf." Now Valley boys who play golf are traitors to their class. But Nails Morton was worse. Nails was an enemy of the people — of the people that is, in the back room of Paddy the Bear's saloon. He came back from the First World War with a medal for bravery under fire and went on firing until he was well established in the hard-beverage business. Then he moved away from the Valley and on to the Gold Coast, where the Valley heard that he was drinking whiskey *with seltzer water in it*. Worse than that, he was wearing fancy tight pants and riding horses — not anywhere in particular, just around in the park. Nails invented the one-man one-way ride when his horse threw him in Lincoln Park one day and killed him. The view of this melancholy event in the Valley was that that is what happens to swells in fancy pants, and Nails's competitors closed out his business (and some of his business associates) for him. But one of his associates, Louie Two-Gun Alterie, lived long enough to go to Lincoln Park the next day, rent the same horse, ride him to the same spot, and kill him.

Back in the 1890's in the Valley, Policeman James Touhy, an immigrant from County Sligo, was an upright man and an honest copper at seventy dollars a month. Roger was the youngest of six boys, with a sister older and a sister younger. Policeman Touhy, a hard Christian man, beat his kids until the neighbors intervened. Mother Touhy, a soft Christian woman, herded her children to Mass. Roger was her baby boy, and he was ten when his mother was burned up in her kitchen in 1908. Policeman Touhy retired from the force on pension to move his motherless brood to the country and save them from the Valley. But the five older boys wouldn't go. They left home. Roger, growing up with his father and sisters, was valedictorian of his grammar-school class — none of them ever went to high school — and at thirteen he went to work.

Being a Touhy — just being one — was Roger's undoing. Of his five older brothers, four were bad. Two of the four died in the beer wars. Jimmy, the eldest, died in prison. The fourth bad brother was Tommy, who went in and out of the penitentiary so often that there was talk of installing a revolving door. Oddly enough, he's still around, living in Arizona in the loving care of a decent daughter. His swan song was a twenty-three-year stretch (with time off for good behavior) for sorting the mail with a gun in the Minneapolis station of the Milwaukee Railroad. That happened in January, 1933, six months before the Factor kidnaping, and on that occasion Tommy showed up in the papers as Terrible Tommy Touhy. The monicker "Terrible Tommy" belonged originally to an old and close associate of Tommy's, Terrible Tommy O'Connor, who had an appointment to be hanged in the Cook County jail one morning in 1919, as I recall. He didn't keep the appointment, and during the subsequent manhunt, his body was shipped to his family for burial in a sealed casket. It wasn't until after the funeral that the bill of lading for the casket turned up with Tommy's own fingerprints on it.

The "Terrible" having passed from T. O'Connor to T. Touhy, the papers proceeded to hang it on R. Touhy after he was grabbed for the Factor kidnaping. And I mean the papers. Chicago — the Chicago I'm talking about — was built by the papers. The gang wars meant circulation. The gangsters were "over the fence," outside the law; they weren't going to sue a paper or plug a reporter. You could hang absolutely anything on them you wanted to. When I went down to the penitentiary a few weeks ago to see Roger, we had a long talk, in the course of which he suddenly turned plaintive and said, "Who do you suppose invented that 'Terrible Touhy?' Nobody ever called me that in my life. What makes them do that to a fellow?"

There was one monicker in Chicago that was old when Scarface Al was new, and that was Jake the Barber. John or Jack he called himself, but it was as Jake the Barber that he was known long before 1923, when he was indicted in Chicago for selling low-tide real estate in Florida. And Jake the Barber he remained through his wonderful career — or at least until November 8, 1933. I was in St. Paul that day covering the trial of Roger Touhy *et al.* for another kidnaping, that of William Hamm, Jr., a brewer. Selection of the jury had just begun when there was a flash that Touhy *et al.* had been indicted in Chicago for the kidnaping of Factor. Filing my story to Chicago that night, I referred to the new indictment concerning Jake the Barber and to its prejudicial effect on the Hamm jurors. But the reference came out in my paper the next day as "John Factor, wealthy speculator," and it came out in all the other Chicago papers the same way. I went on filing it as Jake the Barber but it kept coming out John, etc. After the jury acquitted Touhy *et al.* in the Hamm case — Alvin Karpis was caught three years later and confessed — I returned to Chicago to cover the Factor case, and I asked the telegraph editor what the idea was of the "wealthy speculator" gag. "Oh," he said, "Mr. McCarthy wants to see you." Mr. McCarthy, the managing editor, had never wanted to see me before, and I perspired in the December heat as I crossed the green carpet to Mr. McCarthy's desk. I still remember that green carpet. "Nice work in St. Paul," said Mr. McCarthy, "but this matter of Jake the Barber. State's Attorney Courtney was up here, and he's asked the papers to use the expression 'John Factor, wealthy speculator,' so as not to prejudice prospective jurors in the Touhy trial." "But," says I, "Jake's not a speculator, he's a swindler." "Well," said the managing editor, "swindlers speculate, too." I was going to resign then and there. But I didn't. I'd just got a raise, to $32.50 a week.

Jake the Barber, alias Spencer, Walker, Wise, Guest, etc., had, as I say, a wonderful career. In releasing Roger Touhy from the penitentiary, Judge Barnes made some observations on the credibility of the witnesses who, during that six-year hearing from 1948 to 1954, had been before him. Of Jake the Barber, the complaining witness in the conviction of Roger Touhy twenty-one years earlier, the court said:

John Factor has an extraordinarily agile mind — certainly the most agile mind of anyone the court has observed in connection with the case. He has had very little formal education, but he has nevertheless had an exceeding broad and thorough education. He has learned all that a boy and man can learn as a bootblack, washroom attendant, newsboy, barber, high-pressure stock salesman, Florida land salesman, bucket-shop operator, and confidence man — except to be honest. . . . [His] appearance and demeanor on the stand . . . and the testimony of all witnesses who dealt with him all indicate that Factor was eminently well qualified by character, ingenuity, mental resourcefulness and experience to devise and perpetrate a kidnaping hoax. Furthermore, he had money which he was willing to spend. Finally, he had a motive. He was in real trouble. He faced a long prison sentence when he went back to England. . . .

For two years — prior to his supposed kidnaping in 1933 — Factor had been fighting extradiction to England, where he was wanted as the ringleader of the great Broad Street Press stock fraud. At least three and a half million of the eight million dollars the Factor ring got away with came back to America with Jake the Barber in 1930. It was traced through New York and Chicago banks. Originally a fugitive on the extradition warrant, he surrendered to the United States Marshal in 1931. His lawyers were the highest-priced lawyers in America — among them former Senators Glenn of Illinois and Jim Reed of Missouri plus former Secretary of War Newton D. Baker. On May 29, 1933, the United States Supreme Court ordered his extradition set for argument. The rest of the members of the Factor ring had been taken back to England and convicted. Jake's goose was apparently cooked — unless something happened to stay the proceeding. Now if Jake the Barber were a kidnap victim, and therefore a material witness in a capital case, the extradition warrant might be stayed.

He had a motive, and he had a friend. His friend was an old Valley boy himself, Captain Dapper Dan Gilbert, chief investigator for the state's attorney's office. Dan had gone to work as a wagon boy at eleven, and in 1913, after a campaign in which his opponent was shot on Christmas night, was elected secretary-treasurer of the Baggage and Parcel Delivery Drivers Union's Local 725. Dan served on the governing council of the Chicago Teamsters Union until 1917, and then he went on the police force and rose like a meteor. But he never, as they say, lost touch with Labor.

The Chicago Teamsters Union — twenty-three locals with twenty-one thousand members — was not a labor union. It was a strong-arm racket and had been a strong-arm racket since it left the AF of L's International Brotherhood of Teamsters in 1908. One by one and killing by killing, the teamster's locals fell into the hands of the outlaws and inlaws who controlled the owners' association, the Chicago Truckers and Transportation Exchange. Nobody really cared what happened to the orphan unions — nobody, that is, except the working stiffs, the teamsters. When the stiffs tried to get into their own halls to vote they found the halls filled, and if they insisted on getting in, they found themselves in a ditch.

So Jake the Barber, who did not want to go to England, had a friend in Captain Dapper Dan Gilbert, who was a Friend of Labor at a time when Labor was being transferred, in a friendly way, to the Capones. But Roger Touhy was an obstructionist.

Late in 1930 one Marcus Studdy Looney came to see Roger and offered him a set of unions if Roger would cast his lot with the Capones. Roger said no, he was doing all right in the beer business.

He had the northwest part of Cook County, where the police would direct traffic by day and drive Roger's trucks by night. He was making $50,000 a year or so, and the hundred free barrels he provided for every Republican and Democratic picnic were a drop in the vat. There were no guns and no killings and Roger didn't want any part of the Capones.

But the Capones wanted part of Roger. Roger heard that Bill Rooney, a Valley boy who had shot his way into the "legitimate" ownership of the Sheet Metal Workers Union (and the part ownership of a few others), was going to be shot by the Capones; his offense was having some money in his union treasuries that the Capones wanted. Roger told Rooney, and Rooney, sure enough, *was* shot, fatally. While Roger was wondering whether he might be shot fatally, the remaining "legitimate" teamster leaders moved out to Park Ridge, a suburb that Roger more or less owned, convoyed by a flock of bodyguards provided by Roger's brother Tommy. Roger, whom the besieged bosses trusted, served as treasurer of the siege, and when the boys came for their money, they came to Roger's basement, which was fixed up, in case of a rumpus, as a rumpus room. The treasury that Roger disbursed consisted of $75,000 contributed by Dan Tobin, president of the International Brotherhood of Teamsters, and $50,000 kicked in by the union bosses who were besieged. Tobin sent his international vice-president, Paddy Berrell, an ex-con, up to Park Ridge along with the money, and when Paddy got careless and went for a ride with one of his bodyguards, he and the bodyguard were both machine-gunned. One by one the Capones were picking off the beleaguered bosses, and the bosses got scared. Then Roger was invited down to Capone headquarters for a talk, and he got scared. Finally the bosses surrendered to the Capones and turned back what was left of the money — $40,000. It cost Tobin's organization another $350,000 and several years to clean up the Chicago unions.

So Captain Dan, the friend of Jake the Barber and the Friend of Labor, was not a friend of Roger Touhy. "To put it mildly," wrote Judge Barnes,

Roger Touhy was not an acceptable person to Captain Gilbert. Relations between them had been unfriendly, dating back to an altercation in the Cragin Police District in Chicago in 1923, when Gilbert wanted $5 a barrel for every barrel of beer delivered in the district, even though it was near beer. . . .

[But] the old Gilbert-Touhy enmity was not the vital element in the choice of Touhy as scapegoat in the Factor affair. That choice had its basis in the peculiar affinity between the so-called Capone syndicate and the [state's attorney's] office during the early '30's, and Touhy's position on the opposite side of the widespread movement of the syndicate into numerous labor organizations at the time. [The Capone] syndicate could not operate without the approval of the [state's attorney's] office, which at that time was [State's Attorney] Courtney and [Chief Investigator] Gilbert. They did continue to operate and thrive without interference from Courtney or Gilbert. The relationship between the State's Attorney's office, under Courtney and Gilbert, and the Capone syndicate, was such that during the entire period that Courtney was in office [twelve years beginning in December, 1932], no syndicate man was ever convicted of a major crime in Cook County.

There we were, then, in Chicago, the night that Jake the Barber Factor either was or wasn't kidnaped. That was June 30, 1933, around midnight, as Jake was leaving a Capone roadhouse in the northwest suburbs after an evening of gambling. The next day Captain Dan announced that the Touhy gang had done the job — an announcement all the more wonderful in that no law-enforcement official, high or low, paid a call on the Touhys in the days that followed. The faint odor of fish that was detectable even then was not dissipated by the insistence of the British consul in Chicago and the attorney for the British Crown that the kidnaping was a hoax designed to prevent the missing Factor's extradition.

On July 12 the wealthy speculator was picked up on the streets of La Grange, a very respectable suburb, by a very respectable policeman named Bernard Gerard. Jake was bleary, bearded, and bloodshot of eye. He said he had just been released after twelve days of "unmerciful torture" in a filthy and bug-ridden basement. He had, he said, paid $70,000 ransom. Policeman Gerard testified some six months later for the defense in the trial of Touhy and described Factor's appearance to the court and jury this way:

Well, his tie was in place . . . and he was wearing a light linen suit, which was clean. His sleeves were wrinkled. His pants were somewhat wrinkled. His shoes were quite clean, no marks of dirt on them; no marks of dirt on his hands. He also had a white handkerchief, which was very clean—wrinkled, but no marks of dirt on it. His nails and hands were perfectly clean, cleaner than mine, and I have just cleaned them. . . . The cuffs of his shirt were pressed and clean. His collar was straight, in place and—well, that is about all.

Nearly sixteen years later, in 1949, Bernard Gerard, since promoted to lieutenant (and since then promoted to chief of police of River Forest), testified before Judge Barnes that when he left the stand in the Touhy trial he was seized by two state's attorney's policemen, taken to Captain Gilbert's office, cursed by Gilbert and Factor, accused of being in Touhy's pay, and later tried before the Civil Service Board at the demand of State's Attorney Courtney. He was acquitted.

Jake said he could not identify his kidnapers, and the Touhys were left strictly alone for a while. Roger went fishing in Wisconsin with two gunmen named Wee Willie Sharkey and Gloomy Gus Schaefer and an old labor skate named Eddie Father Tom McFadden. Wee Willie, who with Gloomy Gus was guarding Father Tom, got the Indians drunk on the Flambeau reservation and had them doing war dances. Roger fished by himself a few days and then called the trip off. On their way home their car skidded into a telephone pole in the village of Elkhorn. They were flagged down and fined, and while they were settling up, the hick cop looked in the car and found it filled with small-bore cannon. The travelers were arrested and held five weeks in Milwaukee without being indicted for anything. They were shown to Factor by both the police and the FBI, but Factor could not identify them. One day during the five weeks two gentlemen in plain clothes entered Roger's cell, knocked his teeth in, ruptured him, and fractured a vertebra. Finally, the prisoners were indicted for the aforementioned kidnaping of William Hamm, Jr., the brewer.

Now I was a nice boy and I didn't like gangsters and kidnapers. And I was a law-abiding boy and I trusted the United States. But I am frank to say that after the United States put Walter Bowick on the stand in St. Paul I never fully trusted the United States again. Hamm himself had told me he could not identify the defendants, and Harold Nathan, the field chief of the FBI, who had been sent to St. Paul to supervise the case, told me off the record that the government's case was weak. Then the government sprang its witness Bowick, and Bowick identified all the defendants. He had, he said, seen the kidnaping. Within twenty-four hours after Bowick left the stand, the defense, with the aid of a two-bit detective agency, proved that Bowick had never lived where he said he was living and was working in Chicago the day he saw the kidnaping in St. Paul. The government's case collapsed, and the jury acquitted Touhy *et al.* Defendants McFadden and Sharkey, after five weeks of being rolled in the tan, sat stupefied throughout the trial. Mc-Fadden was placed, voluntarily, in the funnyhouse afterward, and Wee Willie, the war dancer, hanged himself in his cell after the acquittal. Meanwhile the defendants had all been indicted by the State of Illinois for the kidnaping of Factor, and one day during the Hamm trial the front row of the courtroom was roped off and Jake the Barber was ushered in, accompanied by an entourage including Captain Dan.

As soon as the indictment was returned in the Factor case, State's Attorney Courtney, a prominent Democrat, armed with a good argument against extradition — that Jake the Barber was a material witness in a capital case — hopped the rattler for Washington, to call on an even more prominent Democrat. The even more prominent Democrat conferred with his subordinate, United States Attorney-General Homer S. Cummings, who in his turn talked to Secretary of State Cordell Hull, who thereupon refused to execute the extradition warrant for Jake the Barber.

Roger Touhy *et al.* were tried twice for kidnaping Jake the Barber, and I covered the business from start to finish. At the first trial, which began January 11, 1934, Father Joseph Weber came up from Indianapolis to testify for the defense. Touhy had been visiting Father Weber in Indianapolis the day Hamm had been released in St. Paul, and Father Weber had visited Touhy in Chicago while Factor said he was in the hands of his kidnapers. According to Judge Barnes, Father Weber had told the FBI that "the Touhys are being railroaded for the Hamm and Factor kidnapings; that the government [of Chicago] is corrupt, the judges are wrong, and the Chicago Police Department is dominated by the Capone syndicate."

But somewhere between the FBI and State's Attorney Courtney, Father Weber's statement got mislaid.

Father Weber, a parish priest, was famous for his social work. "I've seen him take out his handkerchief and wipe a little kid's nose on the street," Roger told me a few weeks ago. "He tried to help my brother Tommy when Tommy was in trouble about a department-store safe in Indianapolis. That's how I got to know him. It was at the time of the Klan, and Father Weber was after the Klan, too. I knew some fellows down there who were able to get the Klan's membership list for Father Weber. He never knew how they got it, but it broke up the Klan. But his big pitch was this rehabilitation, like they call it, rehabilitation of criminals. He supported everybody in his parish, it was the poorest in town. Me — oh, I was his 'collector.'" The Terrible Touhy grinned as he used the gangster term. "I'd go to fellows I knew and tell them that I had to have money for something that had nothing to do with beer, and they'd give it to me and I'd give it to Father Weber. I never been very religious, you might say, but I know religion when I see it, and he had it good."

While Factor was wherever he was between the night of June 30 and the night of July 12, Father Weber had been at Roger's house and telephoned him half a dozen times. He had done so at the request of Factor's private bodyguards, who claimed they wanted Roger to act as contact man with Factor's kidnapers. Roger, who knew that Factor's bodyguards were Lieutenant Leo Carr of the Chicago Police Department, on sick leave, and a Capone hood named Murray the Camel Humphreys, declined the invitation and had a temporary falling out with Father Weber. When Leo Carr was last heard of, many years later in California, he was still Factor's bodyguard and still on sick leave from the force.

Roger had other alibi witnesses in the first Factor trial, witnesses whom Judge Barnes accepted as truthful when he heard them twenty years later. But Jake the Barber, whose profession was swindling, was, as you may imagine, the perfect witness in every detail. From the plan of a house some of Touhy's men had rented in the suburb of Glenview, Factor identified it as the one he'd been held in. He was blindfolded all the time, he testified, but after he had been held seven days, the blindfold was removed "for a few minutes" so that he could write his wife a ransom letter, and it was then that he got a glimpse of Roger Touhy. The defense presented a medical expert who testified that a man blindfolded for seven days would not be able to recognize faces for four or five minutes after sudden exposure to light.

The jury was unable to reach agreement after the first Touhy trial, and the judge set the retrial for eleven days later. William Scott Stewart, Touhy's lawyer, presented affidavits from himself and Touhy asking that he be relieved as counsel. The judge told Stewart that if he wasn't in court to represent Touhy he'd go to jail for contempt. Twenty years later Judge Barnes held that the trial court's refusal to let the defendant be represented by counsel of his own choosing "deprived [Roger Touhy] of a fundamental right going to the essence of a fair trial. . . . this one error was so fundamental as to vitiate the entire proceedings from a constitutional standpoint." What had happened — Judge Barnes learned twenty years later — was that Roger wanted to testify in his own defense both in the Hamm and the Factor cases. But Stewart, who represented all the defendants, had been opposed: If he had let Touhy (who had no criminal record) testify, the other three defendants (who had bad records) would be jeopardized if they didn't testify. Stewart was a smart criminal lawyer, but, whether he wanted to or not, he represented what the law calls "adverse interests," and the trial judge refused to solve his dilemma.

The second trial looked like a repeat performance of the first except for two significant changes. One was that the state did not submit the plan of the Glenview house or ask Factor where he'd been held. Twenty years later Judge Barnes discovered that a dumb but dutiful copper had found the real house where Factor had held himself during those twelve days and had phoned in to Captain Dan to tell him all about it. Captain Dan had told him to keep away from it. There was a significant change in the defense, too. The advance list of defense witnesses for the second trial did not include the name of Father Weber. All by myself, and without disturbing my city editor, I telephoned to Father Weber in Indianapolis and asked him if it was true that he was not going to testify. He told me to talk to the bishop of Indianapolis. The bishop said that no parish priest could participate in public affairs without the consent of his ecclesiastical superiors and that that was all he had to say. When I asked State's Attorney Courtney about it, he said he knew nothing about it.

And then — as the state was closing its case in the second trial — a surprise witness was called to the stand. Isaac Costner, or Tennessee Ike, said that he had participated in the kidnaping with Roger Touhy and the other defendants and he wanted to confess and atone:

> Q. Do you see Roger Touhy in this courtroom?
> A. (*Pointing.*) That's him.

To support Tennessee Ike's story the state produced Basil the Owl Banghart, who testified that while he had not been in on the kidnaping proper, he and one Charles Ice Wagon Connors, whereabouts unknown, had muscled in on Tennessee Ike's attempt to collect $50,000 in supplementary ransom after Factor was released. When Basil Banghart stood trial a little later on for his own confessed part in the alleged kidnaping, his lawyer asked, "What is your occupation, Mr. Banghart?" "Thief," said Basil. "What was your last place of permanent residence?" "601 McDonough Boulevard, S.E., Atlanta, Georgia," said Basil, "but it wasn't permanent." It wasn't until the next day that we found out that 601 McDonough Boulevard was the street address of the federal penitentiary from which Basil had filed his way out awhile back. ("Stone walls and iron bars do not a prison make, just like the poet says," Basil once told me, and he ought to have known; he had left four penitentiaries "without," as he put it, "permission.")

After Tennessee Ike stepped down from the stand, the reporters scrambled for the door. Who was he? He was a habitual criminal, with a record as long as your arm and halfway back. He had lived on the lam, in and around Knoxville, where he was hiding from the revenuers when he and Banghart were picked up for knocking over a mail truck in Charlotte, North Carolina. Over a week end between the first and second Touhy trials, Captain Dan and Jake the Barber had gone to Baltimore, where Jake had identified Ike

as the "good man" among his kidnapers, and they had all come
back together to give Ike the opportunity he craved to testify in the
interest of justice. Twenty years later, a deposition from Tennessee
Ike made in Leavenworth Penitentiary was read into the record of
Judge Barnes's court, along with the deposition of a dozen people
in Knoxville who had seen and done business with him on every
one of the twelve days that Jake the Barber had been out of circulation twenty years before. Tennessee Ike deposed that he was
in Knoxville, all right, and not in Chicago at the time of the kidnaping and that he did not know Roger Touhy. According to Costner's deposition filed with Judge Barnes, he faced a thirty-year rap
for the Charlotte mail job, and the assistant attorney-general of the
United States, Mr. Joseph B. Keenan, had promised him a break
if he testified against Touhy. He got the thirty years anyway, and
he was very disappointed in Mr. Keenan. "A completely spurious
witness," said Judge Barnes. But the jury is the judge of the facts
in a lawsuit, and if perjured testimony is presented by the State of
Illinois, the victim must go to the State of Illinois with the evidence
and get a new trial. If, however, the State of Illinois *knowingly* ob-
tains a conviction on perjured testimony, then the victim obviously
cannot get a fair trial from the State of Illinois and he must go to
the United States of America with his evidence and ask for relief
from an unjust state. "The evidence discloses," wrote Judge Barnes,
"and the court finds that Factor, the state's attorney's office, and the
Department of Justice, once the publicity and notoriety originally
set in motion by Factor started to avalanche, worked and acted in
concert to convict Touhy of something, regardless of his guilt or innocence . . ." Just in passing, the judge had an unkind word for the
FBI. The court said that "the Department [of Justice] did evince an
astounding disregard for Touhy's rights and indulged in practices
which, in due regard for the administration of justice, cannot be con-
doned." Some questions were raised: Why was Touhy held, part of
the time by the FBI, without being charged with anything? Why did
the FBI continue its activity in the case long after it knew that the
crime, if any, was not in its jurisdiction? Why did an FBI agent
threaten to send an alibi witness for Touhy to prison if he took the
stand? Why did the FBI suppress the statements Factor made im-

mediately after his release and also those he made when he saw Touhy in custody and could not identify him?

Well, sir, Roger the Terrible Touhy went to prison for ninety-nine years in February, 1934. In October, 1942, when all his petitions for a rehearing had been denied by the state courts, he got so discouraged that in company with six other discouraged parties (including, of course, Basil the Owl Banghart) he worked his way over the wall of the Illinois State Penitentiary and into a handy automobile. Eighty days later the truants were all either killed or captured. Roger was captured, and that, you would suppose, was curtains for Roger. The Illinois law provided no penalty for prison-breaking when Roger broke prison, but it provided (under a statute which Judge Barnes called "medieval cruelty" and unconstitutional besides) that a prisoner who aided and abetted the escape of another should receive the other's sentence in addition to his own. This statute, Judge Barnes held, violated the Fourteenth Amendment to the Constitution of the United States, which requires *equal* protection of the laws. Roger Touhy was doing ninety-nine years, and Eddie Darlak, who escaped with him, was doing one hundred ninety-nine years; when they were recaptured, Touhy was convicted of aiding and abetting and was given Darlak's one hundred ninety-nine year sentence in addition to his own; Darlak, who had aided and abetted Touhy and given him a gun, was not even indicted. Who cared what they did to Roger the Terrible Touhy?

When Roger went to prison, there was something like $50,000 in the family. For five years Clara Touhy retained good fee-taking lawyers and then in 1938 she too got discouraged. She took what was left and moved away to bring up her two boys under another name. It was hard on Roger, but she thought she was doing the right thing, and I think Roger thought so too. The last lawyer she went to was the venerable Thomas Marshall, who had prosecuted Governor Len Small and Senator William Lorimer. Marshall took the case over the vehement protest of his gentlemen's-club associates in the Chicago Bar Association. He got a batch of affidavits from state's witnesses who admitted they had perjured themselves. But the state courts refused to hear the case on its merits, and that was that.

There was another eminent lawyer in Chicago. Thomas McConnell, who had represented investors in England in the case against Factor. McConnell, a big corporation lawyer, was a member of the Chicago Literary Club, one of those sociable little affairs where somebody reads a paper once a month. In 1945, McConnell read a paper on Factor and afterward had a discussion with Charles P. Megan, another club member, in which he disclosed that Factor had admitted to him that he could not identify Touhy. Megan subsequently used this information in an action for Touhy, and McConnell accused him of abusing privileges of the club. But he testified on Touhy's behalf when the case came before Judge Barnes.

When Megan called me one night late in 1945, I was flattered as well as mystified: Megan, just about the most respectable lawyer in Chicago, was president of the bar association. He asked me what I thought about the Touhy case, and I told him what I subsequently told when I was in the witness chair in Judge Barnes's courtroom.

There was no money left when Roger's younger sister Ethel persuaded Megan to take the Touhy case. Later on Roger got a $15,000 libel settlement from the movie company that made "Gangster Touhy," which, incidentally, Roger's older son, Roger, Jr., saw one night as entertainment for the GI's invading Italy. Later on, the administrator of the United States courts put up the paper-work costs — another $15,000 — out of a fund provided for indigent appellants. In 1948, Megan died, still fighting the hopeless case, and Robert B. Johnstone took it. I knew Bob Johnstone in college. He was one of those bright-eyed boys bent on a noble profession. He wasn't going to get rich — and he didn't. He's had one big client for seven straight years now: Roger Touhy, indigent.

Arguing against Judge Barnes in the Court of Appeals, the State of Illinois finally admitted last summer that maybe the testimony that convicted Roger *was* all perjured, but it argued that State's Attorney Courtney and Captain Dan hadn't known about it; therefore there was no "federal question," and Roger should go on addressing his appeals to the State of Illinois.

Meanwhile, Courtney had become a state judge. Captain Dan rose in the world, too, before he fell. In 1950 he was running for sheriff of Cook County when the Kefauver Crime Committee came to town and talked to him in secret session. A *Chicago Sun-Times* reporter walked into the printing plant that was printing the Senate committee's records, asked for a copy, and got it — just like that. The records disclosed that Captain Dan, with an annual salary of $9,000, had paid taxes on an income of $45,000 in 1949. The Chicago Crime Commission had protested his reappointment by each of Courtney's successors, always in vain. It wasn't until he was beaten for sheriff in 1950 that the "world's richest policeman" left town.

Jake the Barber didn't do badly either. After the Touhy conviction, the extradition warrant to England was allowed to lapse at the suggestion, it is said, of a very prominent person. In 1940, Jake applied to the Federal Alcohol Commission for a permit to run a distillery, and guess who appeared as his character witness? Captain Dan. Well, the Commission wasn't impressed, and it denied the permit on the ground that "John Factor is an individual who cannot be believed under oath." Two years later he was convicted in a federal court of the fraudulent sale of other people's whiskey warehouse receipts and sent to Leavenworth for ten years. He's living in Beverly Hills now, in a $75,000 hovel, and the government is breathing down his neck in the matter of $479,093.27 income taxes for the years 1935 to 1939.

When Judge Barnes released Roger in 1954, Jake was interviewed in Beverly Hills:

I took my life and the lives of my family and friends into my own hands when I testified in court about my kidnaping. Does that sound like it was a frame-up?

I was told by friends the odds against my ever going on the witness stand were 100 to 1 and that I might fear the worst. Yet Judge Barnes condemns me in his decision. I shouldn't have been condemned . . .

It wasn't so much Touhy and his gang that was on trial at that time. It was kidnaping in this country. If those men had gotten away with that crime God knows what they would have gone on to.

That's why I risked my life to go to court and testify. Maybe fate singled me out to rid the streets of Chicago of that mob.

Roger the Terrible Touhy has spent twenty-two years in prison for something he didn't do. He did plenty, but there is no evidence in or out of court that he ever committed a capital crime — or that he wouldn't, of course. Judge Barnes observed, in his written opinion, that Roger was a family man and had never been convicted of a felony or placed on the Chicago Crime Commission's lists of public enemies. It's true that he wasn't legitimate and that he kept very bad company and that he broke a lot of laws. But all that doesn't add up to kidnaping, or to two hundred ninety-eight years in prison (ninety-nine with time off for good behavior).

Like Jake the Barber and Captain Dan, Roger was a Valley boy. Seen from the Valley, he might have been worse, much worse. He had never done anything illegal until he was twenty-three, and then he found that his garage business, which was a success, would be even more successful if he used it for beer. He married a decent girl when they were both Western Union operators, and his kids were decent and don't even drink, and there they all were, twenty years afterward, Clara and the children, to claim him for their husband and father in Judge Barnes's courtroom.

The United States Court of Appeals reversed Judge Barnes's decision last summer on the ground that Touhy had not exhausted his remedies under the Illinois statutes. In 1943 he had filed a petition for a writ of habeas corpus in the United States District Court on the ground that he shouldn't have been incarcerated in the first place; but he had neglected to attack the constitutionality of the escape statute itself. This, said the Court of Appeals last summer, he must do before he could seek relief from a federal court. In 1954 Judge Barnes held that Touhy *had* exhausted his remedies in Illinois because the Illinois Supreme Court had sustained the constitutionality of the escape statute in another case. On this point, which the lawyers call a "nice" one and the laymen go to sleep on, the proceeding may go round and round a while longer. In reversing Barnes last summer, the Court of Appeals dodged the question of the fraudulent kidnaping entirely, saying: "If either of the judgments of conviction under which Touhy is presently serving is valid, there is no need to test the validity of the other." The escape conviction is valid — i.e., binding upon the federal courts in the absence of a Constitutional challenge by Touhy in the Illinois Supreme Court. The Court of appeals did go out of its way to add, as an appropriate comment on the "so-called" escape statute, that "it shocks the conscience when one considers that under the terms of this Act, one escaping prisoner can be sentenced to 199 years while another of the same group may be sentenced to a year or two." In the meantime Roger the Terrible Touhy stands condemned to serve a sentence of one hundred ninety-nine years for escaping from a penitentiary in which he was unjustly confined for ninety-nine years in the first place.

Twenty years is a long, long time. The old clippings under "Factor, John (Jake the Barber)" and "Touhy, Roger (Gangster)" in the reference room of my old paper fall apart when you unfold them now, and so do I. But Roger, when I saw him in prison a while ago, was full of beans. "I been reading a lot of law books," he told me, "and I got hold of a book by this Voltaire and I read it seven times. That boy's hard to beat."

You know, a fellow doesn't get a chance to read more than one or two really good books in twenty-two years, no matter where he's doing his time. I got to read one recently by a man named Arnold J. Toynbee. This Toynbee says that one way of judging a civilization is by what it does with its convicted criminals.

. . . Judge Douglas is especially horrified at the thought of the mixing of blood by the white and black races. Agreed for once — a thousand times agreed.

—ABRAHAM LINCOLN, 1858

The integrationists say that the issue is equal educational opportunity. The segregationists say that the issue is sexual intercourse of Negroes with whites and the consequent amalgamation of the races. When the Supreme Court ordered public school desegregation in 1954 the Jackson, Mississippi, *Daily News* said: "White and Negro children in the same schools will lead to miscegenation." As long as the integrationists go on saying that the issue is nothing but civil rights, they will be talking to themselves.

Miscegenation is the way the segregationists have always defined the issue. This is the way it was defined by Stephen A. Douglas in 1858. Lincoln disagreed; like the present-day integrationists, he insisted that the issue was simply legal equality; and he protested against "the counterfeit logic which concludes that, because I do not want a black woman for a slave, I must necessarily want her for a wife." After the Civil War the Knights of the White Camellia said in their constitution that "social equality would soon be the fruitful source of intermarriage between individuals of the two races; and the result of this miscegenation would be gradual amalgamation and the production of a degenerate offspring."

Social equality leads to miscegenation. What constitutes "social equality"? Anything and everything; in the old days emancipation from slavery, today desegregated schools and buses, restaurants and

From the *Progressive*, September, 1959.

198

housing. Gunnar Myrdal, in his monumental *American Dilemma*, found that "the very lack of precision allows the notion of 'no social equality' to rationalize the whole system of color caste in America." In the segregationist's logic, every deprivation of rights (at least where those rights bring Negroes and whites together) is justified as resistance to miscegenation.

The consecrated taboo in America is, of course, intermarriage and not miscegenation at all (unless the miscegenation involves a white woman against her will). When the segregationist rails against "race pollution," he does not necessarily care how much the race is polluted or how much his ancestors have done to pollute it, as long as their legal wives were white. When he cries "mongrelization," he doesn't ordinarily mean that he objects to the production of mongrels by himself or the males who listen to him, just as long as the producers, good religious people that they are, are married *only* in the sight of God.

"I was addressing a girls' school recently," says Negro attorney William Kelley, executive secretary of the Milwaukee Urban League. "My subject was the Supreme Court's outlawry of the 'separate but equal treatment' doctrine in public education. In the middle of the question period a girl got up and said: 'Do you believe in miscegenation?' I said the only thing I could think of: 'Do you mean *miscegenation*, or do you mean the *solemnization* of miscegenation and the assumption of the legal, moral, and religious responsibilities that such solemnization entails? If you simply mean miscegenation, you're asking about an accomplished fact, and there's nothing to be said about it. There are several million Americans called Negro whose pigmentation ranges from sepia to pomegranate to ochre, from milk-chocolate brown to daffodil yellow, and they didn't get here by any "separate but equal" treatment.' "

The segregationist's trump question is, of course, "Would you want your daughter to marry a nigger?" Many liberals, having tried (and failed) to avoid answering that question, have tried to answer it. I am one of them. My answer, "Not unless she was in love with him," is no answer. Neither is another I've heard given southerners: "*Your* daughters have always married Negroes; it's *your wives'* daughters you're worried about." The only actual answer I've ever heard was the one given by a Jew: "No, I wouldn't. I wouldn't want her to marry *any* of you Gentiles."

There is almost no Negro-white intermarriage in America. The highest rate ever recorded was 1.2 per 100 marriages in Los Angeles between 1924 and 1932, and this figure represented the intermarriage of whites with all other races in an area with a comparatively high proportion of Latin Americans, Filipinos, Orientals, and Indians. In 1948 the California statute forbidding interracial marriages was invalidated, and in 1951 there were .56 such marriages per 100 in the state — about one-half of 1 per cent. Five years afterward John H. Burma reported in the *American Journal of Sociology* that "no significant trends as to increases or decreases by months or years were observable."

But miscegenation is something else. Its popularity, especially in the segregated South, is attested by the fact, no longer disputed, that at least 70 per cent of all American Negroes have one or more white ancestors. Segregation in the South has always been what proud Negroes bitterly, and proud whites jovially, call "daytime segregation." Twenty-eight states — including all of the South and some of the West — have laws vividly forbidding intermarriage, but only four penalize interfornication, and these four make no enforcement effort. Even before the War (Civil, of course) such statutes were dead letters in the South because a Negro could not testify against a white. Intermarriage, on the other hand, is just as sternly resisted by law today as it was in slavery; more so. Until 1910 it was permitted in Louisiana, where for a hundred years, French Creoles had married wealthy Negro girls. (*Before* Emancipation one-fifth of the property of New Orleans was owned by Negroes or part-Negroes, many of whom had Negro slaves.)

Miscegenation has flourished in America as in no other country. Negro and white indentured servants were thrown together in one common depreciated class before the reduction of the Negro to slavery in the eighteenth century. Intermarriage was legal and not infrequent. After slavery was established, the slave girl was not only at the mercy of her master; it was to her advantage to be his concubine and to the master's to breed the highly valued mulatto. (Breeding slaves was cheaper than buying them.) And before and since Emancipation (and since the beginning of the world and until the end) there have been two compulsions to miscegenation. One, particularly strong in America, is the challenge of forbidden fruit; the other is the piquancy of variety or, as the French say in another (but related) connection, *Vive la différence!*

The white man's traditional repugnance toward miscegenation — Lincoln said he felt "disgust" at the idea — is not southern. It is American, "remarkably similar," Myrdal found, "throughout the country." And in a truly miscegenated populace like ours — composed of all the racial stocks of Europe — the Negro is the one distinguishable outsider, the most obvious and ubiquitous "other." True, the northerner does not appear to be thinking about miscegenation, perhaps because he doesn't dare to. But the southerner isn't thinking about anything else. "They don't build a federal government big enough," says school segregationist Ace Carter of Alabama, "to integrate my daughter with niggers."

Is it the white man's fault; or is it his history's? He is preconditioned. He cannot help *discriminating* the Negro; how can he help discriminating *against* him? And his country's peculiarly puritanical tradition, sensitizing him to sex, focuses his discrimination on miscegenation. The northerner's prejudice against actual propinquity seems to be much stronger than the howling southerner's; many old southern cites have no residential segregation, and Professor E. Franklin Frazier, an authority on race relations in the post bellum South, found very few northern soldiers among the white ancestors of part-Negroes. "Northern soldiers," he says, "had an aversion to close intimate contacts with the blacks, an attitude that was lacking among Southern whites." As well it might have been, among a people who as children had played and eaten and slept with Negro children and, as infants, may even have been suckled by a Negro "mammy."

On the surface the Negro is as firmly opposed to miscegenation as the white — but not for the same reason. White and Negro scholars agree that the Negro's race pride is a defense reaction or response to white prejudice, a "secondary attitude." Common as this pride is among Negro chauvinists, it is, says Myrdal, "a white, not a Negro, argument." Negroes know that their race is not pure. They know it by looking at themselves. And for two hundred years they have had a social stratification among themselves based upon their knowledge of their racial impurity: a "good complexion" is a light one; "good hair," straight; a "good nose," thin-nostriled.

Does this mean that the Negro favors miscegenation? In a negative sense he does; he would be inconsistent if he didn't. But what he wants is the repeal of racist marriage laws — not merely because they insult him and deny his civil liberty, but because of their effect in encouraging illegal miscegenation, with its abuse and exploitation of the Negro woman and the legal impunity of the gallivanting white man.

A harder question is whether the Negro actually shares the white man's "natural disgust" at the idea of miscegenation. The answer — impossible to come by statistically — would seem to be that he doesn't. Repugnance requires a sense of superiority. Equals may hate those who subjugate them, but they do not find them categorically obnoxious: the man who is excluded from the country club because of his race or religion has no primary feeling against intimate association with the members. Similarly, the Negro who considers himself the white man's equal would seem to have no primary attitude toward miscegenation, any more than, say, Pennsylvania boys react to Ohio or Michigan girls. People tend to fall in love with "their own kind" — nationally, religiously, or racially. Negroes assume they will marry Negroes; and nearly every last one of them does.

There are two kinds of reality — the reality of things as they are (or may be) and the reality of things as people see them. The two realities may coincide, but the white man's hostility toward miscegenation and his dread of amalgamation arise strictly from three realities of the second kind.

First, he sees that there are such things as races and such a thing as a pure race.

As far as science now knows, there aren't and there isn't. In the middle of the eighteenth century the "father of anthropology," Blumenbach, concluded that "no variety of mankind exists, whether of color, countenance or stature, etc., so singular as not to be connected with others of the same kind by such an imperceptible transition that it is very clear they are all related or only differ from one another in degree." Two centuries later the eminent Krogman, in *The Concept of Race*, summarizes the present state of our knowledge: "Below the level of the species definition is uncertain, persistence is doubtful, and transmission is variable. In other words, the breakdown of *Homo sapiens* into subgroups is zoologically very risky business. . . . We are all far more alike than different. . . . [There are] no fundamental differences . . . biogenic potentialities are shared equally. . . ."

There *are* observable and measurable physical differences that enable us, simply for purposes of superficial classification, to distinguish human groups. How did these differences come about? The only possible assumption, says Krogman, is that "the basic *sapiens* population from which modern races developed was relatively homogenous, and that via mutation, isolation, selection, and recombination diverse gene-populations emerged." Physical traits, bred into geographically isolated groups, show signs of adaptation to the conditions of environment. Says Huxley: "The dark skin, which characterizes most of the people living near the tropics, is almost certainly the result of elimination by natural selection of the fairer types of pigmentation less fitted to afford protection against the actinic rays of the sun. The greater number of sweat glands in the Negro and the reduction of their number among the yellow-skinned peoples, are probably adaptations to hot and to dry conditions respectively. . . . A white skin is a disadvantage in the Tropics and a wide nostril in the Arctic."

The "pure race" — if it could be found anywhere on earth — would have utterly isolated for ages, culturally primitive, technologically backward, and undeveloped in the arts of civilization which the crossing of cultures has produced. We shall never know how "impure" the first American settlers, black *or* white, were when they got here; we know that African soldiers invaded Britain with Caesar two thousand years ago, and, boys being boys, one thing certainly led to another. We know that Europeans, especially the Portuguese, were frequent settlers in the West African ancestral areas of most American slaves. And we know that in America free intermarriage

The Issue Is Miscegenation   203

between white and Negro indentured servants was not prohibited until 1691, in Virginia, and that prior to the reduction of the Negro to slavery the "poor white's" hatred of him was unknown. How much Negro-white miscegenation there was between 1619 (when the first Negroes reached Virginia) and the Civil War is suggested by Ray Stannard Baker's calculation in 1908 that three million of the country's ten million Negroes were mulatoes, or half-whites. Wirth and Goldhammer, in *Characteristics of the American Negro*, tell us that "contemporary observers, on the whole, tend to leave an impression that no likely-looking Negro, or especially mulatto, girl was liable to be left unmolested by the white males [in the ante bellum South]; that few of the young white men grew up 'virtuously,' and that their loss of virtue was scarcely to be attributed to cohabitation with white women."

The rate of miscegenation continued to rise in the South even after the Civil War. (The original Klan required its members to swear only that they would not *marry* a Negro.) After her emancipation the freedwoman could move about, and into the white man's cities; but she was still defenseless against him. "Father Abraham" had made her his equal, but Father Abraham wasn't down in Dixie in the seventies and eighties. Besides, concubinage with a white man was, if anything, more than ever economically better than marriage to a Negro. And the mulatto's high value — as the white man's sex object and the white woman's servant girl — was still an incentive to "breeding" half-bloods. The reduction in miscegenation probably set in in the nineties or shortly afterward; no one knows. Urbanization would tend to increase it (especially in the North) and so would the sexual laxity of the twentieth century. But that same sexual laxity made white women more readily available to white men, and would therefore tend to reduce "mixing." The decisive factor in reduction was doubtless the rising status of the Negro and, with it, rising pride and moral dignity. But there is no *un*miscegenation. The "white" and "Negro" blood that was mixed at the pleasure of the by-gone southern gentleman is mixed forever. If there is no pure race now — and there isn't — there never will be.

Second, the white man sees the Negro as a race, to which an individual either belongs or doesn't.

As long as the white man defines Negro simply as "Negro" (as he does in the marriage laws of West Virginia and Colorado), he is safe from contradiction, if not from redundancy. As long as he talks (as he does in the Oklahoma law) about "any person of African descent," he is safe, providing, of course, that he doesn't mind excluding some whites of African descent and some Negroes of non-African descent. As long as he says (as he does in Nevada) "any person of the Ethiopian or black race" or (in South Dakota) "members of the African race," he is all right, providing the agrees that a nation or a continent is a race. But the minute he tries to make more sense than any of this, he gets into trouble. If he prohibits the intermarriage of "persons having one-fourth Negro blood," as he does in Kentucky and Oregon, he seems to have decided that a person with 24.99 per cent Negro blood is a white — a very difficult decision, especially when Florida, Indiana, Mississippi, Missouri, Nebraska, South Carolina, and North Dakota have decided that persons having 12.50 per cent (or one-eighth) Negro blood may not marry whites. The 24.99 per cent man appears to be white in Kentucky and non-white in Mississippi. The Mississippian with 12.49 per cent Negro blood is eligible to marry the Natchez Magnolia Queen — but he'd better not let the sun set on him in *this* town if he has 12.50 per cent. In Alabama we draw the line just a little bit finer than we do in Caroliner. We don't fool around with percentages. We cal'ate in *drops*. Persons having "one drop of Negro blood" are interdicted; should such person be waylaid en route to his wedding with the local Cotton Queen and, in the ensuing confusion, lose one drop of blood, and that one turn out to be the Negro drop, he could proceed with his now honorable intentions. But not in Georgia or Virginia, where "any ascertainable trace of Negro blood" puts a man beyond the palefaces. Now everybody knows that a trace is less than a drop; thus Georgia and Virginia must look upon Alabama (not to say Mississippi and Carolina) as a hotbed of "mixing."

There is, of course, no such thing as "Negro blood," in any quantity. Human blood can be differentiated only in one way — by the four common groups found indiscriminately in all human stocks. During the Second World War the American Red Cross (then a semiofficial agency of the government) first refused Negro blood donors. A howl went up, and the Red Cross thereafter accepted "Negro blood" but segregated it for transfusion to Negro soldiers only; you may remember (if you are old enough) that the Americans' enemy in that war was Nazi racism.

Third, the white man sees not only that there are Negro and white races but that the white race is superior.

Because the mulatto's white father prized him for his "white blood" — even educating and occasionally freeing him — the full Negro of slave times accepted the mulatto as a superior kind of creature, a sort of *tertium quid*, below the white but above himself. This acceptance by the Negro of the white man's theory of racial superiority has descended in the Negro social mythos to the present day. But there are signs of a change, although the successful or attractive Negro still tends to "marry light" and is more readily hired by Negro employers. The mulatto myth always involved envy and resentment among full blacks anyway, and it is now beginning to lose its status with them. They know that, belatedly given opportunity, they are as capable as mixed-bloods.

With the abolition of slavery, the white man's new race hatred of his newly legalized equals compelled him to relinquish one of his favorite arguments for white superiority, namely, the obvious superiority of the mulatto over the "pure" Negro. (The argument, of course, ignored the fact that the mulatto had always enjoyed superior advantages.) Today the prejudiced white sees Negroes, dark *or* light, as indiscriminately inferior. And they *are* inferior, on the average, in their occupations, their housing, their education, and their achievement in almost every field.

"The American," said Bernard Shaw, "compels the Negro to black his boots and then says, 'He's fit for nothing but blacking my boots.'" To say that all, or most, or many, or some Negroes are found among lowly placed, or unskilled, or uncouth people is simply to say that whatever it is that makes people that way also makes all, or most, or many, or some Negroes that way. But to say that the Negro race is an inferior race is to say that every Negro is born that way and will die that way, no matter what his opportunity. Myrdal, though he found the northerner more polite, more "tolerant," could find no substantial difference among whites of different regions or classes on this one fundamental belief — that the Negro is *somehow* racially inferior. The white man's aversion to miscegenation requires that he believe the Negro inherently subhuman. Even a Lincoln, seeing nothing but the then condition of Negroes, recorded his conviction that "in some respects he certainly is not my equal." In what respects he doesn't say — few whites do. And if a Lincoln, why not you and I? If the "nigger" were your equal, you would want your daughter to marry him.

The Negro's racial inferiority is something the white man knows in his bones, or in his viscera — in other words, a prejudice, which, like all prejudices, may with equal likelihood be true or untrue. When, under some duress, the locus of the inferiority is specified, it is invariably in one or more of three areas — biological, intellectual, or cultural.

One. — The Negro's racial inferiority is proved anatomically and physiologically — that is, he is constructed differently and, as an organism, functions differently from the white; and the differences are hierarchical, lower-higher, like those of the ape and man.

Scientifically this supposition is wholly discredited. Of the four characteristic features of the "typical" Negro — dark skin, broad nose, wooly hair, thick lips — the first two are a *little* closer to the ape than the white man's while the white's hair and lips are *much* closer to the ape than the Negro's. As for "primitive" and "advanced" stages of evolution, all morphological evidence indicates that man evolved only once. We have already seen that there is no such thing as "Negro" blood. It is equally impossible to determine by examination of the human brain whether its owner was black, white, or pimento. True, the ideal Negro type tends to dolichocephaly — or longheadedness — and to a degree matched by only one other human type: the ideal Nordic. By all other standard indexes, such as fertility of mixed mating (even the fox and the wolf cannot mate fruitfully) and comparative harmony-disharmony of parts, there is no evidence of hierarchy.

In the late nineteenth and early twentieth centuries the facts of biology and psychology proved that Negroes *were* different from whites, not just in visible and measurable bodily features, but in higher susceptibility to disease, in lower mental ability, and in greater personality disorder. The rise of social research in the 1920's began to complicate the picture. And if there is anything that people who have simple scientific facts to sustain their prejudices do not like, it is complications. The findings of social research were facts, too, but they had the disadvantage (in the layman's view) of being come by without microscope or stethoscope. They were facts about environment — housing, diet, climate, clothing, medical care, and educational and occupational opportunity. But the new facts coincided with new medical knowledge. Pellagra, syphilis, and nephritis were now known to be environmental, not constitutional. The Negro's notorious susceptibility to tuberculosis declined as his living conditions improved. A study which showed that Illinois Negroes had a dementia praecox rate three times as high as whites had to be reinterpreted — or rather, interpreted for the first time — in light of the facts that Illinois Negroes were concentrated in cities (where the over-all rate is twice as high as in rural areas), that Illinois Negroes were concentrated in those age and income groups with the highest rate of d.p., and that most Illinois Negroes were recent migrants, whose mental disease incidence, regardless of color, is much higher than that of natives. In every area where social research was correlated with the biological facts, the inference of racial superiority has been undermined or exploded.

Two. — The Negro's racial inferiority is proved intellectually — that is, he is unable to think as well or learn as much as a white man.

Less than twenty years ago a *Fortune* survey found that a majority of whites, ranging from 60 per cent in the North to 76.9 per cent in the South, thought that "Negroes now generally have lower intelligence than white people." The percentage of those who regarded the difference as due at last in part to heredity ranged from 55.5 to 79.2. The Negro's actual inferiority was obvious, and, besides, the new intelligence tests showed that the average Negro I.Q. was 20 to 25 per cent lower than the white. But was it — again — *bcause* he was a Negro?

Intelligence tests tried to measure the innate capacity of the subject to learn. But nobody knew then (or knows now) if mental capacity is an innately determined quantum or if the tests we have yet been able to devise operate prejudicially in connection with the subject's environment. Complications again — and the I.Q. figures were so nice and simple. As a matter of fact, the rug had already been pulled out from under the superior intelligence superstition (a superstition confirmed by scientific facts!) in 1921, with Yerkes' classic monograph, "Psychological Examining in the U.S. Army," published quietly in the *Memoirs* of the National Academy of Science. In the Army Alpha test of 1917, a language-based test given only to literate recruits, Negroes as a whole had scored much lower than whites, but northern Negroes had scored much higher than southern whites, and the same thing was true of the non-language Beta test. The median scores for Negroes from New York, Illinois, and Ohio were 45.02, 47.35, and 49.50 respectively; of whites from Mississippi, Kentucky, and Arkansas, 41.25, 41.50, and 41.55. Either northern Negroes were innately more intelligent than southern whites, or the education of southerners was so poor that northerners, white or Negro, appeared to be innately more intelligent than white or Negro southerners. Which was it? The answer was obvious: Environmental conditions made southern whites *look* as if they had been born less intelligent than northern Negroes.

Before the I.Q. fad subsided at the end of the thirties, it was found that one group of underprivileged Negro children in Tennessee had a score of 58; another group of privileged Negro children in California had a score of 105. The Los Angeles public schools tested five hundred Negro children with the whites in fifteen elementary schools and found the median I.Q. slightly higher for the Negro group. Successive types of testing have all demonstrated that group biological differences, however real, do not account for group intellectual differences.

Three.— The Negro's racial inferiority is proved culturally — that is, by his inability to develop an "advanced" society or keep pace with the one he is in.

Of the three race dogmas this is the hardest to investigate. It requires the impossible — an objective definition of culture. People who cut off their enemies' head with machetes and people who cut off their friends' heads with two-toned convertibles both regard their cultures as advanced. Still the fact (at least *a* fact) remains. The

American Negro as a whole is backward in terms of American cultural standards in science, art, morals, and manners. This anyone can see must be true. But is it because he is a Negro? Even before the development of social research this particular dogma was shaky. True, the racist saw the shiftless, "worthless" Negro all around him; but he also saw the Frederick Douglass, the George Washington Carver, the Booker T. Washington, indubitable Negroes of indubitable genius. Carver could not be a Negro and still save the "goober" economy by his plant research — but he was and he did.

There was something else, something that the southern racist did not see. That was his own culture. The behavior he ridiculed or condemned in the Negro was his own. The Negro was a southerner. The lazy, good-natured, romantic, immoral, profligate, shabby, violent Negro reflected traits that are so common in the South that the foreign visitor (not to say the northerner) calls them all southern traits. What produced them in many or most southern whites produced them still more prevalently in the most depressed southerner, the Negro. Climate, soil, boll weevil, poverty, defeat — in a word, environment.

Still the fact remains: "*Negro* culture" is inconsequential. The *Negro's* sole contribution to American culture is American music, which is tom-tom primitive. But we don't ask what the Swede's contribution is, or the Pole's, or the Irishman's, or even what American culture is, or how much there is of it. If there were only one "pure" Negro who was a genius or a saint (instead of hundreds or thousands), the white man could not say truthfully that "the Negro" is culturally incapable or that only white men develop a culture. In deference to the "exceptions," the white modifies his generalization, then, and says that most or many Negroes are backward; and the next thing he knows (or doesn't), he has forgotten the qualification and talks about "the Negro."

However "culture" is defined, cultures rise and fall; we have only to think of ancient and modern Greece. The Negro slave's ancestral culture may well have been much higher than his first American master's; several premedieval African cultures (notably Ethiopia's) were more advanced, even by present Western standards, than any of contemporaneous Europe's. But the black man's culture was beaten out of him with the lash. He was separated from his kinsmen and countrymen so that he could more easily be brainwashed. And for two hundred years he was fixed in his degradation. Literacy, property, and human rights were forbidden him by law until 1863 and for another half-century denied him in fact. He is just now emerging from all the indignities that can be visited upon a man. And unlike the Japanese- or Chinese-descended Americans, he has no culture other than America's to call his own, no other basis for group pride, no memory (so immutably tied to language) of another civilization. If he has got to be a second-class American, then he has got to be a second-class man, because an American is all he is.

Like "Negro intelligence," "Negro personality" and "Negro character" appear to be the product of environment; at least, other persons and groups of people in the same condition act, never uniformly, but, like the Negro, on the average, in the same way. Summarizing a vast Carnegie study in *Characteristics of the American Negro*, Klineberg writes: "What differences there are appear to depend on existing discrepancies in the opportunities afforded to the two groups." The popular concept of the "marginal" man originally described the individual of one culture who had to live in another as the "cultural hybrid." When the individual is racially, as well as culturally, marginal; when, in a word, he can be distinguished not only by background but by appearance, his maladjustment is, axiomatically, intensified. That a culturally and racially "marginal" man should ever achieve "normal" behavior might well be viewed as something of a superhuman achievement, a sign of individual, if not racial, superiority.

When we submit the arguments against white superiority to our enlightened neighbor, he says, "Of course, of course. I've know that for years. There's nothing really inferior about Negroes. Why, I know a Negro college professor who. . . ." We must interrupt him at this point and say, "Would you want your daughter to marry a nigger?" He rocks on his heels, and while he is still rocking, we ask him, "Would you want niggers" — we are very careful here to say "nigger," not "Negro" — in your golf club?" As soon as he recovers sufficiently to begin sputtering, "Why — why — why ," we must in-

terrupt him again and say, "Why not?" It is only then that we come
to the heart of the issue. It doesn't matter whether Negroes are innately inferior, equal, or superior, temporarily or permanently.
What matters is something so profound that no argument touches
it, no evidence speaks to it. Our enlightened neighbor, who is long
since convinced that there is no such thing as racial superiority, is
ourselves. And like ourselves he is moved by a mechanism hidden in
the deepest recesses of the heart. He has rejected every argument
against segregation — which means every argument against miscegenation. But the hidden mechanism still functions. He is a racist. You
are a racist. I am a racist. Why?

The Christian has the easy answer: the Devil. The Devil has
planted in all of us the love of unearned increment, of something for
nothing. If, without lifting a finger, I can be superior — well, why
not? If, however worthless I may be, I can be worth something by
having been born white, or American, or the eldest son of the Duke
of Marlborough, I will cherish the worth all the more mightily. It's
my one absolutely inalienable possession. I may forfeit my good
name; my purse, my home, my family, my job, my health, my liberty,
and my life may all be taken from me. But nobody can take my
whiteness away from me. I'm *in*.

When a few members of what the sociologist calls the out-group
come (unwillingly, in the Negro's case) to live among the in-
group, they are depreciated — the depreciation ranging from the
city man's ridicule of the yokel to the native white's dislike of the
foreigner or the Negro. As long as the out-group are few (or are
held in subjection as they increase), they are not thought of as dangerous. But when they increase and are no longer legally subjugated,
they are no longer merely comical or obnoxious but dangerous, and
the in-group's sense of security requires their segregation.

The white man who has never directly injured a Negro may nevertheless bear the unconscious guilt of chattel slavery and hate the
cause of his vicarious wrongdoing; while the white who has directly
injured a Negro (merely, for example, by living in a "restricted"
neighborhood) may have a still heavier guilt to justify by hatred.
Deeper buried still: Man, the impure, wants to be freed from his impurity — from impure flesh and blood and bone, from impure occu-

pations and associations, from impure thoughts and desires. He wants to be "washed," "cleansed," "white as snow." And the Negro is black—the color of evil and dirt and the dread unknown.

Acceptance of this racist mystique, below the level of rationality, is not confined to yahoos and legislators. Learned men of the greatest consequence, judges, South *and* North, low *and* high, have generally upheld the racist marriage statutes of the states and their opinions ring repetitiously with the characterization of mixed marriages as "unnatural," "productive of deplorable results," "conducive to a degeneration of the public morals," and detrimental to the "moral and physical development of both races and the highest advancement of civilization." The documentation of such assertions from the bench is invariably missing; white judges turn out to be white men. Four years ago the "liberal" Virginia Supreme Court, upholding that state's statute, found that "there is no requirement that the state . . . must permit the corruption of blood [which would] weaken or destroy the quality of its citizenship."

Does the "social equality" which the segregationist says leads to miscegenation actually lead to it? It was the social inequality of slavery and the segregationist South, reinforced by laws which forbade interracial marriage and even interracial fornication, that led to miscegenation on a colossal scale, while the relative social equality of the North led to intermarriage on a minuscule scale. The racist's ready invocation of white southern womanhood and its protection suggests that he is preoccupied with rape; but it would not seem to be rape that he has on his mind when he asks, "Would you want your daughter to marry a nigger?" And rape accounts for almost no miscegenation; voluntariness is of the essence of the evil (if it is an evil). The question has often been asked of the whites who enact laws against intermarriage: If their white women do not want to marry Negroes, why is it necessary for them to pass laws forbidding them to do so? The question is a mean one.

It would be a little more decorous to discuss miscegenation without reference to sex, but it would also be a little more difficult. To begin with, the fascination of the repugnant, in any area of life, is a commonplace: "I simply couldn't take my eyes off it," whether the "it" is a murder on television or a monster in a sideshow. It not only rivets the eyes; it unrivets responses we normally try to repress. And the fascination and the repugnance both seem to spring from the same aspect of the object: its difference from ourselves and what we know. Deep stuff, perhaps, but the soul is not a shallow saucer, and sex is an emanation of the soul.

Whether white women are more attracted to Negro men than white men to Negro women is undetermined and, probably, undeterminable. The few (and necessarily inadequate) studies of intermarriage, in Boston, Philadelphia, Chicago, and Los Angeles County, reveal a great preponderance of Negro husbands and white wives. But this fact, even if it is universal, is not conclusive alone. The human male is the aggressor; it is he who does the courting and proposing. And most intermarriage is in northern cities, where the proportion of unattached Negro males to females is high. In addition, intermarriage in America nearly always involves "emancipated" individuals, among whom there are many white and few Negro women. A considerable percentage of white female–Negro male marriages certainly involves a degree of "protest" on the part of the white females — protest against the sexless preoccupation of the modern white American male with "getting ahead" or against their own fathers.

But sex rears its beautiful head in the midst of these pedestrian speculations. Both classic and modern historians confirm James Baldwin's assertion, in *Notes of a Native Son*, that "darker races always seem to have for lighter races an aura of sexuality." The rapist of the southerner's nightmare — or dream — is the "buck nigger," big and black. The Nubian slave of high romance was a Negro. And the chronicles of explorers abound in their coming to rest (at least temporarily) by the side of a dark-skinned girl. Whether tropical peoples are more interesting sexually than non-tropical peoples may be debatable; but it is generally observed that they are more languid and more excitable — qualities that in combination are not unpraised by the poets.

There is no doubt, however, that the southern white preferred the mulatto slave girl to her full-blooded Negro sister as the object of his passion. The storied "quadroon ball" of early New Orleans, the commonplace marriage of French Creoles to mulatto girls in the same city, and the well-developed *placage* system there, in which white men established a permanent contractual relationship with mixed-blood girls, whom they courted and whose parents' permission they asked, all suggest that the nearer to white a "Negro" girl was, the more desirable she was to white men. Why? She was more "white" than her black sister but, above all, rarer, and rarity, like variety, is said to be spicy.

Sex is the opposite of the weather; everybody talks about the weather and nobody does anything about it. The role of sex in miscegenation is more obvious than the way in which the role is played. There are some things that Professor Kinsey despaired of learning, and should have. But Myrdal was willing to say that "the South has an obsession with sex which helps to make this region quite irrational in dealing with Negroes generally. . . . The sadistic element in most lynchings" — often involving emasculation of the victim — "also points to a close relation between lynching and thwarted sexual urges." It was out of this unpenetrated and perhaps forever impenetrable complex of non-rational drives that the South's "third sex" was born — the "flower of southern womanhood." The origin of this "woman on a pedestal" may in part (but only in part) be explained by the Puritan strain in American culture, South and North; the Negro slave girl, defenseless in any case, was uninhibited by the blessing of a puritanical upbringing. The white wife was absolutely unable to avoid knowing of the carryings-on of her husband — and of her father and her son. And the northern abolitionists were loud against it. The southerner's answer to both his wife and the Yankee was the construction of a beautiful fiction. "On the one hand," says Wilbur Cash in *The Mind of the South*, "the convention must be set up that the thing simply did not exist . . . and on the other, the woman must be compensated, the revolting suspicion in the male that he might be slipping into bestiality got rid of, by glorifying her." The southern gentleman was able to convince himself, as he found his way down to the cabins by moonlight, that his wife was a paragon. She may have had little occasion to be anything else.

Miscegenation certainly can't impurify the race unless it produces offspring. And even then, unless the offspring miscegenates, the impurity, if any, dies with him. But the inferiority of the Negro and the superiority of the white ought both to be apparent in the half-breed. He ought to be superior to his Negro parent and inferior to his white. The proof of the mixing is in the mulatto. Unless the mulatto is inferior to the white — and not because of environment — the Negro is not inferior to the white and miscegenation cannot be condemned on the ground of racial corruption.

We know a little about the mulatto. We know that, at least until recently, he was generally the intellectual and cultural superior of the unmixed Negro. But was it because he had "white" blood? Social research does not say no; it simply says that the mulatto has always enjoyed (until very recently) an immense superiority of opportunity over the "pure" Negro. But the rate of antisocial behavior among mulattoes was also high. It has declined radically, as the mulatto has shared the increased opportunity for Negroes generally and as his once intense resentment of being peculiarly *déclassé* has faded with time and color; with greatly decreased miscegenation in the past half-century, the mulatto has been disappearing. (Of course, the white racist who cited mulatto criminality or immorality was arguing against himself; if mixed-blood Negroes are inferior to pure-blood Negroes their inferiority must be the consequence of their "white" blood.)

You would rather be a hybrid than what the Kluxers call a mongrel — but there isn't any difference. Cross-fertilization has produced "mongrel" agricultural stocks of such superiority that the pure strain has in many instances been abandoned altogether. But the superior plant or animal hybrid is produced by controlled experimentation, while the consequences of random cross-fertilization in humans can only be observed. The studies of miscegenated groups — the Rehobother Bastards (a cross between South African Boers and Hottentots, as divergent a pair of "races" as can be imagined), the Polynesian-white descendants of the mutineers of the "Bounty" on Pitcairn Island, the Chinese-Hawaiians in Honolulu, white-Negroes in Brazil, and Indonesian-whites on the Timor Archipelago — all support the theory of heterosis, or hybrid vigor: the offspring of the cross tends to be larger in size, more active, more fertile, and with improved vitality and longevity. Scholars generally agree with Benedict, in *The Races of Mankind*, that "as far as we know, there are no immutable laws of nature that make racial inter-mixture harmful." Of course the human hybrid will usually re-semble each of his parents in some physical respects, but Hooten in the Harvard *African Studies* discovered that "Negroid features seem to be attenuated, rather than intensified, by successive gen-erations of inbreeding of mixed types." "While *two* parties with Negro blood may very occasionally have an offspring with somewhat more Negroid features than themselves," say Wirth and Goldham-mer in the Carnegie study, "it is not possible for a white person and a person with some Negro ancestry to have an offspring more Negroid than the partner with Negro blood." The "black baby" of melodrama — the spawn of the young aristocrat and the beautiful brunette whose telltale shadows on her fingernails nobody ever noticed — is a complete fiction.

If there is no other reliable basis for determining race, the only thing left is appearance. And here, as elsewhere in this life, ap-pearance is deceitful. It is estimated that thirty thousand part-Negroes a year "pass" into white society permanently and that many times thirty thousand might but refuse to because of pride or family ties. And many "pass" without ever knowing they have done so. Unlike the "black baby" of fiction, the white baby of real life is often part Negro. Occasional instances reach publication; a few years ago a good "white" farmer in Mississippi named Davis Knight was convicted of miscegenation when a family feud disclosed (to him, as well as to his wife) that his great-grandmother had been a slave girl. In *A Study of Some Negro-White Families*, Day of Harvard found that "dominant mulattoes and five-eighths [-white] individuals are frequently mistaken for foreigners of various na-tionalities, or for white Americans. . . . I know of no case of a quadroon [one-fourth Negro] who could not easily 'pass' for white. . . . In the few cases of octoroons [one-eighth Negro] which I have studied, I have been able so far to see no traces whatever of Negro admixture." Of thirty-five intermarried Negroes who "passed" for white, Day found sixteen quadroons, fifteen three-eighths Negroes, *and four mulattoes.* On the Von Luschen skin-color scale a study of mulattoes showed absolutely "white" pigmentation in 12.55 per cent of the males and 20.6 per cent of the females.

Nearly all of us know nothing of our ancestors beyond our great-grandparents. The shadow sinister may be just beyond the far side of our limited acquaintance with our forebears. And although most race marriage laws stigmatize Indians as well as Negroes, it should be observed that in Virginia, where a trace of Negro blood pollutes, a trace of Indian makes a First Family; intermarriage of whites with persons of one-sixteenth or less "Indian blood" is permitted in the Old Dominion, in deference to the proud racist descendants of the one good Indian who wasn't a dead Indian — Pocahontas. Will Rogers and Vice-President Charles Curtis were proud of their Indian ancestry; it is only the Negro who is irredeemably inferior.

Once appearances have been shown to be deceitful of race, the ground begins to give way under the marriage statutes and the Red Cross "white blood" bank, and all the processes, legal, non-legal, and illegal, of racial discrimination totter on their single foundation. You may think you wouldn't eat with a Negro — or your daughter marry one — but for all you know you do and she has. You may cry up the protection of the white race without knowing that you don't belong to it. You may lynch your own half-brother on the charge that he plucked the flower of southern womanhood — and the flower may have been a black one.

And if the preservation of the supremacy of the white race depends on the preservation of its *looking* white, the supremacists should turn their attention immediately from the "nigger-lovers" to the biochemists. The doom of white civilization may be foretold in the following words of Professor John A. Kenney in the *Journal of the National Medical Association*: "Lerner has shown [in the *Archives of Biochemistry and Biophysics*, 1952] that mercury will compete with copper ions in tyrosinase which in turn inactivates the enzyme which catalyzes melanin formation. Once this has occurred, the reaction is only slowly reversible." It should be added that melanin is the black pigment present in the skin of all human beings except albinos. Almost any Negro — whose skin is not allergic and whose spirit is willing — can use a variety of standard formulas to whiten himself. The Citizens Councils should smash the pharmacist's jars of monobenzyl ether of hydroquinine and p-hydroxypropiophenone, the most effective devices against melanin formation.

Most Negro-white marriages (and courtships), if not secret, are at least furtive. Unless the two partners have already cut themselves off from their backgrounds, their marriage will ordinarily do it for them. The relatives, friends, and business associates of the white partner will be the more hostile; the white is "marrying down," the Negro "up." Not that the Negro's circle will approve of the marriage — it won't — but it will be readier to forgive and to accept the white partner on the basis of merit. Negroes may be inferior, but they seem to be a little more human.

Thus the newlyweds move immediately into isolation — or into the Negro world. But there they are also uneasy. Negroes generally look upon the white bride or groom much as the whites do: There must be something wrong with a white who marries a Negro (or a Negro who marries a white). An occasional Negro — and a rare white — will marvel that two people could be so much in love as to have been willing to make the desperate sacrifices that intermarriage entails. Either partner, but particularly the white, is liable to lose his job if the marriage becomes known. So the tendency to keep it secret, or at least, "close," abides. Their friends are other intermarrieds (if there are any); in New York and Chicago there have been informal clubs of such couples. The intermarried pair ordinarily lives just inside the boundaries of a Negro neighborhood in a large city.

Something like half of the estimated ten to twenty thousand Negro-white couples in America are politically or artistically "advanced" individuals, people whose social and economic sanction does not depend on the church, the P.T.A., the Legion post, and the luncheon club. Among the other half of the intermarrieds, white immigrant males of low social status (and low native race prejudice) are common, especially since there is ordinarily a shortage of their countrywomen among them. (With immigration almost cut off, this source of intermarriage is disappearing.) Then there are native white males of low status, often personally unattractive to white girls. Probably because of the immigrant and the unattractive male, the marrying age of interracial couples is very high; in the Los Angeles study, for instance, it was thirty-nine for the white grooms. The proportion of divorced persons intermarrying is also very high, especially among the whites involved; in Philadelphia thirty-four out of eighty intermarried persons had previously been married to co-racialists; it would seem that an unsuccessful marriage is broadening. Attractive white girls marrying Negroes are usually college graduates and daughters of prominent parents, apparently from the "protest" category. Like white males of such standing, Negro girls with high status almost never intermarry, partly, no doubt, because of pride, partly because it's polite for a girl to wait until she's asked, and partly because they can "marry up" to a light-skinned Negro of position. Three times as many white women marry Negro men as Negro women marry white men.

The intermarriages that make news usually involve a Negro artist — Lena Horne and MGM Musical Director Lennie Hayton, Sugar Billy Daniels and Martha Braun, Sidney Bechet and Elizabeth Taylor. When Stuart Outerbridge of *the* Bermuda Outerbridges married Royce Wallace, a singer at his night club, he was thrown out of the Royal Bermuda Yacht Club and, he said, completely ostracized. Only once in a great while does a Negro leader "cross the line": diplomat Frederick Douglass did, and so did NAACP Secretary Walter White.

The wars of 1941 to 1945 and 1950 to 1953 added something new to American miscegenation — the white war bride, German, French, or English, brought back to America by the Negro soldier, and more significantly, the Japanese or Korean war bride. Asians, especially Japanese, have a strong aversion to intermarriage (with whites *or* Negroes). Prior to the Second World War there was almost no intermarriage among Japanese-Americans with any "outgroup." It is very slowly increasing now, with whites, but almost no Mongoloid in America ever marries a Negro — yellow *plus* white racism. Europe has a fine new crop of mulattoes, Germany in particular; the French and American Occupation commands were more than benign in their attitude toward the Moroccan and Negro "debasement" of Hitler's Aryans.

Half of the Negro-white marriages in America are barren, and the other half produce remarkably small families, often one child, rarely more than two. The late age of the marriage combines with the unwillingness of the couple to subject children to the fearful strains of their position. More important, as regards amalgamation: interracial mating is almost always limited to a single generation, the reason, of course, being that the American mulatto is accepted only in the Negro world. The worst sufferer is the child whose white parent wants him accepted by whites.

If the American Negro is marginal, the mulatto child is sub-marginal. In his early teens he is likely to be called "bastard" or "miskeg" by Negroes, and in his childhood he may be taunted by his Negro playmates for the same reason that Negroes are taunted by whites: for being different. I knew a ten-year-old Negro boy during the Second World War with very light skin but no sign of the epicanthic eye fold common to Orientals; his black schoolfellows called him "Jap-eyes." The last stanza of Langston Hughes' poem, "Cross," though its setting is the old South, portrays the mulatto adolescent everywhere:

> My old man died in a fine big house
> My ma died in a shack.
> I wonder where I'm gonna die,
> Being neither white nor black.

Wherever he dies, the chances that he (or she) will die married to a white are almost nil. The world (the American white world) says he's a Negro. He may hate being a Negro; but if he does, he hates the world that made him a Negro still more. Marrying Negro, he will introduce a little more "white" blood into the next generation of blacks but no more "Negro" blood into the white. *If* he marries. The tensions of his childhood may make a criminal (even a suicide, rare among Negroes) of him — or a genius; the well-known Negro journalist, George Schuyler, married the daughter of a white Texas banker, and their thirteen-year-old daughter's *Manhattan Nocturne* was premiered by the New York Philharmonic.

Racial equality has come about — like miscegenation — without benefit of clergy. It is said that in America there is more racial segragation between 11:00 A.M. and noon on Sunday than at any other hour of the week. The church has been moving since the

1954 school segregation decision; the Roman Catholic church rapidly, the Protestant (with spectacular exceptions) slowly. But on the segregation of would-be wives from would-be husbands, it is as silent as it is on war. It no longer quotes scripture, as the "Bible-bangers" of the old South misquoted it on the inevitable slavery of the "descendants of Ham, accursed of God." (It was Canaan, not Ham, who was cursed, and it was Noah, not God, who cursed him.) On the ultimate, last-ditch issue of racism — miscegenation — the church today says nothing. A very rare clergyman speaks, at his peril, like the Reverend Kelly Barnett of the Episcopal Seminary of the Southwest, who, testifying against school segregation before a Texas legislative committee, was (of course) asked by State Senator Wardlow Lane if he believed in intermarriage. Barnett said that, while he thought it "sociologically inadvisable," he believed that "the right of marriage is a personal right." A few days later Lane leaped to his feet on the senate floor and shouted: "Why, these preachers want to mix colored and white. That's what Dr. Barnett said. He said it's all right for nigger and white to intermarry, but if one of my East Texas niggers married Barnett, I would feel sorry for the nigger. I want that clear: For the *nigger*."

The Lanes will not let the church remain silent indefinitely. And the church is the church that preaches the brotherhood of man under the fatherhood of God; that preaches the parable of the black Samaritan in answer to the Pharisee's question, "Who is my neighbor?"; that preaches the Ten Commandments received from the hand of God by the man who married an Ethiopian woman; that preaches the disciple who said, "God hath made of one blood all nations of men," and the apostle who said, "He who does not love his brother, whom he has seen, how can he love God, whom he hath not seen?" The church is the church that preaches Christ crucified that "they may be as one . . . one flock, one shepherd."

One of the strongest statements made in support of the Supreme Court's school decision — a statement the *Christian Century* called "a model of clear-thinking insight" — was made by seventy-four Atlanta ministers. They quoted the golden rule and went on, after saying that Negroes should have the *full privileges of first-class citi-*

zenship, to suggest that they should have all the privileges but one: "We do not believe in the amalgamation of the races. . . ." They did not say whether God does.

It is not just the church that trusts in God; the national motto commits every American to that trust, and the national creed proclaims that all men — not all white men, or all Negroes, but all men — are created equal. But nowhere in the Western world today is a caste system of rigid inequality so vigorously expressed in law as in America. (Even the Nazi "Aryan marriage" laws were more liberal than Virginia's.) Perhaps the belief in the inferiority of the Negro race alone enables us to square our racism with our American creed of equality: American Negroes must be inferior creatures — otherwise American whites are inferior Americans. Nor is it our creed alone that confronts us; the fact that our country is the great melting pot confronts us, too. We are proud of creating an "American tribe" out of the most diversified of the world's populations except Russia's. We are fanatical, not only about American equality, but about Americanism. We mistrust things foreign and alien; everything and everybody that comes to America has got to be Americanized. The American dream is the dream of complete assimilation — except for the Negro. When novelist Erskine Caldwell says, "Eventually you'll have an amalgamation of the two races in the South," he would seem to be trying his hand at science fiction. What the sociologist calls assortative mating — like marrying like — tends to keep intermarriage from spreading. There will, of course, be more "white" blood in the Negro population, as part-whites marry non-whites; but the six million part-white Negroes will, the present pattern indicates, continue to marry non-whites. The Negro population as a whole will become a little lighter and more homogeneous in color; but that is all.

The racist marriage statutes have become more numerous and more rigidly enforced against Negroes in the past fifty years. They stand court tests because marriage has been held to be within the power of the separate states. But so is education. The 1954 decision in *Brown et al.* v. *Topeka Board of Education* did not place education within the power of the federal government; it simply forbade, under the Fourteenth Amendment, unequal protection of the state's public school laws. That decision overturned *Plessy* v. *Ferguson*, the famous case in which the Supreme Court upheld "equal but separate" railway accommodations in Louisiana. In 1896 the Louisiana statute was upheld on the ground that it enjoined members of *both* races from sitting together in railroad cars; it was therefore equal treatment. The state laws against intermarriage likewise forbid Negroes and whites to intermarry. But Justice Harlan said, in his historic dissent in Plessy: "If a white man and a black man choose to occupy the same public conveyance on a public highway, it is their right to do so, and no government, proceeding alone on grounds of race, can prevent it without infringing the personal liberty of each." What if two persons, one white and one black, choose to marry? Can a government prevent it, proceeding alone on grounds of race? The California Supreme Court said no in 1948. The case at bar involved a Catholic couple, one white, the other Negro, who sued on the ground that the California marriage statute forbade them the sacrament of marriage in violation of the religious freedom clauses of the state and national constitutions. This argument, together with the equal protection finding in *Brown* v. *Topeka*, indicates that the statutes of all twenty-eight states forbidding intermarriage will be swept away in one U.S. Supreme Court decision, and the present attack on the Court has been said to involve that consideration. A couple of months ago, after Harry Bridges, who is always up to *something*, discovered that he could not marry a non-Caucasian in Idaho, that state quietly erased its intermarriage statute.

But it is doubtful, in view of the California experience since 1948, that such changes will affect miscegenation or intermarriage except in principle. The big change is already taking place — a bigger change than any law will ever induce: The Negro is at last rejecting the white man's doctrine of white supremacy. Not resenting it, or complaining of it, or defying it — rejecting it. It was his acceptance of this doctrine that spread miscegenation; his rejection of it will speed the rate at which miscegenation is declining.

The Negro is completing the half of his emancipation that he has had to achieve himself. His hands and feet unshackled, he is climbing Jacob's ladder. He is deserting the white man's racism as he climbs from a sense of inferiority to a sense of equality. From there to a sense of unconsciousness of race is a long step — a step that will take a century or two for the Negro and at least that long for the white man. Along about then, or another century or two thereafter, amalgamation of the races will be a conceivable possibility. But along about then nobody will care.

PART
FIVE

DANGEROUS
MEN

PORTRAIT
OF A
DANGEROUS
MAN

Moody finished his sermon — the Colossal Campaign to Reduce the Population of Hell by One Million Souls was under way — and Sankey stepped forward to render "The Ninety and Nine." It was the 1876 Revival, Boston's Biggest Ever. The Giant Mixed Choir had pressed into service for the occasion some very small, mixed giants, and as Sankey mourned for the sheep that was lost, and the audience wept, one of the smallest of the mixed giants in the choir tugged at his mother's sleeve and whispered, "What are they crying for?" His father, on the other side of him, merely said, "Hush," but his mother, unable to resist the evanescent opportunity, bent down and looked hard at him. "They are weeping," she said, "for *you*, Bobbo."

Seventy years have passed, and they are weeping for Bobbo Lovett still. More in sorrow than in anger, the United States Congress cut off his salary as government secretary of the Virgin Islands. A decade earlier, and no less mournfully, a committee of the Illinois Senate demanded his dismissal from the faculty of the University of Chicago. Streaming with evangelical tears, the Bureau of Naval Intelligence found him, still earlier, "the primary factor which loyal Americans must contend with"; the *Chicago Tribune* called him "a pacifist, bolshevik, communist, and pale pink radical"; the chief investigator for the Dies Committee held him responsible for more Communist "fronts" than any other man in America. And the FBI groaned in apostolic agony as it disclosed that Bobbo belonged to four hundred organizations, all of them (with the possible exception of the Red Cross) engaged in overturning the republic.

From *Harper's Magazine*, July, 1946.

229

Others, however, have insisted that, far from not being found, he is one of the few sheep that have never been lost. The first to take this hopeful view was President Eliot of Harvard, who wrote of him in 1893, "Lovett is a man by whose character and later achievements Harvard is willing to be judged." Exactly half a century later the *New York Times* could not think of "any act in his life inconsistent with the purest patriotism"; Harold Ickes called him "an American who has never had any thought except to help other people and to serve his country"; and the municipal councils of the Virgin Islands, in joint assembly, proclaimed him "an American gentleman, a patriotic citizen, a humane administrator, and a symbol of the American flag for which our sons are fighting."

On balance, it would seem that the Boston Revival, the FBI, and the Dies Committee were right. Certainly the evidence is abundant that the *New York Times*, President Eliot, and the Virgin Islands are wrong. Robert Morss Lovett, no less innocent-fronted at seventy-five than he was at five, has a lifelong record of vicious associations, some of which are even yet to come to light. (The FBI, for all its unremitting diligence, never discovered, for instance, that *the only decoration he ever received* was that of the German Red Cross.) He has a record as a jailbird; he has been photographed with Negroes who resisted eviction even though they had not paid their rent; and he has been brought to justice with a thief on either side of him. He has gone bail for at least one Nazi and no end of Communists; he encouraged young men, as long ago as the twenties, to take the "slacker oath"; and as recently as a few years ago, he used his powers as acting governor of the Virgin Islands to stay the execution of a condemned murderer, asserting, with the same disingenuity that he displayed in the choir, that his act was motivated not by the fact that hanging was unthinkable to him as a member of the Committee against Capital Punishment but that the execution was set, as chance had it, for Bunker Hill Day *and to hang a man on Bunker Hill Day was unthinkable to a member of the Sons of the American Revolution.*

In spite of his offenses against public safety and public decency, this admitted enemy of certain American traditions remains at large — and not only at large, but at large in a post of public honor and influence. He is now finishing his second year as professor of English, and his first as acting chairman of the English Department, at the University of Puerto Rico, a public institution supported entirely by the government tax on rum drunk by the American public.

It may be recklessly supposed that a man of seventy-five is not much of a menace, either public or private. (Informing his friends last year of the birth of his first great-grandchild, Lovett announced, with a touch of arrogance, "Now I'm an ancestor.") But his show of genteel senility has been a deceit for years. As long ago as 1933, a policeman testifying against him as a rioter told the court, "And when I went to put him in the wagon, the old gentleman there, he held the door for me." The extent to which his air of ancientness "otherwise influenced the native mind" (a charge made by the United States Congress) was disclosed when Special Agent Willis of the FBI reported that none of the natives he interviewed in the Virgin Islands knew that they had been subverted and that all of them, on the contrary, declared that Lovett was "a wonderful old man," "a kindhearted old man," "a kind and gentlemanly old man," and "a fine old man and a loyal American citizen."

The impression of solid old age is effected by a more than solid portliness; by a Humpty-Dumpty head reminiscent of W. R. Hearst's; by a double-breasted sack coat, a little too short and a little too tight, worn until Mrs. Lovett throws it away in the night; by the indiscriminate courtliness which amazed the Chicago policeman; by an invariable façade of solemnity which has earned him the sobriquet, among others, of the Buster Keaton of the saints; by a high, wrinkled, and wispy (where it isn't barren) gray dome; and by a long, cleft upper lip, which, whether he is annoyed, amused, or embarrassed, moves up and down like a rabbit's to the accompaniment of the blinking of an owl and the pouting of a pigeon.

His deafness is acute in the presence of public lectures, musicales, and Latin American tyrants; but he seems to hear the whispers of beggars and troublemakers. Sleepiness invariably overtakes him at formal functions but never when he's paddling around in the Caribbean or trotting through the hills around San Juan. He has the greatest difficulty in placing certain statesmen whom he has often met, and in fine company finds that he cannot remember a single stanza of "Abdul Abulbul Ameer," whose fifty-six stanzas he sang in a low crowd the evening before.

He has been called a fanatic with a sense of humor, a chuckling martyr, a crusader without a compulsion. But there is no sign whatever that he knows how much evil — some would say good — he has done, or that he has ever known what he was doing when he did it. A Hearst reporter, who was assigned to "smear" him, wrote in the diary that all Hearst reporters keep:

One of the flash pictures I will carry in my mind until I die is that of Professor Lovett, as the big policeman hurried him from the filthy, hot cell. . . . He was neither ashamed, nor was he proud. He was just there. . . . He looked at me as if I were another human being, at the slumping colored boy on bench as if he were another human being, at the policeman who stepped up beside him as another human being — all just alike before him, and, consequently, all made conscious of their being human. He thought he was no better than anybody else, just as he thought that nobody was better than he.

This misspent life began on Christmas Day — itself a deceptive auspice — in Boston in the year 1870. Unlike so many troublesome persons, Robert Morss Lovett never knew either the want or the superfluity of either ancestors or bread. His father was an insurance man, and his mother had been a teacher. "My childhood," he says, "was not unhappy, but uncomfortable. My parents took an unwholesome interest in my life." What they did was try to inoculate him with the Christian, the bourgeois, and the manly virtues. It was simply no go.

Prayer was a thrice-daily performance in the gaslit Lovett home, and Bobbo had to memorize a chapter of the Bible every morning. "I took it right after my codliver oil." His mother tried unremittingly to convert him, but all signs of grace were lacking. His grandfather was a member of the Congregation, in distinction from the Church; he had made no public profession of faith. "I admired Grandpa, and I couldn't believe he wasn't saved." He finally believed himself converted, however, by the hymn beginning, "I love Thee, my Saviour, for Thou first lovedst me." The spirit of *quid pro quo* appealed to him, but when his mother gave him a dollar for remembering the Commandments and his aunt gave him ten dollars for remembering not to pick his nose, the spirit failed him. The private prayer he best remembers is, "Dear God, please cut out the begats."

If he resisted the Christian virtues, he positively crusaded against the bourgeois. Sent to dancing school, riding school, and the Boston Conservatory of Music, he came home hating them all. In school he was put in the non-singers' group. Years later, at a party, he was pressed to sing "Abdul," and when he agreed to, as he always did, the hostess asked Rudolph Reuter to accompany him. The great pianist tried, but Lovett shifted key too fast. At the conclusion, Lovett turned to Reuter and said miserably, "I was a non-singer in school." "Did you say 'non-singer?'" Reuter replied. "I would have said 'anti-singer.'"

"As a child," he says, "I was pleasantly contentious." But his contentiousness did not extend to the field of the heroic pursuits. He couldn't fly a kite or flop a sled. True, he was captain and pitcher of the team he organized; true, also, he owned the bat and ball. The day of the big game, the team advanced him to the rank of umpire. The fact that he had to spend three years trying to manipulate a gun in the rear rank of the worst company at English High School may have lost the country a general comparable, in other respects, to Robert E. Lee.

But there were other kinds of war for pleasantly contentious young men, and one of them was going on at Harvard. The Harvard of 1888 was torn between the Old Guard, representing the traditionally smug, narrow, and remote "education of a gentleman," and President Charles W. Eliot, the man who, probably more than any other, accounts for Robert Lovett. Eliot's steady, self-assured struggle to overturn Harvard appealed to a natural-born lost sheep. The courses, characterized by the treadmill routine that Eliot was fighting, were pipes. Maintaining a *summa cum laude* average was easy for Lovett, and he had time for other things, especially the newly established *Harvard Monthly*. Norman Hapgood liked his stories and asked him to write for it. He became an editor and met Hutchins Hapgood, George Baker, George Santayana, and the two contemporaries who became his closest friends, Robert Herrick and William Vaughn Moody.

There were men on the faculty then like Everett, Toy, and Kittredge; but, by and large, the teachers and the teaching were, to Lovett, fantastically unreal. He recalls that in Child's famous Shakespeare course "a whole year passed without any mention of the fact that Shakespeare had a personal history and wrote for the Elizabethan stage." By the time he left Harvard, Lovett's central intellectual conviction — that literature is life and life literature — possessed him. Half a century later he formalized his *raison d'oeuvre* in the Hapgood Lectures at the University of Michigan: "The material of literature is derived from humanity and human experience. It returns, revitalized and reinterpreted, to be received again by human beings and to become once more a part of their experience. In this process the artist is mediator and agent. Surely, neither artist nor art can profit by being divorced from the great community which is for both, and in a double sense, the source of life."

In his *Monthly* editorials he crusaded against "Harvard indifference," in all its most honored forms — antifeminism, empty orthodoxy in religion, and the habit of describing the great community, when it was described at all, as "teeming." A further hint of the dangerous man to come is to be found in the Class Poem of '92, which proclaimed that "the upward struggle is itself salvation / And only faithlessness is real disgrace." The poem ended, "Fair Harvard, we who are about to live salute thee." Its author, back from a summer in Europe with Norman Hapgood, was saved from choosing between divinity and law by an assistantship in English at Fair Harvard.

He who was about to live was in agony when, the following year, Herrick asked him to come along as an instructor at the new University of Chicago. He wanted to love Harvard as Newman loved Oxford; to live there, and, if not in God's own time, then in Harvard's, to die there. At twenty-two, he was much readier to contemplate death than life, antiquity than modernity, completion than adventure. The upward struggle, to which he had borne testimony at twenty-one, and of which the Dies Committee found him guilty at seventy-one, did not appeal to him. He insists he has always loved "decay and the end of everything." His favorite line is "The sooner 'tis over, the sooner to sleep."

The Chicago of 1893 was no place to sleep. President Harper

took the occasion of the October convocation to assure the faculty of the University that the payroll would be met. Chicago was tough, and the little coterie of tough men who ran it were, in the panic, tougher still. The collapse of Pullman paternalism in the great railroad strike reduced Chicago to the anarchy that its millionaires thought they had hanged after the Haymarket. Into this hungry, bloody, muddy, and bitter Chicago came the young man who wanted to love Harvard as Newman loved Oxford — into this, and more.

William Rainey Harper, for all his great scholarship, was a man after Chicago's own heart. Storming that he couldn't run a university and be hampered by a budget, he bulldozed Rockefeller out of infinite millions. The chubby little "steam engine in pants" never stopped for or at anything. Rockefeller gifts were celebrated like football victories, and football victories like the Second Coming. The great history professor, Von Holst, delivered an oration in defense of the Oil King; the faculty accepted a champagne dinner (along with an observatory) from the traction boodler Yerkes.

Only in innovation did the bustling, backslapping Harper resemble the patrician Eliot. He introduced the quarter system, the junior college, the summer quarter, university extension work, and the university press. And he peopled his new university not only with mighty names like Michelson, Whitman, Nef, Loeb, Shorey, Chamberlin, Salisbury, and Small but also with comers like Ferdinand Schevill in European history. From Harvard, along with Herrick, the young novelist, and Lovett, the young critic, there arrived in the English Department Moody, the young poet, and John Matthews Manly, the young Chaucerian.

The bachelor life, with Moody and Schevill, was legal, if not always exemplary. An occasional grape was pressed; a semioccasional rose was flung; a continual story was told. There are rumors still — but let the FBI track them down for itself. In the summer of 1895 Lovett and Ida Mott-Smith, of Radcliffe, who had helped him break down the Harvard indifference, were married. Bimbles, Doodoo, and Beebee (Robert, Jr., Ruth, and Beatrice, on their birth certificates) were born, the two latter in Europe, where Lovett, on long sabbaticals *en famille*, sampled vast quantities of books, cathedrals, and Burgundies; discovered he wasn't a novelist; led his young son over

Tyrolean passes where angels trod; and was converted to lifelong *avant gardisme* by men like Berenson, Russell, and Dolmetsch.

Realism was becoming a word in France, in Italy, and in realistic Chicago, and Lovett spent much of his time and still more of his heart with the local renaissance, personified variously by Fuller, Garland, Herrick, Dreiser, and Moody, and later by Anderson, Masters, Sandburg, Dell, and Hecht. It was they who broke the new ground; but it was Lovett, pushing all of them on, who was surer than any of them that new ground must be broken. Still more of his time, and most of his heart, went into his students. Frank Norris was one at Harvard; and then, in the early Chicago days, came Maude Radford Warren, Anna Louis Strong, Samuel Harper, Howard Mumford Jones, Vardis Fisher, Helen Hull, Dorothy Scarborough, Ruth Cross, Carl Van Vechten, Harry Hansen, and Burton Rascoe. Later there were Glenway Wescott, Elizabeth Maddox Roberts, Nathaniel Peffer, Vincent Sheean, and John Gunther; and later still, George Dillon, Sterling North, Albert Halper, and Meyer Levin. A crazy wild Irish kid who always talked big and did nothing came in one day with a short story. Lovett read it, pouting and blinking, and said, "We can stretch this into a novel." The story was *Studs Lonigan*.

Hundreds more who call themselves "Lovett men" came under his spell in the University Poetry Club, which he organized; or the University Dramatic Club, which he urged to the first American productions of Yeats, Synge, and Gregory; or in *Poetry*, the first magazine of its kind in America, which he helped Harriet Monroe establish. His fifty-dollar annual prize was a spur to kids who had wondered if anybody cared about new poetry; but the goad was the Lovett Sunday evenings, the Lovett classes, and the Lovett office, where anybody who wondered if anybody cared about anything new at all found Lovett caring. "Let's try it; let's see it; let's go ahead with it; let's send it around," was what he said.

He had grown middle-aged very gracefully and not at all dangerously. But wasn't he, contrary to his own doctrine, somehow "divorced from the great community?" What had he meant by the upward struggle in the poem he wrote at Harvard? Was it to be found within the newly ivied walls of a university or between the boards of a book? There had been fleeting glimpses of the struggle — he remembered being shocked, for instance, when he learned that Spain had yielded to the American demands the day before America attacked — but he had grown middle-aged much too gracefully for a dangerous man.

The mentor of so many pacifists, the idol of so many more, and the defender of them all has never been a pacifist. Like Wilson, he opposed America's entrance into the war, and for Wilson's reasons. He lent his name to every peace group; who, in 1914, '15, and '16, didn't? But as 1917 came on, the peacemakers melted away. It was April, and then war. The peace people held meetings to demand a statement of war aims. On the last Sunday in May came the big meeting in Chicago's Auditorium. There was a committee, including Lovett. The committee, like the peacemakers before them, melted away. The speakers couldn't come. At the last minute Lovett stood on the platform alone. He began: "This meeting has been called for the sole and explicit object of representing to the Administration the general desire that as soon as possible, the war aims of the United States be set forth, together with the terms of the peace which represent their fulfillment. This meeting is not held to pass any criticism on the course of our country in entering the war."

Outside the packed hall were hundreds of people who couldn't get in, and police. The papers had warned the community that the pro-Germans were going to meet to obstruct the war effort. Outside the hall somebody pushed somebody else, and the police went into action. The next morning the papers reported an antiwar riot. The following day the streets around the University were covered with leaflets calling upon patriots to lynch Lovett in effigy in front of his apartment that night. The professor was scheduled to give a doctoral examination and was torn between the two attractions, when his friend Bill Chenery (later, editor of *Collier's*) called him and protested that without the victim's presence the lynching would be a dud. He went and watched unnoticed. There were clergymen in the mob, and professors; there were not many students.

It was the virginal morale of a country's first man-sized war, and the tub-thumpers included a large section of the University faculty, marching fatly with wooden guns and proving that they were men and not just professors. A secret meeting was called in the faculty to demand Lovett's dismissal. It began and ended when Henry Gordon Gale, eminent All-American, eminent physicist, and in 1917, the most eminent tub-thumper of them all, got to his feet, looked silly, and finally managed to say it: "If Lovett goes, I go too."

The lynching was the trauma of Lovett's life. It taught him the meaning of Samuel Butler's statement that of three misfortunes — loss of money, loss of health, loss of reputation — the last is by far the least. Now he knew where the upward struggle was. Now he was free to fight it.

With almost every male member of the English Department scurrying to Washington to fight the war, Lovett, when he was asked what he was doing to help, replied, with his usual dead pan, "I am carrying on with the ladies." But more and more, as patriotism turned to persecution and persecution spread to village and farm, he found himself in the great community, testifying for "draft dodgers," that is, pacifists, and for "Bolsheviks," that is, socialists. He defended the American rights of people with German names. He crusaded against a prison terror that sent murdered pacifists back home in Army uniforms. He fought for Scott Nearing, for the leaders of the Non-Partisan League, for Max Eastman, and the editors of the *Masses*. His historic defense of the IWW's before Judge Landis may have contributed to their conviction by a jury of professing Christians. Lovett suggested — and counsel proclaimed — that "there is a ritual of violence and a ritual of Christianity, to which the subscribers, in both cases, pay lip service without in the least intending to put them into practice."

On May 7, 1918, the telegram came. The night before, Lieutenant Bimbles, who had volunteered from Harvard, took a patrol in Belleau Wood. It was a brass hat's bonehead mistake; the patrol walked into the enemy and was wiped out. Lovett was away a few days in Boston, where his brother Sidney walked into the parental home to find him weeping with his father. It is the only display of emotion larger than a frown or a chuckle ever reported of the man. He returned to Chicago, taught his classes, went on with the upward struggle.

The shooting ended and the war began. He attacked Versailles, America's abandonment of the League, the Bristish massacres in China, and the French invasion of the Ruhr. He became president of the Friends of Freedom for India, a member of Oswald Garrison Villard's committee to go to Ireland to investigate the Black-and-Tan outrages, and a lobbyist against American intervention in Mexico and the Caribbean. He joined the Anti-Imperialist League and the Committee to Aid China during the hopeful days of the Christian General.

His long career as a thoroughly conscious fellow traveler of the Communists began with the Russian Revolution. Even pacifists like Jane Addams saw the bloody rise of Russia as a dent in the iron curtain that fell all over the world right after the war. His hopes for liberal nationalistic capitalism sinking, Lovett followed the counterrevolutionary activities of the Allied governments — including his own — everywhere in the world. As chairman of the Committee for the Relief of Russian Women and Children, he was softly informed by President Livingston Farrand of the American Red Cross that "we are unable to work with the Bolsheviki, but we're right behind Wrangel's troops." Undaunted, his committee, which included Presidents Eliot and Nielson, organized a ten-dollar-a-plate dinner at the Waldorf. They made the mistake of printing the menu: black bread and thin soup, the standard evening meal of a Russian child. The shimmering guests had bought all the tickets, but when they saw the menu, they drifted into the Waldorf dining room and failed to return for the speeches. Normalcy had come to America, and Lovett discovered how few of his countrymen were morally willing, or psychologically able, to have any truck with the upward struggle.

The few, then, had to do it all. Lovett the imaginative writer had already passed with the failure, decades before, of his novels *Richard Gresham* and *Winged Victory*. Lovett the scholar passed with the Auditorium speech in 1917; none of his half-dozen subsequent textbooks came up to the prewar *History of English Literature*, written with William Vaughn Moody and known still to hundreds of thousands of children as "Moody and Lovett." Lovett the critic passed when he ended his year's editorship of *The Dial* in 1919, where he launched Malcolm Cowley and Lewis Mumford as reviewers. Back in Chicago, Lovett the dangerous man was forced to be born.

In the postwar trample toward normalcy, his name was on every defense committee, usually in the flattering, if thankless, role of treasurer. The Lovetts, if not the law, would have to preserve the principle that ten guilty men should escape rather than one innocent man be punished. A German writer, imprisoned as an enemy alien at Fort Oglethorpe, wrote Lovett for help, proclaiming himself a pacifist and describing the torture to which he had been subjected. Lovett got Norman Hapgood to intercede with Attorney General Palmer. The German wanted to meet his benefactor, and Lovett invited him to the Harvard Club in New York, where Hapgood recognized him as a notorious pro-German agitator. The man hopped the next boat to Germany, where, says Lovett, "he at once became an ornament of the Nazi school of literature."

The "Red raids" took their toll in the higher learning as everywhere else. When a German-born student named Louis Wirth — now a distinguished sociologist at Chicago — criticized the Treaty of Versailles at the Student International Club, the sacrilege was at once reported to President Judson. Judson called a faculty meeting to consider witholding Wirth's college degree. Lovett made the only speech. He wanted it understood, he said, that he had no objection to withholding Wirth's degree, providing that President Judson would thereafter include approval of the Treaty of Versailles in the entrance requirements of the University. It was the end of the witch hunt at Chicago, with a single victim: Lovett. His resignation was requested as dean of the junior college. Judson was reported to have said that Lovett was a dangerous man: "he knows anarchists, socialists, and Lesbians." Lovett resigned as dean, refusing to defend himself, and his three assistant deans resigned the following day.

As an active editor of the *New Republic*, where, for a decade beginning in 1921, he spent six months a year, he found himself caught in the wheels within wheels (or pinwheels within pinwheels) of the third-party movement. The "Committee of 48," with Amos Pinchot, Dudley Field Malone, Lovett, and their likes as the leaders, held a "nominating convention" in Chicago for the 1920 campaign. The labor groups, also convening, refused to unite on a reform platform, and the platform as adopted was repugnant to the reformers' candidate, Senator La Follette. Amid the chaos, Lovett found "new parties being born throughout the Morrison Hotel. In the lobby, we started and plunged as the word was whispered, 'Judge So-and-So of Nebraska has a new party in Room 445.'" But four years later the mugwumps polled a staggering five million votes for La Follette and Wheeler. La Follette gave Lovett the foreign policy plank to write and asked him to take the presidency of the University of Wisconsin. "A Christian like you wouldn't last a week," Professor John R. Commons informed him from Madison, and Lovett declined to be a candidate. The post went to Glenn Frank.

His *New Republic* career began with book-reviewing. He brought in young Edmund Wilson to help him and went out to look at "the great community." Called to Washington to testify before the President's War Policies Committee, he announced his conviction that "the way to take profits out of war is to take them out of peace." He went to Boston to cover the Sacco-Vanzetti case and wound up chairman of the Sacco-Vanzetti League. (The "worst dereliction" of his life, he says, was his failure to raise the $50,000 which a member of the gang that actually did the killing was willing to take for the actual story.) He went to Cleveland to speak on disarmament and discovered himself conducting the struggle against Newton Baker and the New York Central-Van Sweringen Terminal deal. He was one of the founders, with Roger Baldwin, of the American Civil Liberties Union, and from then on, wherever there was trouble, he turned up in person or pen: Centralia, Bisbee, Tulsa, Harlan, Herrin, Brooklyn, Passaic, New Bedford. Whenever and wherever nobody else would write or speak or sing, there was Lovett. Somebody had to.

Van Wyck Brooks complained that "Lovett writes better than any of us" — a lover's exaggeration, perhaps, like everything ever said of him by his friends — "and spends his time doing everything but writing." But Lovett had long since decided that his time wasn't worth anything. The end product of man's life was man, not words. If a man had words, he should use them for man. His articles are more pedantically written than Brooks suggests, easy and long, until their implications are irresistible inferences, and without rancor. He is devoted to Ruskin, and with reason.

If capitalist man is, as Maritain says, man in a hurry, Lovett was a Communist indeed. His colleagues at the University knew that if they got sick Lovett would take their classes. Either as an official witness for the Civil Liberties Union, or simply because he had read about the case in the paper, he sat for days on end in neighborhood police courts. Discovered thus sitting one day by one of his friends, Lovett explained, "I am fixing the court with my eye in an effort to intimidate it into a carriage of justice."

Jane Addams was "the only person I have known whom I would follow into social conflict blindfolded," and she needed help at Hull House. Lovett moved in with his family in 1921. Along with the rest of the residents, he took his turn tending the door and the switchboard two nights a week. He conducted classes for immigrants. But his greatness at Hull House, as everywhere, lay, as Jane Addams put it, in his being there. People came to him heavy-laden.

One who came to him needs to be remembered: a Russian refugee, who had written an autobiography exposing Soviet corruption. Lovett thought the book was important, if not too well written, and succeeded in persuading a publisher to get it out. The book was not a success, and its author accused Lovett of sabotaging it in behalf of the Soviet government. Lovett, with more courtesy than the situation demanded, replied, in a scribbled note of consolation, that he himself "did not care whether the book reflects on the Russian Government or the United States Government or any other — all in my opinion being rotten." A decade later the scribble appeared as Exhibit 19 in the files of the Illinois Senate committee which, demanding his dismissal from the University, stated, "If all the exhibits offered in evidence against Professor Lovett were disregarded except Exhibit 19, proof of his disloyal conduct is conclusive." Still a decade later, Exhibit 19 was produced by the United States Congress. But Robert Lovett still scribbles careless notes of consolation to young writers when their books don't sell.

The associate of so many Communists, the defender of so many more, and the tool of them all has never been a Communist. Robert Lovett's whole life has been at odds with principles and practices inseparable from communism — violence, intolerance, expediency, self-interest, and materialism. And no one who knows him doubts that if he were a Communist, he would have joined the Communist party. Yet, of the four hundred organizations which the FBI connected him with, it is safe, if a little conservative, to name three that were not, at any time and in any degree, infested by Commies — the Pulitzer Prize Committee, the National Institute of Arts and Letters, and the Harvard Club of New York.

If he often found himself working with them, it was not because of his early faith (somewhat wilted since) in the Russian Revolution or his conviction (subsequently adopted by the American government) that the Soviet Union was here to stay. It was because the Communists, like the Socialists, were willing to work, whatever their ends, for immediate causes which found respectable liberals frigid or impotent. If the Commies were fighting the Mooney and Scottsboro cases to provoke the class struggle, Lovett was fighting the same cases to rectify injustice. If the Communists were using him for their purposes, he was using them for his; and the ancient question of who was doing what to whom is still to be answered.

He was too innocent in his heart to be an innocent front. He knew the Communist pattern of control-or-destroy. He knew he would be, as he often was, reviled, as "literary looker-on," "Trotskyite," "capitalist stooge," whenever his own estimate led him to break with them. But the estimate was always his own. "I have never been as afraid of liberals going Communist," he says, "as I have of their pulling out of liberal organizations when the Communists, with their discipline, their persistence, and their eagerness, threatened to seize control."

Persons who value either their purses *or* their good names above trash will never understand men like Lovett. Harold Ickes, defending him before Congress, said, "Most of us would be more critical and discriminating in our associates. I, for example, would refuse to join any organization if I knew that it contained a large number of

Communists, whatever its professed objective might be. But I am a far more suspicious man than is Mr. Lovett. He has, for the seventy-three years of his life, found it difficult to think ill of any man."

But there were those — professing Christians all — who regarded latter-day associations with publicans and sinners as strictly un-American. In term of length, the record of Robert Morss Lovett in Mrs. Elizabeth Dilling's *Red Network* made him the most dangerous man in America; and with the death of Jane Addams and Ramsey MacDonald, whose records were longer than his, he rose to undisputed eminence as the most dangerous person in the world. He had attracted, meanwhile, the attention of more formidable patriots than Mrs. Dilling. One of these patriots did not think much of professors in any case and thought highly enough of Hermann Goering to publish his articles in a chain of powerful newspapers. "I have never understood," says Lovett, "how I first offended Hearst. It is true that I called him Public Enemy No. 1, but everybody else had a list of Public Enemies and I didn't see why I shouldn't have one of my own."

The New Deal was on; the New Deal was the Brain Trust; and the Brain Trust was a wire-whiskered idiot with a bomb in each hand and a mortarboard on his head. The steady hammering at "Red professors" was one facet of the attack. One evening the publisher of Hearst's Chicago *Herald & Examiner* was entertaining his most important subscriber, Charles R. Walgreen. Mr. Walgreen remarked that his niece had heard a lot about communism at the University of Chicago; even, said Mr. Walgreen, whose drug stores did not advertise contraceptives, about free love. The publisher did not have to be reminded of the Chief's order to "get" Lovett. Mr. Walgreen withdrew his niece from the University and demanded, exclusively through the Hearst papers, a legislative investigation of Communist teaching at the University. The next thing the poor druggist knew, he had retained a lawyer, who, as chance had it, was also counsel for the *Chicago Tribune*.

The great investigation — consisting of a series of jammed public hearings — was one of the most delirious events of our time. (One witness, with a distinguished record as a labor spy, anti-Semite, and vigilante, testified that the Red flag flew over the University on May Day.) There was, of course, no pretense made of supporting the charge of Communist teaching. When Lovett offered to recite the lectures in his courses in seventeenth- and nineteenth-century English literature, counsel for Mr. Walgreen asked him if it was true that he approved of the "slacker oath against our country." "If," said Lovett, "you refer to the so-called Oxford oath not to bear arms, I regard it as the individual equivalent of the Kellogg-Briand Pact by which the United States gave up war as an instrument of national policy. I am opposed to violence, including violent revolution. My son was killed in Belleau Wood, and I do what little I can to save similar young men from a similar fate."

When the smoke blew away and the papers blew themselves out, the University awaited the verdict. The legislature had the power to tax its property and bankrupt it. When the legislative committee "acquitted" the University but found that Lovett had "pursued an unpatriotic course of conduct for eight or ten years," President Hutchins, who had thus far conducted himself like a gentleman, wrote a violent statement. Professor James Weber Linn dissuaded him from issuing it. "But, Bob," said Linn, "I'll tell you this. If the trustees fire Robert Lovett, you'll receive the resignations of twenty full professors tomorrow morning." "Oh, no, I won't," said Hutchins, "my successor will."

The University sat tight while the wolves howled. "We've got to stand by Lovett," said Professor Gale to Hutchins, "but he's cost the University millions." "Oh, I don't know, Henry," said Hutchins, "this last time around he brought in about four million." The Rockefeller Foundation had given the University $3,000,000. A letter offering to be "of whatever service for which you may wish to call on me" had been received from a resident of Long Island, Marshall Field. And a miserable little man had gone to Professor Charles E. Merriam with a $250,000 proposition. "I don't know," said Merriam, "you've hurt Lovett's feelings." The little man advanced the ante to $550,000, and the University announced the establishment of the Charles R. Walgreen Foundation.

The morning the legislative committee demanded Lovett's dismissal, Dean Edith Foster Flint called the Lovett apartment at Hull

House. Lovett was out of town, and Mrs. Lovett was obviously uninformed of the committee's report. Thinking to soften the blow, Mrs. Flint began telling Mrs. Lovett what a wonderful man her husband was and how much everyone loved him. "Edith," said Ida Lovett, interrupting her, "is Robert in jail again?"

The Chief died hard. Daily the Hearst papers demanded that Lovett be fired. There was only silence, until one day the *Herald & Examiner* announced: "Under pressure of the demand for his ouster, the University of Chicago has decided to drop Professor Robert Morss Lovett from its faculty, according to authoritative sources. The University administration contemplates retiring him on Christmas Day. At that time Professor Lovett will be eligible for a pension." That afternoon the University announced that Professor Lovett, who would reach the retirement age of sixty-five on December 25, had been persuaded to remain on the faculty.

He wanted to retire; he "loved decay and the end of everything." He wanted to sit in the sun; he wanted, he said, to read a few of the books on which he had lectured so eloquently for forty years. But the upward struggle carried him on. He went to Flint, Michigan, and was escorted into the sit-down-struck plant. Holding his five shares of General Motors stock above his head, he informed the grinning strikers that "my management is mistreating my workers, and I am here as one of the owners of the corporation to tell my workers that I am behind them."

Blandly going his way, seemingly unaware that he was a "must" on the list of men whom powerful forces — in, as well as out of, the government — were determined to destroy, he took to the hustings against the massacres incident to the Little Steel Strike. He denounced Roosevelt's failure, under the Neutrality Act, to recognize war when there were a million Japanese soldiers in China and a whole Italian army corps in Spain. As late as the spring of 1939 he pleaded for limiting American intervention to economic sanctions. But after the Hitler-Stalin pact and the partition of Poland, he gradually advanced to the position, in 1940, of calling for "all possible aid, even if it involves war with the aggressors."

That a man who was willing to follow Jane Addams blindfolded — who had often said, "I have always been opposed to violence," and was fond of saying that "blood is the milk of old men" — should go overboard may have shocked his pacifist friends. But there was no real inconsistency in his record. He had not opposed the first war; he had opposed the basis on which it was fought. The Fascist attack on civilization was, as he saw it, the concerted, climactic assault against the upward struggle. His defense of dissenters was no less wholehearted than it was the time before. "I am not," he said, "against war under any and all conditions. I live on a lower moral level than many men I admire."

It would be an offense to judge this feelingest of men as a political, economic, or even literary thinker. If he has been consistent, his consistency has been an accident. There is a higher consistency in him. He is Plato's "man of right opinion," who get where a man ought to go without knowing how he got there. He moves by the heart, and it is men's hearts, not their heads, that he moves. After forty years of teaching English literature, he says that the one thing he knows for sure about English literature is that it cannot be taught. His lecture courses were ineffably dull; "Robert hangs up his personality," Professor Philip Schuyler Allen said, "along with his hat in the cloakroom." Asked what Lovett's "teaching technique" was, Meyer Levin replied that it was the same as that of the great teacher of painting in Paris who was never known to have done anything except pass behind his students' easels and mutter, "*Continuez, continuez.*" James Weber Linn may have come closest of all when he said, "Robert doesn't teach; he warms."

It was the summer of 1939, and Lovett, crowding seventy, was *really* ready to retire. He had taught three emeritus years at Chicago and two summers at Northwestern University and the University of Colorado. He had spent the summer of 1938 on a lecture tour for the League for Industrial Democracy, the Socialist organization of which he had so long been president. Now he and Mrs. Lovett were touring the West, visiting James Westfall Thompson and Upton Sinclair in California and moseying around Arizona, where John Manly, Ferdie Schevill, and Sherwood Anderson all had sunny places. The Lovetts thought they would stay.

"It seemed perfectly natural," says Lovett, recalling his invitation that summer to a White House dinner for Rachel Crothers. "Miss Crothers was the cousin of my dentist." The day after the dinner, his old friend Harold Ickes asked him to go to the Virgin Islands as government secretary. "What we need," Ickes told Lovett, "is a greeter." What they really needed, it tourned out, was a governor. The governor was absent most of the time in Washington, where it was an open secret that he was trying to get rid of Lovett, whom the natives idolized. Lovett spent more than half his four years in the Virgins as acting governor. Mrs. Lovett tried to get him to buy a new suit; he agreed to buy a new hat, which he argued, was the most important part of a Caribbean governor's costume, since it was always being held conspicuously over the heart at receptions for visiting dictators.

On February 1, 1943, Congressman Dies denounced Lovett on the floor of the House as "an irresponsible unrepresentative, crackpot radical bureaucrat." Thoroughly frustrated by the fact that only four of the more than eleven hundred government employees he had denounced had been fired, Mr. Dies demanded that "if there is no other way to get rid of these people, we should refuse to appropriate money for their salaries." A subcommittee of the House Appropriations Committee, with Congressman Kerr (Dem., N.C.) as its chairman, was created to take up where Dies left off. On April 14, 1943, Lovett, then in Washington, was handed an "invitation" to appear before the Kerr committee less than twenty-four hours later. He was denied access to the charges and the right of counsel. Even the solicitor of the Department of the Interior was excluded from the hearing. The transcript of the hearing was never shown to Lovett, to the Department, or even to the House of Representatives, which voted his conviction.

The Kerr committee reported that Lovett was "unfit to continue in the employment of the United States Government by reason of his association and membership in organizations whose aims and purposes have been subversive of the Government of the United States." The committee failed to observe that among others guilty of association and membership in one or another of the organizations they listed were Thomas E. Dewey, Wendell Willkie, James Farley, Cordell Hull, and Justices Frank Murphy and Robert Jackson.

The House attached a rider to an appropriation bill providing that no part of the appropriation was to be used to pay the salaries of Lovett and two employees of the FCC similarly pilloried. Letters in defense of Lovett poured in, not from radicals, nor merely from the entire population of the Virgin Islands, but also from Chairman Thomas Lamont of J. P. Morgan and Company, President E. E. Brown of the First National Bank of Chicago, Judge Learned Hand, and the senior partners of the largest corporation law firms in both Chicago and Washington. Men who hate each other have one thing in common, their love of Lovett. "Robert is the damnedest fool I have ever known," said one of the country's most conservative (and ungrammatical) millionaires once, "but when I say his name I feel like I'm in church."

Signing the appropriation bill, with the rider attached, Mr. Roosevelt said, "I have been forced to yield to avoid our delaying the conduct of the war. But I can not so yield without placing on record my view that this provision is not only unwise and discriminatory, but unconstitutional." Harold Ickes, who was always mad, had known Robert Lovett, who was never mad, for all of forty-five years. Ickes insisted on fighting. Preliminary suit, for recovery of the interim salary, was filed in the United States Court of Claims, which, in a unanimous decision, awarded Lovett his back salary of $1,996.

The issue over the lost sheep of the 1876 revival is not, in 1946, an issue over $1,996. It is the issue over the encroachment of Congress on the executive. It is the issue over due process of law. It is the issue over one of the basic causes of the American Revolution — the bill of attainder, a law against a man. It is the first such law in American history, and Lovett's reaction was typical. "It was by attainder that Parliament cut off the Earl of Strafford's head," he observed. "Our advance in civilization is shown by the fact that it is only my salary that has been cut off." On March 25, 1946, the Supreme Court of the United States agreed to hear on appeal the case of the cutting off of Robert Lovett's salary.

Something appeared in a leafy place called Emancipation Garden the night of March 28, 1944. It was the United Citizens Organization, comprising every subcommunity (including the churches and the businessmen's association) of the Virgin Islands. It existed to say good-by to the Lovetts and to give them a surprise in the form of the Robert Morss Lovett Charity Fund, to be used as Lovett might direct. The Joint Municipal Councils of the Islands blubbered about "his upright, just, and sympathetic administration"; the St. Thomas *Daily News* bemoaned "a great and noble American, whose name, long after he has gone, will be uttered here as a synonym for tolerance, integrity, honesty of purpose, and distinguished service." Lovett said, "When I come back, I want to find a new hospital, a new high school, better housing, and a decent water and sewage system."

When Chancellor Jaime Benitez invited him to come to the burgeoning University of Puerto Rico, Lovett asked what he was to do there. "Just be here," said Benitez. His two last remaining Chicago cronies, Ferdie Schevill and Percy Holmes Boynton, were teaching in the sun, and Lovett went. "If he stays *here* four years," said Governor Rex Tugwell, with characteristic conservative horror, "he'll be elected king." But this year, he says, he's going to quit. His "love of decay and the end of everything" has had to wait for thirty years. He is going, at last, to pursue it, "in the form," he says, "of my autobiography." But there may be another wait; according to word from San Juan, he is up to his ears in the upward struggle for the four freedoms for Puerto Rico.

They say that Jesus saw the multitudes heavy laden and faint of heart, and they say that he sorrowed and said to his disciples: "The harvest truly is plenteous, but the laborers are few. Pray ye therefore the Lord of the Harvest, that he will send forth laborers into his harvest." That's what they say.

And the disciples prayed and prayed — that's what *I* say — and many laborers came to the employment office of the American Friends Service Committee and the Church World Service and the Catholic Worker and offered to labor in the harvest. And they were all young and their eyes shone with ardor and they went out to labor. And then they grew older and got married (or didn't get married) and got an offer at Socony Vacuum or Macy's or Time, Inc., and the ardor went out of their eyes and they saw, for the first time, the sign above the door of the employment office: Abandon all hope of getting rich and respectable, ye who enter here. And they turned away.

Pray ye therefore the Lord of the harvest, that he will send forth laborers into his harvest for keeps. For the laborers, when the young men and women grow older, are few and far between, and when you look to see whose long bent back that is, whose step that is that staggers under the sheaves, you see that it is Red Schaal's, growing old in the harvest, his eyes shining with ardor. And you say to yourself, "Now where do you suppose the Lord got Red Schaal, and where will he get more like him?"

Red was — as he is — running the Peace Section of the American Friends Service Committee for the Middle Atlantic states. One night after he and I did a stand in Baltimore, we cadged a ride in to Philadelphia and landed outside the Reading Terminal with five minutes

From the *Progressive*, January, 1955.

to catch the rattler to Binghamton or somewhere. We each had a suitcase. And we had three big cases of books besides, for where Red goes his "literature" tables (on which he nets 40 per cent) go with him. Red was — as he is — a sick man. I wasn't. I got the two suitcases under one arm and a case of books in the other and howled for a porter to carry the other two cases of books. The porter came hotfoot, but Red had got hold of the two cases of books and he wouldn't let go; he wouldn't pay out four-bits of the Service Committee's money. He ran tottering to the train with those cases and caught it half-dead.

That's how I see him, and that's how I'll always see him, toting those cases. I've seen kids in Europe who grew up with blood and bone because the Service Committee shoved four-bits worth of milk or medicine into them when they needed it most. The Service Committee got that four-bits out of the blood and bone of Red Schaal. I see him pinching fifty cents in Philly; another fellow sees him squandering fifty dollars in Pittsburgh, in the manager's office of a hotel. "I'd like to know," Red is saying to the manager, as he's about to sign for the Green Room for a weekend conference, "if the hotel takes Negro guests." "Not ordinarily," says the manager, "but we'll make an exception in your case." "Thanks anyway," says Red, putting the pen down, "but we'd rather you didn't make an exception in our case. We'll go somewhere else." So he signs up for the Lavender Room across the street, at fifty dollars more of the Service Committee's money. The Lavender Room takes Negroes ordinarily.

Another fellow sees him leaving the office at five o'clock with a long-distance call unmade that he ought to have made before he left the office. Now Red's a meticulous administrator, a clean-desk man; but he has to call Erie, and the night rate to Erie is fifty cents cheaper, so Red's going to call from home after six o'clock and save the Service Committee's money. One fellow sees him pinching fifty cents on the phone rate; another sees him squandering fifty dollars in Pittsburgh. One of Red's speakers, at a conference in Syracuse, is quoted as having insulted the flag. The fur is flying and Red gets a letter from a contributor to the Service Committee demanding that the speaker be disowned. So Red dictates a letter, which reads, in full: "I am sorry that you have decided to discontinue your contribution to the Committee, but there are many equally worthy agencies and I hope that you will contribute to them."

One sees him one way, one another, but everyone who has seen him, in his thirty-five years in the harvest, has been changed. Not for the better but for the greater consciousness of his own shame. Take me. Before I saw him packing those cases of books through the Reading Terminal that night, it never occurred to me that I couldn't spend fifty cents of the Service Committee's money rather than break my back. Since that night I still spend the fifty cents, but I see Red packing those cases, and I'm ashamed. It takes a long time for shame to eat its way to the bottom of a man's heart, but watch me.

I talked to three ministers about Red, three ministers of the Gospel according to Matt., Mark, Luke and John. The first one said, "He makes a man ashamed of himself," and when I said, "You, too?" the minister said: "Many years ago a 'Y' secretary got into the kind of moral disgrace that people won't tolerate. He was a good man, too; you know how those things are. I was on the committee that had to decide whether we'd keep him on. I felt we couldn't; we had to think of the organization; you know how those things are. So we decided to fire him, and as the meeting broke up, somebody said, 'I wonder what Red Schaal would say,' and somebody else said, 'I don't know what he'd *say*, but I know what he'd *do*, and it wouldn't be what we have done.' That was twenty years ago, and I can't see Red Schaal, or even hear his name, without remembering that meeting and being ashamed."

The second minister I talked to said (and I quote him verbatim), "He must have a very deep faith." "But haven't we all?" I said, meaning, "Haven't you?" "Oh, of course," said the minister, "but Red's must go down deeper, the way he stands up to things."

The third minister said, "Red? I've known him for twenty, twenty-five years. I guess I know all there is to know about him — there isn't much to know about him, really — except one thing. I don't know what he does when he gets discouraged. I wish I knew."

There isn't much to know about him, really, and that's what makes the question so hard: Where do you suppose the Lord got him, and where will he get more like him to send forth into his harvest? I can tell you what he looks like and how he lives. I can tell you where he was born, and to whom, and what he did after that. I can show you the finished product, the ingredients, and the process. But I can't figure out the formula, and I'm glad that that's the Lord's problem and not mine.

He looks like the man who, in college, was voted Least Likely to Succeed. A lanky, bucktoothed hayseed, with weak eyes, big shapeless features and a grin that, given his teeth, he just can't help. He's about six feet long, his feet are too big, his arms are too long (and stick out of his sleeves), and the total impression is that of his color — sandy. (They say he was first called "Red" when he was "Y" secretary at Johns Hopkins, not because of his hair but because of his radicalism. His real name is said to be Eugene; he signs himself E. A. Schaal.) That's about what the finished product looks like. In one word: ungainly. In another: unprepossessing. He could drink himself silly and they'd never hire him to pose for Calvert's. He doesn't drink. He doesn't smoke. He doesn't swear. "Doesn't he," you say, "have *any* redeeming features?" Hardly any, to tell you the truth. If integrity is a redeeming feature, he has that one, but I don't mean anything much by "integrity." I mean merely what the word used to mean before it got dressed up like a Christmas tree; I mean oneness. What he thinks he says, and what he says he does. That may be a redeeming feature, but it doesn't make friends. It influences people, though.

I've told you what he looks like. Now I'll tell you how he lives, and that won't help you answer the question, Where did the Lord get him? either. He lives with Esther Schaal — their three daughters are grown and gone — in a house in Lansdowne, Pennsylvania, Philadelphia petit bourgeois suburbia. The Schaal house looks just like all the other houses in the block and is furnished just like them, and Red thinks it's wonderful. Outside stands the car, which looks and is just like all the other cars in the block, and Red thinks *it's* wonderful too. The Schaals own the house and the car free and clear; that's Red's estate.

If the house and the car are petit bourgeois, just wait until you see the man. He is the only man I have ever known who would be caught reading *Redbook*. He reads *Redbook* every month and the *Inquirer* every evening. When he isn't reading *Redbook* or the *Inquirer*, he is looking at low comedy on television. When he isn't looking at low comedy on television, he is playing bridge, and when he isn't playing bridge, he is playing canasta. And that is the man the disciples prayed and prayed for and the Lord sent forth. I am not kidding. That's the man: You can tell him by his necktie. It's the necktie that is absolutely identical with everybody else's. I've told you what he looks like and I've told you how he lives. You'd die laughing if you hadn't seen him bringing in the sheaves in the harvest of the Lord. Where do you suppose the Lord got him, and where will he get more like him?

The Lord got him on a farm in Gillett, Wisconsin, the youngest of nine children. The elder Schaals were "Forty-eighters" from Germany, but they were Methodists and they never missed a Sunday. Red saw Esther Christiansen in church, where she sang in the choir. The Christiansens, whose farm was six miles from the Schaal's, were Danish Lutherans, but Esther was working for a man in Gillett who was a Methodist, so she had to go to the Methodist church. Red married her and made an honest Methodist of her.

Red's father never got past the third reader, but he believed in education. When his oldest son got big enough, his father wanted him to go to high school and college, but the boy wanted to farm, so his father gave him a $2,000 farm and set aside $2,000 for each of the other children to go to high school and college. When he got old and his wife died, he sold the main farm and gave each of the children $1,000 and put the rest of the money into a perpetual trust, from which any of his descendants can draw $300 a year for two years to help them through high school or college.

That's where the Lord got Red. "Pa," says Red, "had a liberal streak here and there, and now that I think of it, he read the *Christian Century* in his late years." But Red never heard of pacifism or socialism or nonracism in Gillett or in Appleton, where he attended Lawrence College. He began hearing things when he subscribed to Bryan's *The Commoner* and *La Follette's Magazine*. He was still in high school, and he cannot, for the life of him, remember how he got started reading dangerous literature. But he overcame the danger, and after working on the farm summers and spending his senior summer in college raising money for the "Y," he went to work for the "Y" at Camp Funston, in September, 1917, while he waited for his draft number to come up.

The "Y" workers wore uniforms, and one day on a train Red got talking to the man next to him. Red introduced himself and the man said, "So you're from where that damned La Follette comes from," and Red, who has never got over being tactless, tactlessly told the man what he thought. A week later Red was summoned before the camp inspector and a colonel, put under oath, and given the charges made against him by the United States Department of Justice. The charges were (1) that he had said that he thought La Follette was sincere and (2) that he had said that some people were making money out of the war. The colonel asked him if that's what he'd said, and Red said it was. The colonel said that if he'd recant he'd have the charges quashed and everything would be all right. Red, who didn't go for either cant or recant, said he wouldn't, and the camp inspector fired him and told him to turn in his monkey-suit at once. Red turned in the suit and went home. The next day he joined the Navy and came out an ensign. The Navy convinced him that you can't make a good man out of a bad system and the military system was a bad system.

But he wasn't yet against war; he wasn't a pacifist. Then he went to Northwestern University to get his master's degree in religious education and from there to American University in Washington to get his doctor's degree. It was at the student "Y" convention of 1920, at Lake Forest College, when a bunch of the delegates moved out of a dormitory where Negroes were, that the young liberals revolted under Sherwood Eddy and the man who became the greatest single influence in Red Schaal's life — Kirby Page.

In 1923 he went to Johns Hopkins as "Y" secretary, and there he remained until 1936. His student forum was the toughest in its time in this country, with speakers like Norman Thomas, Bishop McConnell, Harry Laidler, Sherwood Eddy, and, of course, Kirby Page. Tough; tough Christians; "full gospel" men. Red came out of it — his board tried to kick him out, but the students rebelled — a "full gospel" man himself. The Young Men's Christian Association couldn't — and still can't — go along with Christ on race, on war, and on the economic order, and Red thought he'd like to go along with Christ. So, when he met Ray Newton, another "full gospel" man, at the American Friends Service Committee in Philadelphia, and Ray asked him how he'd like to raise money for the Emergency Peace Campaign, Red said fine. He raised the money, but the country went roaring down the road to war, and after that Red wasn't so sure any more about emergency campaigns. It looked like a long pull, a lifetime of labor in the harvest of the Lord of the harvest. The Service Committee wanted the laborer, but it had no money. Red said he'd organize a peace education program in the Middle Atlantic states and raise his own budget. That was all right, but he couldn't go to regular contributors and take money away from relief work. That was all right with Red. He went from town to town ringing doorbells and avoiding regular contributors. His budget was $1,000. Now it's $40,000.

Some of the Quakers didn't like Red's money-raising, especially his taking an offering at meetings and especially if the meetings were in a Quaker meetinghouse. The first time I sat on a platform, having shot my cuffs on a very high level, and listened to Red tell the customers that he had to have money. I blushed myself. I don't blush any more. I rejoice to sit on the platform and see the laborer go through the people's pants for the gleanings. Red wants money, every nickel you've got. The nickels — he thinks it's good for the poor to give, because when they give it hurts — add up to $40,000 a year. He wants more.

Always more. One day we were driving through the Alleghenies in the snow — we had to make four hundred miles that day to a meeting in Buffalo — and at noon Red said, "Lunchtime. We might as well make a pastoral call while we're at it." We pulled in at the coffee shop of a small college. I was going to order the blue plate, but when Red ordered a cheese sandwich, I ordered a cheese sandwich, and then the proprietor of the coffee shop came up and said, "Glad to see you, Dr. Shaw, always glad to see you. I like the Friend's Society, always glad to see you," and he hollered into the kitchen, "Two steaks for Dr. Shaw and his friend," and then he went out in the back. A few minutes later he reappeared with two checks, each for $50. "I figured the Friends' Society could use some money, Dr. Shaw. I like the Friends' Society, but I've just redecorated the place" — "It's right pretty," said Red — "and I'm a little short, so I made out one of the checks for today and one for a month from today. I haven't a pen. Is pencil all right?" "It certainly is," said Red, and off we went. "And a free lunch, too," said Red, as we got into the car. He wrote "Free lunch" down in his expense book, and I wrote "Free lunch" down in mine.

The next day we were going through Utica at lunchtime, and Red stopped and said, "Pastoral call." "Restaurant?" I said. "No," said Red, "minister." We left the parish house with $25, and Red said, "I know a good place to eat," and we went there and got the cheese sandwich. The sandwich was terrible. "I thought you said this was a good place to eat." "It is," said Red. "It has a good race policy. I didn't say the food was good."

He's not unfunny, exactly, but his humor is, like him, self-effacing, laconic, sly, and dry. With his inflexibility about things — and his sense of fairness to an audience — he begins his meetings on time and stands up behind, and then alongside, the speaker after forty-five minutes. I've seen him flag down Eleanor Roosevelt, and that takes some flagging. Once, with Gladys Walser as the speaker of the evening, Red announced, as he usually does, that the meeting would open with a few minutes of silence. Gladys, who was going through her notes on the platform, didn't hear him, and as soon as he sat down, she got up and started talking and went on until Red finally got her to quit after fifty minutes or so. "First time I ever saw a speaker run over at *both* ends," he said.

Inflexible as he is, rigid, and, as they say in Gillett, sot in his ways, he has a hard time seeing sense in innovations of any kind. If his associates insist on trying a new technique, Red yields with an air of mild impatience combined with the conviction that it isn't techniques but the same old labor in the same old harvest that counts. I've heard him called aggressive, but he isn't aggressive; all through the war he talked pacifism to anyone he met but without the hot fervor that annoys people. He's stubborn. He's playing for keeps, at croquet, at bridge, at the "full gospel."

I wouldn't say he speaks sweetly — never. But he speaks simply. He finds it easier to practice than to preach. He spends hours, days, with his local loyal committees in the Middle Atlantic communities. He works on them earnestly, yields to them democratically. When he knows he can't yield, he tells them so in advance. He will stand on principle anywhere, and anywhere includes the American Friends Service Committee. He loves the Service Committee; it's his life. "Imagine," I once heard him say, "being *paid* to associate with people like this." But he'll fight it on anything. His heart's on his sleeve, his resignation on the table. None of his superiors — they don't call them "superiors" at the Service Committee — would dare criticize his selection of radical speakers.

A few years ago a great foundation made noises as if it were going to give the Service Committee millions of dollars for peace work. The peace secretaries around the country were told to send their personnel needs to the AFSC central office, so that a salary budget could be presented to the great foundation. One man wanted five assistants, another ten, and so on. Red wrote, "None." The most overworked man on the staff, with no needs. When he was asked if that's what he meant, Red said, "That's what I meant. I can't find enough committed people to fill the jobs we've got now. Why create more jobs?" He wants money, but he wants men worse, and without the men he can't use the money. Commitment is all he cares about, across-the-board commitment. He's the slowest laborer in the harvest, because he doesn't want to bring in the chaff. Some of his friends — and associates — want to get a million or ten million signatures. Lots of people. Mass movement. Red says, "I'm going faster now with more people than I want to. I don't want to play God with people, get them into an institute or conference, like sheep in a gangway with only one exit, pound the doctrine into them, and turn them out converted. It doesn't work. It's waste motion. People's ideas change slowly, their lives slower still."

The harvest truly is plenteous, but it takes its time maturing. In thirty-five years Red Schaal has matured a handful of "full gospel" people in each of one hundred fifty or two hundred communities in Pennsylvania, West Virginia, Maryland, Delaware, New Jersey, and New York. A handful. In each of one hundred fifty or two hundred communities a handful of people *stay* pacifists, *stay* non-racists, *stay* social and economic radicals. Thousands and thousands *get* that way elsewhere, but the winds blow them over. Red's got his eye on the long, long harvest.

So the minister who said, "I know Red, but I don't know what he does when he gets discouraged," doesn't know Red. Red doesn't get discouraged. "We don't have to be successful," said Red, in the only flowery thing I ever heard him say; "we have to be right." What the minister didn't realize is that Red really believes in God. The Author of history will change history when men want it changed; men won't change it. And that's the difference between Red and the reformers, and that's why his back never breaks, and that's why some of his friends (and some of his associates) criticize him for "converting the converted" and make loving fun of Red's "constituency." Laborers in the harvest because Red Schaal converted them and kept on converting them.

He used to be a lot sharper-tongued than he is. His thirty-five years with the Quakers — he's still a Methodist and a "full gospel" thorn in the side aisle of his local church — have softened him some. And have stiffened the spines of the Quakers. He's gentler now when he explains to a fellow Methodist why he can't contribute to the new War Memorial. And a lot fewer Quakers are contributing to War Memorials than were a while back, and a lot more to feeding the victims of the wars that the Memorials memorialize. "Red has learned a thing or two from the Quakers," says Kirby Page "and he's taught them a thing or two — or three."

Young men who mistake age for wisdom come to see me once in a while and ask me what they should do with their lives. I say, "What do you want to do, friend?" If the young man says, "Be a writer," I say, "Write." If he says, "Be a preacher," I say, "Preach." If he says, "Be a professor," I say, "Profess." If he says, "Change the world," I say, "Change the world." But once in a while a young man turns up, bucktoothed and bucolic, long, lanky, and crosseyed, without very much on the ball, and he says, "They voted me Least Likely to Succeed, but I don't want to succeed, I want to be right." Then I cleave to him and say, "My friend, the Lord of the harvest needs laborers like Red Schaal." If he says, "I never heard of him," I say, "You never will. He is laboring in the harvest. You can't labor in the harvest and be heard of, both."

Trotsky was greatly interested in the personality of Muste, asked
me questions about him and entertained some hopes that he would
develop into a real Bolshevik later. . . . Muste's handicap was
his background. He had started out in life as a preacher. But despite
the handicap of this background, he gave promise because of his
exceptional personal qualities, and because of the great influence
he had over the people associated with him; his prestige and his
reputation. He was, you might say, the last chance and the best
chance; and even he, the best prospect of all, couldn't come through
in the end because of that terrible background of the church. . . .
— JAMES P. CANNON, in
History of American Trotskyism

It was a Sunday morning, in the summer of 1940, on the shore
of one of the Finger Lakes in upper New York, and silent worship
was going on. A man stood up, a long stringy man about six feet
high that you'd say had been disjointed and reassembled. He had
a big sloping forehead wrinkled like the back of his pants knees,
a big nose, big ears set at forty-five degrees, a nice wide mouth, and
a nice mop of brown and gray hair. You couldn't say how old he
was; he had the seasoned skin of country men; it doesn't change
much.

"If I can't love Hitler," he said, "I can't love at all." Then he
sat down. Now it's against the Quaker ground rules — this was
Quaker worship — to answer back. In Quaker worship, you testify,
if you are moved to, but you don't answer back. But I wasn't going
to let anybody get away with loving Hitler while I was around; that

From *Fellowship*, January, 1952, published by the Fellowship of Reconciliation.

was carrying a bad thing too far. War, which made Hitler Hitler, and made Hitler worse, and made the next Hitler worse than the last one — war was one thing. Loving Hitler was another. I would take this faker on, whoever he was, as soon as worship was out and it was legal to fight.

I never did somehow. Some seventeenth sense told me that he was out of my class. His voice, maybe; at once soft and precise. His eyes, maybe; clear gray eyes that peered through old-fashioned silver-rimmed specs, peering through and beyond you. But more than that, more than his hands, even, hands like Dürer's, hands that you thought of shaping clay, or dust. What told me he was out of my class was the way he said those ten words, "If I can't love Hitler, I can't love at all." He wasn't preaching or confessing. He was saying something to himself, and his voice had picked it up and amplified it; it came from the very center of the man. He had been moved to testify. I was getting the idea of Quakerism, and of A. J. Muste.

I thanked God (à la Swinburne) that I was not a Christian and didn't have to pretend, much less try, to be one. It was hard enough to be a Jew, even in America, and desperately hard in Germany; but anything was better than having to be a Christian and love your enemies.

Ten years later — in 1950 — A. J.'s sixty-fifth birthday was to be celebrated with a series of dinners across the land. An offering, or collection, would be taken, and it always amounted, by the time A. J. got through with you, to more than you could afford. Those eyes of his peered through those silver-rimmed specs at you and through you like nitroglycerin through a bank vault. A. J. would shuffle disjointedly away from each of those birthday dinners with an old satchel full of money, and when the novitiates whispered, "Won't he even buy a new suit?" the initiates said, "Consider the lilies of the field."

At each of the dinners a union stiff spoke, along with a pacifist, a preacher, a professor, and a politician, each of them telling how A. J. had done more for unionism (or pacifism, or preaching, or professing, or politics) than he himself had for pacifism, preaching, professing, or politics. "All I can remember about A. J. Muste after twenty years," the union stiff said, "is the time I went to the big Paterson strike meeting in the winter of 1931. I was down and out, on strike, and my shoes were so thin I could feel the cold through the soles. All the do-gooders were on the platform to pep us up and raise the relief fund. I was in the first row of the audience, and right up above me, on the platform, was this long, skinny fellow. I never saw such long legs on a man, and he kept crossing them to get them out of the way, but pretty soon they'd start swinging, and I saw the bottom of each of his shoes; the soles were gone and he had newspapers in them. I turned to the fellow next to me and asked him who it was. He said: 'It's Muste. Used to be a preacher, before he went straight.' "

At the age of six, Abraham John Muste went straight from Ellis Island, with his Dutch immigrant mother and father and brothers and sisters, to grand Rapids, and straight from there to Hope College near by, and straight from there, with a year's detour into Iowa to teach within twenty-five miles of Anna Huizenga and marry her, to the Dutch Reformed seminary in New Jersey and into a little New York City pulpit.

He was going straight out of the ministry, as a result of taking some "higher criticism" courses at Union Theological Seminary. As errand boy in the high school library in Grand Rapids, he had got into the forbidden shelf of evolution books. Now he could no longer swallow Calvinist orthodoxy, and he was going to quit, when he was called to the Congregational Church in Newton, Massachusetts. That was 1914, and he had already voted, in 1912, for Debs.

He seems to have had the confidence — it's called security now — that makes the difference between a mere rebel and a real revolutionary. His folks were poor, had always been poor, but they didn't think they were poor and had never been hungry; his father was a good coachman in Holland and a good furniture worker in New Holland. A. J. was the oldest son — "If you weren't an idiot, that meant the ministry" — and in college, besides romping through Bible and the classics and working in the library and dining hall, he was captain of the state championship basketball team, state oratorical champion, and valedictorian. He was Most Likely to Succeed.

At sixty-six A. J. Muste can ride steerage, which isn't torture in itself, without undergoing the torture of envy when he sees the first-class passengers. At sixty-six A. J. Muste can make a $100 or $500 speech for $10 or $25, which is just enough, or not quite enough, for vittles, without envying the speakers who make a $10 or $25 speech for $100 or $500. In so far as choice is given men, A. J. Muste, with all his abilities, could have chosen differently or, simply by refraining from choice, could have been a first-class passenger himself, riding on other men's backs instead of carrying them on his own.

In 1915 and 1916 America was moving to war and preaching peace (as in 1941 and in 1951), and the passengers, in and out of the Christian ministry, were hanging on heroically to the crowded Ship of State. (The Cross of Christ wasn't crowded.) A. J. Muste was no hero, though he was mistaken for one; twenty years later he met a parishioner from those days who said, "You saved my soul; if you had backed down in Newton, I wouldn't have gone on believing in God."

In the Dutch Reformed Church, they read Scripture uncritically; in the Union Theological Seminary, they read it critically; but when it came time to lay it down and choose between the Cross and the bunting, the critical and the uncritical were one with the Congregationalists — and the Baptists and the Methodists and the Presbyterians and the Unitarians — of Newton, Massachusetts. They hung the bunting on the Cross and went to Armageddon (1917 edition).

Little churches don't get big preachers often, and Newton didn't want to lose A. J. So they suggested a leave of absence with some nice Christian war agency like the "Y" or the chaplain corps. A. J. said thanks just the same, he was happy where he was, preaching Christ crucified. But when the first boy from the church was killed in France, Christ crucified was inadequate consolation to the Christian parents, and A. J. resigned. The first of his three children was a year old.

Who — as the Lord demanded of Job — feeds the young ravens? A. J. joined the Providence, Rhode Island, Meeting of the Religious Society of Friends. He served as volunteer parson at the Friends'

Moses Brown School, which gave his family a place to live. He had helped organize the Fellowship of Reconciliation, an international association of Christian pacifists, and he represented the American Civil Liberties Union, which succeeded, at long last, in getting it through the head of Woodrow Wilson that whipping conscientious objectors in prison was a dispensable part of the War Effort.

In January, 1919, (his second child was born that year), normalcy hit the factories in Lawrence, Massachusetts. The AF of L's United Textile Workers' Union was in favor of accepting the boon of reduced working hours — for pieceworkers. In the dead of winter, thirty thousand workers walked out, and the AF of L sorrowfully turned away. Three pacifists named Muste, Rotzell, and Long showed up at strike headquarters, and Muste was elected chairman of the strike committee and organizer (and later general secretary) of the independent Amalgamated Textile Workers.

The Lawrence strike was his first, and then, in the next decade or so, came Passaic, Paterson, New Bedford, Toledo, Minneapolis, Columbus, Allentown, Gillespie, Charleston, and some more. Sometimes they won, and sometimes they lost. Tom Tippett asked every parson in town to preach the funeral sermon for the six strikers who had been shot — all six of them in the back — by the company's private deputies. A. J. had to take time off the picket line to preach the funeral sermon, because the local parsons wouldn't. Beginning at Lawrence, he had to take time off from the picket lines, every now and again, for a stretch in jail.

Jim Cannon, the Trotskyite who found that A. J., "the last chance and the best chance," could not overcome "that terrible background of the church," wrote of him: "Muste went out there" — the Chevrolet strike in Toledo in 1935 — "and exerted a considerable influence on the rank and file leaders of the strike. We got a lot of publicity from his activity, but nothing tangible in the way of organization. That was one of the weaknesses, it seems to me, of Muste's methods. He was a good mass worker, gaining the confidence of the workers very quickly. But he tended to adapt himself to the masses more than a real political leader can afford to do."

How can a "good administrator" and "good mass worker" fail

to produce anything "tangible in the way of organization?" Why, by adapting himself to the masses more than a real political leader can afford to do. "A Trotskyite," said Cannon on another occasion, "will do anything for the party, even if he has to crawl on his belly in the mud." A. J. Muste was a good administrator and a good mass worker, but he could not crawl on his belly in the mud. He could not believe one way and talk another and act still another. He could not believe in peace, and maybe even talk peace, and not be a pacifist. But neither could he believe in social reform and talk social reform and not get out on the picket line. If there is a conflict between pacifism and the picket line — where the picket line means the class war — it is a conflict that comes only to activists, never to talkavists. A. J. Muste could talk better than the rest of us, but he couldn't stop there.

By the time he became the first director of Brookwood Labor College in Katonah, New York, in 1921, he was ready to let pacifism slide for the class war. He had seen four-year-olds spitting blood in the Carolina mills. By 1929, he was committed, however nebulously: He told the Brookwood graduating class that "Brookwood stands on the basis of the class struggle — a school which does not accept the capitalist system." By 1932 he had seen worse things than four-year-olds spitting blood. "I was pretty well convinced that the Marxist-Leninist position was sound; there had to be a revolution."

Poor Stalin! The task of making permanent the "temporary" terror — the "war communism" — in which the Russian revolution was born had been lifted from Marx's shoulders by history, from Lenin's by death, and from Trotsky's by exile. If they had lived, if the revolution hadn't devoured the revolutionaries, the workers' democracy would have come, of course — but the revolution always devoured the revolutionaries. Stalin was to blame — Caesar, Napoleon, Alexander. A. J. Muste was a premature anti-Stalinist, singing, at Brookwood, as Trotsky sang in Norway, of what should have been, could have been, would have been — but never in all history was.

The AF of L first supported Brookwood, timidly, but the students came, as always, from the advanced unions, primarily the needle trades and the miners. Then the AF of L got scared; a little

Roosevelt prosperity was all it needed to go back to its open opposition to organizing the unorganized and to the class war. Vice-President Matty Woll, who wore a wing collar at lunch, got after Brookwood as a Red Menace; Brookwood hung up Gompers' picture next to Lenin's (or v.v.), celebrated May Day (as the AF of L used to do), taught the class struggle. The AF of L disowned Brookwood; contributions dried up; A. J. organized the Conference for Progressive Labor Action, in the first instance to save Brookwood, ultimately to work "toward a revolutionary American labor movement." In 1933 the AF of L directors of the collapsing school threw A. J. (and most of the staff and students) out. It took a few more years for Brookwood to collapse completely. What did the labor movement, with higher wages and shorter hours, want with education, much less with a movement to organize the unorganized, still less with Marxism-Leninism?

The CPLA became the American Workers Party and then merged, originally over A. J.'s protest, in the end with his acceptance, with the Trotskyites. In 1935 the Trotskyites took the "French turn" ordered by Trotsky to infiltrate and control the Socialist parties, which had failed to withstand the rise of fascism in Europe. Again over A. J.'s protest, the Trotskyites split the Socialist party, absorbed the left wing, and left the right wing fluttering around (which it still does) in the New Deal air. Thus the end of the CPLA and the American Workers party — the "Musteites" of left-wing splinter-party history. They had organized unemployed "leagues" (which collapsed when employment came) and, as Trotskyite collaborators (the Trotskyites regarded them as stooges), helped conduct the great automobile and truckers' strikes in Toledo and Minneapolis in the early New Deal.

Out of the welter of it all, the Trotskyites went on with the "permanent revolution," and when the second war came, their leaders went into one of Roosevelt's New Deal prisons. They stuck to their guns — and I mean guns. "The American worker," Trotskyite Cannon said (and Quaker Muste heard) in 1934, "is no Quaker. Further developments of the class struggle will bring plenty of fighting in the U.S.A."

A. J. Muste was, like the Trotskyites, and unlike the Stalinists, the Socialists, and the New Dealers, a true revolutionary. But he was not an intelligent revolutionary. He made the same mistake Marx made: he really believed in Marxism. He saw the workers with a capital *W* as a separate species. He saw Workers' Education, also with capitals, as a separate species of education. Workers would learn the interest of the workers, just as capitalists learned the interest of capitalists. In his Marxian innocence he mistook instinct for both learning and interest. The instinct of the workers was identical with that of the bosses; they both wanted the money, and the bosses happened to have it. The trade unions were no more eager to learn than the trade association; what was there to learn? They both knew, by instinct, all that they needed to know to pursue, in collision with one another, their common objective.

What had become of Christ crucified? He was there, in the mines, in the mills, in the factories, crucified by the bosses in caves, at looms, on assembly lines. He was there, all right. To preach (and to live) Christ crucified means (and it still means and always will) to be a social revolutionary. But socialism, pursuing gold for the many, like capitalism, pursuing gold for the few, crucified its beneficiaries on the cross of gold. The true revolution would divide the gold as a matter of course, but the false revolution would simply transfer the gold and leave all mankind still crucified; that was all that was wrong with Marx.

In the summer of 1935 a troubled revolutionary — troubled by the discovery that oppression no more converted the oppressed than it did the oppressor — went to see the Old Man, in exile in Norway. The Trotskyites' God was really an old man with a beard, to be seen face to face by the faithful, and ever ready with new revelation. The Mustes had never had a vacation, and the inevitable collection, taken by their friends among their friends, overflowed with contributions from people who hated Musteism and loved Muste. His friends saw him — the class warrior — for the last time as the boat pulled out from Hoboken pier with his skinny arm raised in the clenched-fist salute of bloody revolution. His letters from Honefuss, immediately after his meeting with the Old Man, were, even for an enthusiast like A. J., hysterical: "I am completely captivated by him." Trotsky, a little more cautiously, returned the compliment.

The American Marxist revolutionary — who had once been a world Christian revolutionary — had met the world Marxist revolutionary.

Then there was silence, five weeks of silence from A. J. Muste, whose prodigious capacity for continuing correspondence wherever he was had always been a wonder. Then Cara Cook, his assistant, got a "Landed yesterday" postcard from New York and, a few days later, a single-spaced typewritten letter of sixteen pages. "It's not true, it's not true, it can't be true," she kept saying as she read it.

A few days later, in Minneapolis, Vincent Dunne, the Trotskyite teamsters'-union leader, got a letter from a friend. Two years earlier, in 1934, A. J. Muste had been one of the heroes of the great teamsters' victory there, and the union leaders had taken him by force to a clothing store and put a brand new suit on him. Now Dunne read the letter, whistled, and turned to his sidekick, Bill Brown, and said: "Bill, what do you think? Muste has gone back to the church." Brown said: "Well, I'll be damned." Then, a few moments later: "Say, Vince, we ought to get that suit back."

But A. J. Muste had never left the church, and that was the complaint, down the years, of all his labor associates who found him, as Cannon put it, "the last chance and the best chance" but hopelessly incapable of crawling on his belly in the mud. He had never left the church, as his students at Brookwood knew when they heard him say, again and again and again, in the course of their Workers' Education, "On the one hand . . . but on the other. . . ." He had never left the church to become a materialist — the first requirement of Marxism — because he was no more materialist in his heart and in his life than was Karl Marx, who created the fatal fantasy of materialism; he was no more motivated by economic interest than was Karl Marx, who said that all men were so motivated and himself starved in a London slum rather than "make a machine of myself" by grubbing for money.

A. J. Muste had never left the church because he had no more stopped being a pacifist than he had ever started being one. War is only an outward occasion for true pacifism. The true pacifist is pacific in his heart and therefore in his relations in his home, in his work, and among his associates. A. J. Muste was a true pacifist.

He preached the revolution the way so many true pacifists of his time preached it, as if nobody would be used for bullets. That infinitely gentle man never got the hang of hating and never really fooled anyone but himself. "Too much of a gentleman," said Jim Cannon, disgusted at A. J.'s treatment of the "reactionaries" in the Trotskyite movement. One of the other toughies of the revolution said it simpler: "Once a Christer, always a Christer. He's a Christer."

A. J. Muste went back to the Fellowship of Reconciliation, of which he is now executive secretary and the most revolutionary member — leading the picket line in front of the White House and the Soviet Embassy and a Jim Crow restaurant or hotel; fasting all of Holy Week, at the age of sixty-six, in penance for his country's new H-bomb; sending the Collector of Internal Revenue a copy of the Scriptures instead of a tax return; writing a hundred letters a day or reading a thousand, and turning out eloquent little books and pamphlets and articles, arguing the case for labor better than the unions argue it, the case for racial equality better than the social workers argue it, the day's news better, sharper, clearer, deeper than the newscasters argue it, and always arguing peace not quite so well as Christ argued it . . . not quite.

Nobody knows better than A. J. Muste that if he cannot love Stalin he cannot love at all, but he tried to love Stalin, in the labor movement, and he found out how hard it is, He will never be a professional anti-Communist; you will never find him rising with the Budenzes and the Chamberses to tell all (or more than all); but he does not yet see how pacifism, whose spokesman he is, can work with the Stalinists. One of his reasons is irresistible: pacifism must make its witness everywhere and always against violence, war, and tyranny and always make this one witness if it makes no other; and this it cannot do in collaboration with Stalinists if for no other reason than that the Stalinists won't let it. All his other reasons are integrated with the problem of influence and effectiveness, with the danger of "the confusion of pacifism and communism in people's minds." Remember, he speaks now for some 5,000 Christian ministers (besides some ten thousand laymen) in the FOR. Some forty-five hundred of those ministers wish that he would speak a little less loudly as it is, and they shudder a little when he comes to town. With this organizational preoccupation — remember, that was what the Trotskyites complained that he didn't have — A. J. Muste may not argue the case for peace quite so well as Christ argued it.

The voice of A. J. Muste, the voice of a man who is saying what he believes, and always what he believes, and only what he believes, grows louder as the end (of us, not of him) approaches. Young men come to him, as they come to the Quakers, and as the Quakers come to him, to work for him and with him. As old men give him money — and wish (or think they wish) that they were young again — so young men, in and out of the ministry and across the country, gravitate to him in their search for the good, the true, and the beautiful and stay there. The working staff of the Fellowship of Reconciliation is composed, I think without exception, of young and middle-aged men of extraordinary calibre. Some of them are fools for Christ, but all of them are fools for A. J. Muste. And in the smallest town, a preacher who is preaching Christ crucified — and the social revolution that goes with it — is an FOR member.

The letter that Cara Cook got exactly fifteen years ago began:

War is the central problem for us all today . . . and war appears to be imminent. . . . Every day the relations between the great powers grow more tense. Everywhere armaments are being piled up at a feverish rate. Everywhere men wait, most of them, it seems, in a spirit of fatalistic resignation, for the signal to arms to be given. Not a few, their nerves worn with the suspense of waiting for the blow, express the hope that it may fall tomorrow, rather than the next day. And men of the highest standing and intelligence, like people in a panic at a fire, buy pieces of land in remote interior regions and tell you that there a handful of likeminded people will begin to rebuild civilization after the holocaust. . . .

That was exactly fifteen years ago. The letter goes on:

. . . The labor movement has often been proclaimed as the dependable agency to prevent war. . . . The claim has not been substantiated. . . . Nor is there any ground for looking to the U.S.S.R. and the Communist International. . . . It will be said that the official Communist movement has departed from Marxism-Leninism, a contention with which I happen to be in agreement. Would a genuine Marxist-Leninist movement be a dependable agency for the prevention of war? I have become convinced that it would not. . . . So far from combating the idea, which has become increasingly prevalent since the war, that violence is 'the only way out,' it accepts and encourages that idea. . . . It becomes for capitalist leaders an excuse for maintaining powerful armaments, supporting Fascist dictators, resorting to war. . . .

Marxism, claiming its victory to be "inevitable," still demands that its adherents sacrifice everything, including life, for a world they may never see. But "no other designation than God really fits a force working for righteousness and brotherhood which demands complete devotion of men and which is invincible. . . ." Thus, he went on, Marxism without God is an illusion; with God, it is no longer Marxism. The labor and revolutionary movements accent lying and cheating in dealing with the "class enemy," who lies and cheats; it ends in its members' lying and cheating in dealing with one another. It is lying and cheating and what they lead to — violence — that leads to the slaughter of the workers in war and the replacing of capitalism by fascism.

. . . Thus, added experience, observation of the crisis in which mankind finds itself, and arguments which seem to me irrefutable, have brought me again to the position which I held some years ago; namely, that the dynamic we require for life of the individual and society is spiritual, Christian, and the method is, basically and essentially, that of nonviolence.

. . . To take the Christian position does not mean to justify or condone the capitalistic system. Quite the contrary. It provides the one measure by which the capitalistic system stands condemned. . . .

The Christian church failed in 1917. It would not preach, much less practice, Christ crucified; and A. J. Muste left it to work where Christ was crucified in factory, mine, and mill. It took him the best part of twenty years to discover that the labor movement (and the revolutionary movement, which captured a handful of laborers when times were "bad" and lost them when times were "good") would not be anything but a capital movement until it practiced what the church did not, namely, Christ crucified. And so he returned, "to confront the Church itself and its members with the fearful character of the crisis confronting the race and with the demand that they, above all others, square their deeds with their professions, take up their responsibility, gird themselves for the sacrifice necessary to put an end to war and exploitation, and to make the spirit that was in Jesus dominant upon earth."

The Christian church failed again in 1941 and again in 1951. And so did the labor movement and all the other movements. Only a miracle will save any of them — and us — now (and we know it). But the labor movement and all the other movements, except the Christian church, are forbidden to believe in miracles. The Christian church, on the other hand, must believe in miracles or admit that it is not Christian. The miracle of the social revolution — Thy Kingdom come on earth — will work through those who believe in miracles or it won't work at all. All that A. J. Muste has to do is to convert the Jim Crow, capitalist, war-making Christian church to Christ crucified, and his work is done.

PART
SIX

GENTLY
UP THE
STREAM

I want to dilate on the subject of bed, and I don't know who should if I shouldn't. I have had 131,400 hours at the controls, much of it solo, under all sorts of wind and weather conditions all over the world, flying everything from the primitive sleeping bag to the pressurized four-pillow job that they built for Haile Selassie, and another 262,800 hours of ground work, most of it spent getting ready to take off.

Bed as a contribution to human welfare, and especially to sleep, can hardly be overrated, in my opinion. There is nothing that you can't do better in bed. What do you want to do? Sleep? Read? Eat? Drink? Smoke? Talk? Think? Worry? Lie down? Stretch out? Curl up? Cool off? Warm up? Rest? Relax? Twitch? Turn? Toss? Look at the ceiling? Lie on your stomach? You can do them all better in bed.

You can't do any of these things — except worry — in an automobile. But modern Americans spend more for their automobiles than they do for their beds. And this in spite of the fact that they spend almost as much time in their beds as they do in their automobiles. Nor can you do any of these things — except twitch and look at the ceiling — with a television set. Yet modern Americans who haven't got one bed to rub against another go out and buy television sets. Modern Americans don't know what they're missing.

The average modern American spends one-third of his life in bed. One-third of his whole life — you'd think he'd care. But he doesn't. He'll sleep anywhere, and then only when the last dog is hung. He thinks bed is a place to sleep and sleep a waste of time. His idea of a good bed is one near the station.

Nobody should sleep alone, in my opinion, except people who should sleep alone due to circumstances beyond their control. Such

From the *Progressive*, February, 1954.

people should not make fools of themselves, not even for the sake of having someone to sleep with. People who sleep with other people get to know them better, and to know people is to love them. Love is a great thing. There is not enough of it in the United Nations and elsewhere. It is praised by all the authorities — and properly so — but very few take an active interest in it. You take love, year in and year out, and it is just about the finest thing in the world except bed. Combine the two — retaining, as they say in the newspaper mergers, the best features of each — and you have a combo that is hard to beat.

Father Zossima — one of the Russian delegates to the UN — says in *The Brothers Karamazov* that hell consists of not loving. One way to avoid hell is to sleep with somebody. It should be somebody in particular and somebody, if it is a person of the opposite sex, that you are married to. Strange bedfellows do not long remain both strange and bedfellows.

If I seem to be urging the double bed, that is just what I mean to be doing. Twin beds are just one step removed from twin bedrooms, which are one step removed from twin houses. Everything that makes the French more attractive than the Germans may be ascribed to the fact that the French sleep in double beds and the Germans in twin.

You disagree with me about the double bed. You say that people have different sleeping habits. I say, let them have them; what's that got to do with it? Sleeping is only one of the things you can do better in bed. Do they have different reading habits, too? My snoring keeps my wife awake. All right — she sleeps so quietly that I'm afraid she's dead, and that keeps me awake. If you think that the law of compensation does not operate in bed, you have a lot to learn about the law of compensation. You say that one likes to read, while the other wants them both to go to sleep. All right — let the one read and the other want them both to go to sleep. As long as they are in the same bed, things will work out all right in time, and in less time there than anywhere else.

These are parliamentary quibbles of yours. They are like saying that a million dollars is a terrible thing to have because look at the tax you have to pay on it. What's left is still better than nothing, isn't it, *estupidito*? So it is with the double bed, with all its shortcomings.

The advantages of the double bed being myriad, and the short-comings being minuscule, people should sleep together in double beds. My wife likes to work very late at night scrubbing the floors and to get up at six or so to have the children's breakfast hot and the house cleaned up so that she can get to her ironing as soon as they leave for school. All right. It doesn't bother me. When she's in bed I sleep like a log. When she isn't I turn over and sleep like Mark Hopkins.

The minuscule shortcomings of the double bed can be further mi-nusculized by the purchase and use of an oversized double bed. Our family would not be without one. The Italians all have them, and the Italians are wonderful people. The Italians are also numerous, and the king-sized oversized bed can be made up so that it can ac-commodate the whole family. The oversized double bed has every-thing, including room. If the occupants are not on speaking terms, they can occupy the outer sides of their respective halves and ignore each other. It's almost like having two tents to sulk in. And they can always make up without having to go up hill and down dale. If one wants to read, or sleep, or just be let alone while the other is sewing, doing stomach exercises, or praying, neither will bother the other in an oversized double bed.

The double bed is cheaper, too. You can make it up with an ar-rangement of regular-sized sheets which, if you don't slip into the bed carefully, will tie you up in a knot. Write for Auntie Jane's Over-sized Bed-Make for details. Send fifty cents in coin or stamps, and enclose the top off a boxcar. Or you can stitch regular double sheets together and get two oversizes out of three regulars. Send one dollar for Uncle Milton's Pattern Book. Forget the Pattern Book. Just send one dollar. Uncle Milton will know what to do with it.

There are those — I am, I am happy to say, not of their number — who regard the softness or hardness of beds as a matter of what the mainland Chinese call *goût*, or taste, or, as the Swedes put it, *non disputandum*. Beds should not be soft. Marshmallows should be soft. Beds should not be hard. Coconuts should be hard. A bed should have a certain amount of give, but it should have a certain amount of take, too. It should be just right. I lean to the hard, or firm side, myself, partly because of my Spartan background (my grandfather ran Joe's Fruit Stand on the corner of Fifty-first and Prairie) and partly because you can always pound a hard bed soft but not v.v. The same thing goes for abalone.

With the money you save — by buying a double bed instead of twins — you can buy pillows, lots of pillows for lots of purposes and of all kinds except foam rubber, which are terrible. (They are pestproof, but you can keep pests out by not answering the doorbell.)

The bedroom should be big, not only to accommodate the pillows, which should be thrown luxuriously on the floor at night, but also to accommodate large, many-shelved night tables with lamps (selected not for beauty but for utility), vigil lights, vacuum jugs, hot plates, keeper-warmers, snack tins, smoking articles, writing materials, extension telephones (or a pliers to tear them out of wall), small musical instruments (recorders, jew's-harps, and so on — maybe a ukelele), sundials, chemical fire extinguishers to extinguish chemical fires, commodes, macassars, antimacassars, pest repellant (in case they get in after all), smelling-salts and mustard-plasters, salve for burns (from overheated bricks used as foot-warmers, which you should also have), disposable tissues (and a depository for them; don't throw them on the floor with your pillows), the Scriptures (any version but the Revised Standard), Proust, and other *articles de nuit*, or articles of night. The bedroom should be a home in itself. You should be able to live in it, in case of siege. I won't insult you by saying that the darkest possible shades, covered by the heaviest possible curtains, are *de rigueur*. When I am rich I am going to have a wood-burning fireplace in my bedroom and never get up.

Bed is wonderful. Bed is where I want to die and, until then, live. Join me in this great crusade to get everybody in bed as soon as the dishes are done. Leave the dishes until morning, but don't get up to do them. Remember — they aren't getting dirtier just standing there. Don't eat eggs, which, in addition to increasing albumen, dry on the plate and are hard to get off after two or three days.

A final word, for now. I wouldn't touch an electric blanket, especially with a fork. It isn't merely that they may short-circuit — which can be fatal if you get into bed soaking wet — but that you don't know where you stand with them. I once stayed with Keith and Martha Ellinwood in Conesus, New York, on the coldest night of my life. Martha, God love her and rest her, insisted that the electric blanket would keep me warm. I squealed like a stuck pig when she put it over me and I wouldn't switch it on. In the middle of the night I woke up freezing and switched it on. In a few minutes I was warm again and went to sleep. In the morning I learned that it hadn't been plugged into the wall. That's what I mean.

More should be said, written, thought, and done about bed. We are all preoccupied with the unspeakable indecencies of politics, none of us with the innocent splendors of bed. Count Tolstoy said that modern man had found a solution to every problem but the bedroom. The solution to the bedroom problem is to put modern man to bed. Vishinsky should be put to bed with Lodge, and both of them with Mme Pandit. Chambers should be put to bed with Hiss. Dulles should be put to bed and the wool blanket pulled over his eyes. If everyone were in bed, and no one were allowed to get up until an understanding had been reached, there would be a lot less trouble.

What did you get for Christmas? Don't tell me — let me tell you what
I got. I got a lemon tree, from the whole family.

It was just what I needed.

I've never had a lemon tree.

Mommy got it at the Cypress Gardens Nursery, in a two-gallon
tin can with Christmas paper around it. The tree had five lemons on
it. It was a genuine lemon tree.

Mommy talked to Mrs. Cypress about it. Mrs. Cypress said it
should be planted in peat moss in a very warm, protected place and
should hardly ever be watered. Watering, said Mrs. C., will kill a
lemon tree faster than anything else.

All day I admired the lemon tree. In the evening my friend Van
Peski came over to see if we had anything to eat in the house, and
I showed him my lemon tree. "I had one," said Van, "but the darned
fool thing died on me. I watered it and watered it, and still it died."
Van is a Dutchman. He couldn't even hang onto Indonesia, much
less a lemon tree.

When it got to be bedtime, I went to bed. Some people curl up
with a good book. I lie flat and read Thomas Wolfe's *The Web and
the Rock*, which is not a good book. Pretty soon I can't read any
more of it, and then I fumble around for something else. That night
I came up with *The Western Garden Book* and opened it to "Citrus"
on page 352. Here's what it said.

It said that the optimum heat index for a lemon tree is 1900 degrees. You get the heat index by deducting 55 degrees (45 for grapes)
from the average mean daily temperature for March in your area
and multiplying by 31 and then by 12 — and you have the heat in-

From the *Progressive*, February, 1957.

dex. Now I don't know the average mean daily temperature for March in my area, and I don't know where to find out. I asked Mommy, who was reading Proust, and she didn't know. So I decided to skip it unless, during a conversation some time, somebody were to say, "Speaking of good books, let me tell you what the average mean daily temperature for March in my area is." People sometimes change subjects like that, especially at parties and most especially when the conversation lags. I can always get the conversation to lag, so I figured that sooner or later I'd find out what a.m.d.t. for Mar. is in somebody's area. Then, if the fellow turned out to live in my area, I'd be in a fair way to getting started with that part of the operation.

We Western Gardners are pretty informal, and the author of *The Western Garden Book* is no exception. He went on to say that the home gardener ("That's me," I said, mentally) can tinker with raised beds and wind screens, with reflected heat and warm south or west walls, to raise the growing heat far above the level of his local climate. I got up and raised the bed, so as to tinker with it, and Mommy hollered until I put it down. Then I looked at the wind screens in the windows, but they were nailed on. Then I asked Mommy if she would get up and go out and see if the south or west walls were warm. She said to shut up, so I went on reading. This was what it said next.

"A gardener in Santa Barbara, for example, lives in a lemon climate." I don't live in Santa Barbara, but I know people who do, and if I'm ever invited down there, I'll strike up a conversation about their lemon climate and see if one thing doesn't lead to another and maybe get some cogent dope on av. mn. dly. temp. for Mar. "With some minor changes (perhaps a simple windbreak) he can raise an eight-foot square of his garden into a Valencia orange climate." This made me start humming *Valencia*, and Mommy said to shut up again. So I thought about changes, major and minor, and how hard they are to make, and how I went wrong in my youth, in spite of the good advice I got, and how hard it was to change now, and this made me want to talk to Mommy again. But I've read Proust myself, and I know how it is when you're right in the middle of a seventy-five-page description of one hair in the Baron's mustache; you lose the thread when somebody interrupts you. So I turned my thoughts to "a simple windbreak." Just what is a simple windbreak? How does it differ from a complex windbreak? Isn't a windbreak a windbreak? I went on like that, and got to saying "windbreak" so often that the word began to sound meaningless, or worse. So I read on: "By planting in a raised bed, espaliering his tree against a white south wall of his house in front of a concrete patio slab, he might even boost himself out of the lemon climate clear up into the grapefruit class."

I let the book fall. Here was an epic vision! Here was something a man might do! If a Santa Barbaran, merely by planting in a raised bed and espaliering his tree against a white south wall of his house in front of a concrete patio slab might boost himself clear up into the grapefruit class, what couldn't a man do in Carmel, which has a higher class of people, including me.

Clear up into the grapefruit class! The vision blossomed, flowered, fruited. Surreptitiously I pulled the plug out of the wall behind the bed and the lights went out. "Darn," said Mommy, who gets abusive when things don't suit her, "darn that light company. The power has failed again." "I'll get up and phone them," I said. I got up in my little white nightie and pattered out to the kitchen and opened the kitchen drawer to see if there was a grapefruit knife in it. There wasn't. I returned and said, "They said it will be on again in five minutes; so we might as well talk." Then I told her what the book said. "I'll plant it in a bed raised higher than Haman's gibbet," I said, "put two coats of white paint on the wall, and get the biggest concrete slab the Monument Works has got, and we'll boost ourselves clear up into the watermelon class."

Mommy didn't say anything, but I went right on thinking. After a while I said, "Have you ever drunk coconut milk, Mommy?" Mommy said. "There's some light coming in here from somewhere," and she got up and pulled the curtain back and saw that the neighbor's lights were on. Then she came back to the bed and put the plug in, and the lights went on and she resumed her Proust. Never said another word. Never even said good night. She's like that. Her av. dly. temp. is mn., especially when she's crossed.

The next day I transferred the lemon tree to an immense tub that

Dr. Scott Heath (the oculist who told me that *it wouldn't hurt* to rest my eyes once in a while, "at your age") had given me. I didn't have money for peat moss, so I went up the valley to see the Cummings boys at the Valley Lumber Co. They are associated with the Plymouth Brethren and are fundamentalist Christians who admire Billy Graham. Dick Cummings gave me a tract, and we fanned the breeze a while, and then I braced him for a load of sawdust. He was pretty well softened up by that time, so I took the sawdust and planted the lemon tree in it.

That night Dr. Friedy Heisler, the famous psychoanalyst, came by, non-professionally.

"How am I?" I said.

"You're all over sawdust," said she, and I told her what I'd been doing.

"That won't do at all," said Dr. Heisler. "Sawdust is high in carbon when you put it in soil. It draws heavily on nitrogen in the breakdown process."

"Oh," I said, "I'm going to put up a breakdown anyway, either a simple breakdown or a complex breakdown; I haven't decided which."

Dr. Heisler looked at me as if I had undergone some minor changes, and said, "Maybe you'd better look in at the office tomorrow. If the elevator's crowded, use the *escalier*."

"I'm going to use that for my lemon tree," I said.

A YOKEL
AT THE
COUNTY
FAIR

A yokel went to the County Fair.

The yokel was a sober, hard-working, impecunious citizen and a family man. As a matter of fact, he went to the County Fair because his little girl wanted to go, and when she asked him to take her to the County Fair, he could no more resist her than he could when she asked him for anything else.

The yokel had thirty dollars in his jeans, because he had just been paid the day before.

First, he bought his little girl a cone of pink cotton candy for a nickel, and he bought himself one, too. Though his mouth grew dry and his face grew sticky and his stomach grew queasy, and so did his little girl's, the yokel finished the pink cotton candy because he could not afford to waste it. And so did his little girl, and for the same reason.

Next, the yokel and his little girl had their pictures taken, three for thirty cents. The pictures were terrible, but the yokel thought they'd better bring them home because thirty cents is thirty cents, and his little girl agreed with him.

The yokel and his little girl were a pretty spectacle, walking hand in hand, all over pink cotton candy, past the shows and the games and the barkers and the exhibits. A family man, a sober-sided, hard-working family man full of duty, responsibility, and the rest of the homely virtues, is something to see these days, something to see walking hand in hand with his little girl through the dusty hubbub of the County Fair.

There were several shows at which the yokel cast covert glances.

From the *Progressive*, September 5, 1942.

One was called The Follies, another The Female Form, and another Beauty in the Flesh. But the yokel was a family man, and anyway the admission was twenty-five cents plus one cent tax, and anyway the yokel was a family man.

Then they saw the prize-winning animals, the prize-winning vegetables, and the prize-winning flowers, and that was free. They pitched pennies, the yokel and his little girl each pitching five, and they didn't land one in the saucer, and that was another dime gone.

They had eleven cents more to spend, and the little girl, who had reached the age where little girls love babies because they haven't had to mind them yet, wanted to see the two-headed baby. It cost eleven cents to see the two-headed baby, so the little girl went in and the yokel waited outside. While the yokel stood there waiting, a nice man came up to him and said, "I see you're waiting here for your little girl, and I wonder if you'd like to step across the street and take a free roll for an Eastman Kodak." The yokel said he wouldn't mind, and he went across the street, and the nice man got behind the counter.

The game consisted of dumping a tray full of golf balls down a sort of miniature bowling alley. The golf balls landed in holes which were marked with different numbers, and the total of the numbers determined the prize. The yokel dumped the balls and the numbers added up to thirty-one, and the nice man said, "You get a house prize for that, and I'm going to give it to you even though you were playing free." The house prize was an imitation alligator wallet, and the nice man said, "If you'd got thirty or thirty-three, just like this, or any other red number, you'd have won the grand prize. It's a quarter a play."

So the yokel took his thirty dollars out of his jeans and cashed a sawbuck and dumped the balls, and the nice man said, "Congratulations, you hit the jackpot," and he brought out a handsome General Electric radio, opened it up, and put a twenty-dollar bill in the radio, and took out a card and showed it to the yokel. The card said not only that a player who hit the jackpot won the radio and twenty dollars, but that the house had to double, and so did the player.

So the nice man put twenty dollars more in the radio and said to the yokel, "Now you pay fifty cents and hit a red number, and you get forty dollars and the radio." The yokel hit a green number, and the man took out a card which said that a green number meant a free play and a coupon. Three coupons meant the grand prize doubled. So the yokel played the free play and hit another green number, and the man put twenty dollars more in the radio and said, "One more coupon or a red number and you take the whole thing." So the yokel played and hit the jackpot, which meant the house had to double and the player had to double, and there was $80 in the radio and the yokel had to pay a dollar a play, and then two dollars a play, and then four dollars a play, and the radio was full of twenty-dollar bills, and one more coupon or a red number took it all.

But the little girl came out of the two-headed baby show and joined her father, and he thought he'd better quit, but the nice man whispered to him. "I'll tell you something. I just work here on salary, and I'd like to see you win. There's only one way you can miss winning now, and that's what the boss is counting on."

"What's that?" said the yokel.

"The only way you can miss winning now," said the nice man, "is to quit playing. The boss knows that nine out of ten people are fools enough to quit playing at this point, and that is how he makes his killing." So the yokel hit the jackpot again, and the house had to double, and so did the yokel, and the nice man said, "I'll tell you what I'll do, and I'll put it in writing. You take the whole thing if you hit the green, the red, the blue, or another coupon," and he put it in writing.

The yokel was out of money by this time, but he found a couple of friends who lent him five dollars, so he played again and hit the black, and the nice man showed him how he'd have hit the red, the green, the blue, or another coupon if just one of the balls had landed in any other hole than the one it landed in. So the yokel asked his friends for a little more money, and the nice man picked up the game and handed it over the counter to the friends and said, "Just look it over, top and bottom, and tell me if you think it's square"; and the friends looked it over, and they told the man they thought it was square, and they gave the yokel fifteen dollars, which was all they had left. So the yokel dumped the balls, but the numbers added up to black, and when the fifteen dollars was gone, the nice man gave the yokel a practice play free, and it hit the red, but it was just a practice play, so it didn't count; and the yokel said he had no more money, and the nice man gave him two dollars back to get home on.

So the yokel and his little girl went home, and he couldn't tell his little girl, or his wife, or his boss, or anybody else what had happened to him; and he didn't think of shooting himself, but he felt something awful, and he realized he would have to work like a dog to earn the thirty dollars he had lost and the twenty dollars he had borrowed and had lost.

This, my friends, is what happens to the wage earner at County Fairs, to the unsophisticated family man who never drank or smoked or gambled away a nickel in his life. This, mind you, in the year 1942, in a nation enjoying universal education. The yokel had gone to school, and had ridden on the cars, and had been to the city, and had never bought a nickel's worth of gilt-edged stocks. This, my friends, happens every day under capitalism. It happens at County Fair time to thousands of ignorant working men, men who live humbly and honestly, who tend to their work and love their children, who do not pretend to be clever or prophetic, and who do not meddle in other people's business or try to tell anybody else what to do or how to run the country or win the war.

This, my friends, happened to Mayer last Saturday afternoon at the La Porte County Fair.

Like (I suppose) most people, I don't get to Pittsburgh much. As a matter of fact, I never get there, except for a lecture every second year or so, and then — the way one does on a lecture tour, in a town where he isn't closely acquainted — I bounce in and out. I was there a while back, en route from Columbus to Erie, and on the way in from the Pittsburgh airport I saw a sign which read:

SEWICKLEY   2

Sewickley, Sewickley. Come, now — where and when and how had I had to do with Sewickley? I couldn't think, and I let it go. I had an hour to wait for the train to Erie, and I killed it looking in the windows of the secondhand stores across the bridge from the P. & L. E. station. I got a copy of the *Post-Gazette* and got on the train and got something to eat in the diner. When I came back to my seat it was dark and the lighting was bad, so I watched what little there was to watch out the window.

And then I remembered.

I remembered Aix-les-Bains and Dorking Town and Sewickley.

I remembered a day in the summer of 1927, a quarter-century ago. I was nineteen. We were traveling, my mother and father and my older brother and I, from Rome on the *petit grand tour américain*, and they got on the train at Aix, twenty American college girls jabbering English. Of course they saw me from the platform. I was sitting at the window, my chin on my folded hands (and my folded hands on the pearl handle of my Malacca stick), staring emptily out, above and beyond the jabbering crowd on the platform,

From *Harper's Magazine*, December, 1956.

into the empty distance. Of course they saw me: a man still young in years but worn with unutterable sophistication.

Of course they saw me, because they came rollicking through the train to their seats in the car behind us and rollicking back, a little later, to the dining car ahead. I was still staring emptily out, in my pearl-gray spats, and my pearl-gray suit, and my pearl-gray hat, and my stick — a Frenchman, likely, but one of those Frenchmen who belong to no country and to whom every country has, to its edification, belonged.

I was aroused by my father, who said, "Get a move on, boy. This is our sitting for lunch. Have you washed your hands?" My hands were encased in pearl-gray gloves.

"He hasn't washed them since he got those gloves," said my brother.

"Wash your hands," said my mother, "and come on. We'll be in the diner. But for pity's sake — hurry."

Beneath the double-breasted jacket of my pearl-gray suit was a pair of red suspenders, purchased in Rome the day before; the whim of a man whom red suspenders and red suspenders alone would move from an ennui begotten of absolutely every other experience. My father, when I bought them, said, "You're crazy, boy." My mother said, "He'll grow up," and my brother said, "When?" They were my first suspenders, and my brother said, "Don't forget to pull them up after you've been to the bathroom."

I washed my hands and went into the dining car. On my right arm I carried my pearl-gray hat, in my left hand my pearl-gray gloves and my stick, on which I leaned, walking with a loose limp that would hardly deceive anyone who had watched the performance of the dying roué in "The Fool," which had been on the road a season or two before.

The American girls filled almost the whole of the diner, and our table was at the far end. As I entered the car, a falling hush reached my half-consciousness. My face was a pallid mask, my eyes fixed on nothingness — for which the Cinzano advertisement on the farther door of the dining car sufficed. But the hush was broken by a giggle arising from girl to girl and from table to table after I passed. And the incidence of the giggle, proceeding, even as I proceeded, from the back to the front of the car, was not to be mistaken. The pallid mask of my face turned red. As I turned around and sat down, my brother whispered to me, "You forgot to pull up your suspenders."

A week later we reached the Hotel Cecil in London, to spend three days before we sailed on the *Mauretania*. With my stick I managed to get up the broad stone steps, and my brother said to the doorman, "You'd better take his arm. He's in the last stages." In the lobby were two of the American girls who had been on the train from Aix. Coming down in the elevator for dinner were two more. They were all staying at the Cecil.

The first day I didn't go out at all. I explained my behavior to my parents as a general lassitude arising, I thought, from a number of worries, "the worst of which," said my brother, "is that pack of girls who laughed at him in the diner." The second day I had breakfast in the room and went downstairs at eleven, when the girls were sure to be out on tour. One of them was alone with me in the elevator. She said, "Hello," and I bowed from the neck.

"How long are you staying?" she said.

I stared at her. — How long did a man like me, in my condition, know he was staying, and where? — She was the first of the lot I had really looked at, or through. She was not the prettiest. She was very tall (like me), spare, knuckly, small-featured. And nice. Really nice. And pretty enough. "Until Thursday," I said.

"So are we," she said. "Are you going back on the *Ile*?"

"No, on the *Mauretania*."

"Oh," she said, "that's too bad," and then she pulled herself up, the way you do when you might blush, and said, "I mean it's so good to have someone to talk English — American — to," and she laughed a nice laugh compounded of embarrassment and friendliness. I held my stick behind me, and when we got out of the elevator I left it there alongside the car.

We talked some more, and she said that the other girls were out on a rubberneck tour but she hadn't felt so well and, besides, she liked to go places alone once in a while; you never had a chance to when you were in a tour. I understood that, and I said so, and we went for a walk, and when we came back she said, "Thanks for coming with me. I don't really like to go *alone*, and I get kind of scared, even when they speak English. But this is the end of the tour and we've all been together seven weeks."

I asked her what she'd be doing tomorrow, and she said it was their last day and she guessed there would be something scheduled and they'd have to pack and all — and I said, "You can pack tomorrow night. So can I. Why don't you say you're not feeling well at breakfast and I'll meet you in the lobby at ten and we'll go somewhere."

"Where?" she said.

"*Really*," I said, and my pearl-gray limp came back, "there are dozens of places out of London — it's your first time over, isn't it?"

She said it was, and didn't ask me if it was mine.

"Well, then," I said, "I'll arrange something, and we'll be back at five."

I hot-footed it to the American Express Company, and one of the clerks, when I asked him where a fellow and his girl ought to go on their last day in England, said, "Why, Dorking."

So we went to Dorking Town.

I don't know, now, what it was like or how we got there. (By train, I suppose.) I remember a buggy, and village lanes, and a teashop, and that's all. And I may as well say that all of the details of this story (except the pearl-gray outfit; there's a snapshot of me in it) are only what the lawyers, when the witness shakes his head, call "your best recollection, if you please." It was a quarter-century ago, and as bad money drives out good on the market, so bad history, of which we have had a lot this quarter-century, drives out good in the memory.

I remember, as I say, that she was tall and spare. She was dark — at least she wasn't a yellow blonde. I remember that her fingers were long, so I must have held her hand that day — but it may have been only in getting on or off the train. I don't remember what we talked about, except that we didn't talk about the dining car from Aix. She never once said she'd seen me before — she was that nice — and that, I suppose, is why I fell in love with her in the elevator in the Cecil.

I remember that we got back to London later than we intended to, and we said good-by. I must have promised to call her in New York, or to write her, and we must have exchanged addresses. Well — I had a girl back home and she may have had a boy. I know that we never wrote or saw each other again. I don't remember where she was going to school. I don't remember her name. I remember that she lived in a town I had never heard of — Sewickley, Pa.

And what if I went to Sewickley and found her? I'm forty-eight years old and happily married, and I hope she is, too. Besides, 1956 is not 1927, and while we lean people wear pretty well, I'm not the blade I was — or pretended to be. And women wear worse than men. Or at least they act as if they do, and like as not she is no longer lean but gaunt.

Sewickley isn't Chicago, either. It's suburban rich (I've learned) and always has been, and I suppose she's solid, maybe shallow, or even country-club, in all her views (there's no reason that I can think of why she shouldn't be; neither of us had any views at all, in Dorking), and I'm a rheumy old radical. I can get myself shined up for occasions, but what in the world would we talk about? If a real love affair is best ended when it ends, how much more so a day that began and ended in Dorking?

And how would I find her if I wanted to? Go from house to house in Sewickley? And is the impossibility (as I suppose) of finding her the reason that I'm afraid that the next time I'm in Pittsburgh I'll try to? I might advertise in the *Post-Gazette* personals, but how would the ad read? —

> DORKING TOWN. — Will yng lady
> (1927) spent happy day yng man write
> Box 297?

I'd do better to put my ad in the lost-and-found column:

> LOST. — My 19th yr. Sntmntl. value to
> loser. Lib. rwrd. of any 10 yrs. since
> for return of same.

ZILLERTAL
MAN

Hainzenberg/Zillertal,
Tyrol, Austria (*delayed
a couple of months; snow*)

It is at Jenbach that you begin your journey — that my little brood and I began ours — up, up, up into what the Tyrol Tourist Bureau calls, in English, "the much-snug Ziller River Valley," or Zillertal. I think that the Tyrol Tourist Bureau means "much-sung," and not "much-snug," but no matter; the Zillertal is as much snug as it is sung. I snig of Zillertal Man.

I snig of Zillertal Man, but first of the Romantic Narrow-Gauge Zillertal Railway, which takes off, when it has passengers, from Jenbach. "Romantic," retranslated into any European language, means that you'd better wash up while the washing is good and further prepare yourself for the romance ahead by buying a loaf of bread and a whole salami; the Zillertal Railway is not a modern romance.

We were riding the Zillertal Railway, my little brood and I, in order to visit Zillertal Man in the unspoiled beauty of his valley. We could not see much of the beauty, en route from Jenbach, because it was night. But we had the word for it of one of our fellow passengers, who accepted our offer of a bite of salami by biting off half the sausage, that Zillertal Man so prizes the beauty of the valley that passengers of the Zillertal Railway are forbidden to get off to pick flowers while the train is in motion. The little train, packed to the gas jets, made its and our dalliant way up the valley as far as Mayrhofen. There the Zillertal Railway gives out, and we had to change to the Austrian Post Bus, also romantic, for the trip up the mad mountain road of ice to Hintertux at the valley's end.

From the *Progressive*, March, 1952.

But the night Post Bus went only as far up as Lanersbach, and it was flagged at Vorderlanersbach — the Austrian way of designating the town you get to before you get to Lanersbach — by Frau Willi Kirchler, who unloaded us into her house; her brother-in-law, Sepp Kirchler, with whom we were to have stayed at Hintertux, had sent a boy down suggesting that Frau Willi take us in for the night rather than let us climb the last five miles of ice up to Hintertux; Sepp Kirchler took us for softies. Frau Ww. Willi Kirchler was a good-looking middle-aged woman in mourning — the "Ww.," which means *Witwe*, means "widow" and becomes a part of the name of the bereft — and when I asked her about her husband, she told me about the *Lawine*. I had heard about the *Lawine* in the train and the bus, but I couldn't get at my dictionary and so I didn't know it meant avalanche.

The *Lawine* hit the whole Zillertal, along the entire twenty miles or so of its length, at exactly ten o'clock on the night of January 6, 1951. The snow had been mountainously heavy over the Christmas period, and then it had rained the whole length of the valley. The rain, penetrating the snow to the ground, loosened the grip of the snow on the mountainsides. The evening of January 6 the *Föhn* — the soft, wet south wind from Italy — had blown up the valley in a series of little whiffs a half-hour or so apart. That would have been enough to do it; one widespread report is that an instant before the avalanche the motor of a plane was heard through the valley, and the vibration of the motor would have been enough. Not only whole houses, but whole forests came down the northwest wall of the valley. So it was probably the *Föhn*; the snow on the east wall held. It happened the whole length of the valley at once; in three, some say two minutes, the snow was still and the night quiet again.

Zillertal Man doesn't weep and wail; he, and his widow and orphans after him, is soft-spoken, like the snow. Frau Ww. Kirchler said that ten men — she didn't say how many women or children; it's men who count — were killed from the Lanersbach neighborhood. How many had been killed in the Hintertux neighborhood, five miles on up the valley, she didn't know; Zillertal Man's world is his neighborhood. And where his home stood, for a century or two, or five, before the last *Lawine,* there on that spot he rebuilds it and waits for the next one.

There are two reasons for studying Zillertal Man. First, he is dying out; very, very slowly, to be sure, but new roads draw him slowly away to the cities, new wars kill his sons off, new ways draw his daughters from the unchanging work of the land. Second, he is inexpensive to study; my family of five studied him for $11.42 a day, including three meals (plus afternoon tea), cold running water, stone's-throw plumbing, and wood-stove heat.

This was the private home, with two, or even three, bedrooms available, of Ingeborg Brocke, address as per above. Austria is moderately cheap — the only country in Europe that is even moderately cheap — and if you keep away from the cities it is really cheap. When Ingeborg wrote us — and I quote — that "Tyrol is always a bit in front with the height of costs, as the transport of goods to here is so expensive," we didn't understand. Now we do.

We got off the Romantic Narrow-Gauge Zillertal Railway, on its meander back to Jenbach, at the village of Zell am Ziller. Ingeborg was waiting for us at Zell, and we all took the Post Bus up, vertically, to the stop before the ten-family village of Hainzenberg. Below us, two or three thousand feet right below us, was Zell. Above us was a path into the woods — going up.

"Well, here we are," I said in flawless German.

"*Noch nicht,*" said Ingeborg, this being Zillertal Man's quaint way of saying, "Not yet."

"You see," said Ingeborg, a Berlinerin (or female Berliner) who came to the Zillertal in the summer of 1945, trading her clothes for food for her younger brothers, "we don't actually live in the city of Hainzenberg. We live in the suburbs."

There were four heavy suitcases to be got to the suburbs and a still heavier briefcase, two moderately heavy rucksacks, a typewriter (fitted with gun and camera), and one pair of skis for the five of us. Fifty feet up the path, into the sun-shifting snowless pines, there was a house. In front of the house was an assortment of immense woven baskets, built, with shoulder handles, to be carried like rucksacks. Ingeborg said that we would leave the suitcases there and the farmer would bring them up — "up" was the word she used — later. I had to struggle with Ingeborg, who seemed to have no conception of white southern womanhood, for the briefcase and the rucksacks, but imagine letting a woman carry a load like that on her back! Still, when we started up, she had one of the baskets, empty on her back. The woods were lovely, but the path up a little rocky. I thought I would rest a bit, and I did. The little ones were all ahead of me; Ingeborg remained behind me, and when I rested, she rested. Then, as we got higher, the path was muddy, and then it was covered with snow, and then it was covered with ice. I thought I would rest again, and I did. So did Ingeborg. Then I thought I would go on, but I couldn't. "Now, Professor," said Ingeborg, with all the gentleness of a white southern woman, "I take these things," and she did.

The last stretch, going around the shady side of the mountain to the sunny side, where Ingeborg's house was, was the worst. "Now, Professor," said Ingeborg, still behind me, "you must rest again, and then step very firmly on the ice, and do not look down over the edge of the path. The meadow is a little difficult the first time, but step hard on the ice and do not look down over the edge. I will come right behind you and hold you fast if you fall. Or if you become too tired or afraid, I take the things out of my basket and carry you."

That's how I found out why "the transport of goods to here is so expensive." Ingeborg's house is sixty-five hundred feet up in the Zillertal Alps, not "*in* the mountains," but *on* the face of a mountain. And everything in that house — the stove, the bathtub, the tables, the beds — everything in that house that wasn't built there, came up that terrible path, and across the edge of that terrible meadow, on a man's back, or a woman's. There has never been any other way up, nor will there be. Ingeborg's house, called "Krawatten," or cravat, is two and a half centuries old, its square-faced timbers burned black, time out of mind, by the crystal-clear sunshine and the glare from the snow. On this same spot there stood a house named "Krawatten" in 1400, antedating, I should have supposed, the invention of the cravat by the Brothers Brooks.

The place name abides, no matter how many houses or families succeed one another on it. Except for official records — which means birth, baptism, marriage, death, and the rare rental (and rarer yet sale) of a farm — the families are known only by the name of the place. Ingeborg is Krawatten Ingeborg, and down below, between Ingeborg's and the village, is the place "Bischl." One of the sons on the Bischl place is Sepp, or Joseph, known, of course, as Bischl Sepp. It is of Bischl Sepp that I, and all Hainzenberg, sing wonderfully.

Every generation of Zillertal Man produces — no one, least of all I, can imagine how — an archbishop or an artist. The director of the Vienna Philharmonic is a Zillertaler, overheard whistling (not singing, but whistling) as a boy by the director of the Berlin Philharmonic on the Romantic Narrow-Gauge Zillertal Railway. But every generation must produce a Bischl Sepp in every neighborhood, or else the neighborhood, by which I mean the side of a single mountain, would die. Bischl Sepp is the man who can carry anything.

When Ingeborg first came to Krawatten, which had not been occupied for twenty years, she found there a great cone-shaped barrel the height of a tall man. It was open at the top, as if the peak of the cone had been sliced off. What it was, nobody knew, but Hainzenberg supposed that it must have been used, a few centuries before, for making cheese. It was made of wood, not of planks, however, but of square timbers. Its weight was probably three hundred pounds; it must have been built on the mountain. A half-mile above — and I mean above — Krawatten stands, the highest house on the Hainzenberg, except for the hut on the very top where the herdsmen sleep when they take their cattle all the way up to pasture them for the summer. Ingeborg's neighbor wanted to try to build a cellar, for which he needed cement, and he thought that the great barrel at Ingeborg's would be the thing to mix the cement in. But the barrel had to be got up that half-mile. Ingeborg's neighbor sent his son, a famous young carrier, to fetch it where it lay, partly embedded and small end down, on the slope. The famous young carrier could not lift either end, and he went back for his sister, a famous carrier in her own right. Between the two of them they could lift either end, but only either end. They would have to ask Bischl Sepp to help them.

Bischl Sepp is forty or forty-five, medium height, not especially heavy. He has a simple look, like every Zillertaler, and like every Zillertaler, he is not simple. Zillertal Man, if he wants to make a deal with another Zillertal Man, will stand around all day talking to him until the second Zillertaler brings up the subject; then the first has the advantage of not having been the one who was anxious to make the deal. In this way business moves very slowly and very deviously in the Zillertal. And this, together with practical jokes of all kinds (but always of a very involved character), is the way that Zillertal Man passes the winter and even the summer. And Bischl Sepp may say that he will carry a load of four-by-fours up the mountain for you, but not to your door, as he is a busy man, and then leaves the four-by-fours *above* your house and watches you all day, from the woods, pulling them down, one by one, with ropes and skids.

The deal with Bischl Sepp over the barrel — understand that money was not involved — was to be made at Krawatten Ingeborg's one clear winter evening. Present were the neighbor, as party of the first part; Bischl Sepp, as party of the second part; Krawatten Ingeborg, *de facto* custodian of the barrel; and Dr. Werner Schmidt, the distinguished South-Africanist who, after twenty years in South Africa, understands the Zillertal dialect and is always called upon as honest broker in Zillertal deals, since he is a man of the world who has been to Innsbruck, fifty miles away. On all Hainzenberg, only Dr. Schmidt, who lives at Ingeborg's, is called by his full name.

A little schnapps had been drunk — white mule made of mountain pears — and not much said, and nothing at all about the barrel. It was almost ten o'clock, an untoward hour for Hainzenberg farmers, when the neighbor who wanted the barrel said he had better go home now.

"But," said Dr. Schmidt, as non-party to the deal, "what about the barrel?"

"Oh, yes," said the neighbor who wanted the barrel so badly, "the barrel."

Nobody said anything, and the neighbor, supposing the deal was off, got up to go. Dr. Schmidt's instinct is keen, and he decided on direct action.

"Bischl Sepp," he said, "will you help carry the barrel?"

"The barrel?" said Bischl Sepp, who knew that that was why they were there, "oh, if there's a barrel, I'll bring it up later. You" — to the neighbor — "go home now. It is nice here. I'll stay a while."

The neighbor went, and an hour later Bischl Sepp said it was time for him, too, to go home. Dr. Schmidt, whose instinct is keen, said nothing, and Bischl Sepp left. A half-hour later, while Dr. Schmidt was working late over a manuscript, Bischl Sepp knocked at the door.

"What's this," he said, "about a barrel?"

Dr. Schmidt told him.

"Let me see this barrel," said Bischl Sepp, who had seen it, tilted up on the mountainside, small end down, every day of his life.

To tell you the rest of the story I would have to get down on my back, as Bischl Sepp did on the mountainside, just below the smaller open end of the barrel. His head was bent all the way forward on his chest. On his back he wriggled up the mountainside, and up under the smaller end of the barrel, until, resting on Bischl Sepp's neck, it came off the ground. Bischl Sepp kept wriggling farther up the mountainside, farther up the barrel. And then, just beyond mid-barrel, he began to get to his feet.

"You understand," says Dr. Schmidt, "that the barrel rested on his neck — on his collarbone, I should say. He was using his hands —his fingers, rather — to keep it from rolling off."

It took Bischl Sepp fifteen minutes to get to his feet. "And then," says Dr. Schmidt, "he began to trot — not walk, but trot — up the mountain."

A few minutes later, Dr. Schmidt saw from his window that it was beginning to snow. About two in the morning — Dr. Schmidt was still working — Bischl Sepp knocked at the door. Dr. Schmidt opened it. It was snowing heavily. Bischl Sepp stood there, with the barrel on his collarbone.

"Dr. Schmidt," he said, "I want to talk to you."

"Then come in," said Dr. Schmidt.

"No." said Bischl Sepp, with the barrel on his collarbone, "it's all right out here."

"I have an idea," said Bischl Sepp, with the barrel on his collarbone. "When it began to snow, on my way up, I thought, 'Now it's beginning to snow.' So I thought about this all the way up, and by the time I was there, I had my idea." Then Bischl Sepp turned his head, his neck, his collarbone, and the barrel in all directions, to make sure that at two o'clock in the morning, at the top of Zillertal Alps in a blizzard, nobody would overhear him.

"My idea is very good," said Bischl Sepp.

"Ja," said Dr. Schmidt, agreeing that Bischl Sepp's idea was good.

"It goes like this," said Bischl Sepp, after Dr. Schmidt said "Ja." "When I got to the neighbor, I woke him up to ask him where he wanted the barrel in the yard, and then I put it there, and he saw me do it, and then he went back to bed, and then I came down. But I had my idea, already. So I went back up and waited, and thought about my idea, and then I brought the barrel down. Here it is," said Bischl Sepp, as if he were pulling the barrel out of his pocket. "What do you think of my idea?"

"Ja," said Dr. Schmidt, whose instinct is keen.

"When he wakes up in the morning," said Bischl Sepp, "he will go out to see the barrel, and it won't be there. And the snow will be over the footsteps and over the place where the barrel was. And then tonight I will bring the barrel to him — it will snow for a week now — and say to him, 'I have brought your barrel.' And then I will put it down, and he will see me, and then he will go back to bed, and I will wait, and think about my idea, and then I will bring the barrel down the mountain again, and when he goes out in the morning, it won't be there. And then I'll bring it the next night, and if he asks me, I'll say 'No, I didn't bring it before,' and I'll take it down again after he goes back to bed, and I'll do that every night, as long as it snows, you understand, and let me tell you my idea."

"Tell me," said Dr. Schmidt.

"My idea," said Bischl Sepp, "is that he will think that the Devil has got him."

I imagine, but I don't know, that Dr. Schmidt used the Devil to dissuade Bischl Sepp. The Zillertal is, being Austria, and deepest Austria, Catholic. There are shrines along every road, some simple, some grand, and some so primitive that they must be as old as Zillertal Man. There are holy pictures, painted in huge dimensions, and some of them masterfully, on the fronts of houses. Every living room, and sometimes every room in the house, has its crucifix in the principal corner. Religion is as much a part of their lives as sleeping, and since they have been sleeping and praying all their lives, they continue to do so with no consciousness or question in either case. They are not really better than other people, because they are not really more religious than other people. They support the Church not because they have to or want to but because they always have. And if someone suggests, as Dr. Schmidt may have suggested to Bischl Sepp, that they keep away from the Devil — and if their impulse to traffic with him, in a given case, is not too strong — why, they keep away from the Devil.

They, like the Bavarians, who are also Catholics, say *Grüss' Gott* for "hello." When they were told to say *Heil Hitler* for "hello," they, like the Bavarians, went on saying *Grüss' Gott*, and that didn't mean that they were martyrs of the Christian resistance to Hitler. It meant that they always said "hello" the way they had always said "hello."

Dr. Schmidt was telling us about Bischl Sepp the evening of December 24, *Heilige Abend*, and that's why he never finished and we never found out exactly how Dr. Schmidt dissuaded Bischl Sepp from carrying the three-hundred-pound barrel up and down the mountain for a week. The afternoon of December 24 we had all gone slipping desperately down the mountain for the Christmas play at the schoolhouse. After it was over, we climbed back up to Krawatten. The Christmas tree was decorated, and the children had received their presents, as they always do in Europe on *Heilige Abend*, and Dr. Schmidt was finishing the story of Bischl Sepp when there a knock at the door and the young farmer from above — his father is dead now — and his two sisters came in. In their hands they each had two long bunches of twigs woven together and dipped in oil. It was eleven o'clock, and they, and Zillertal Man everywhere in the long valley, were ready to start down the mountain to the great churches — mountain hamlets like Hainzenberg have only chapels. One bunch of fagots, as a torch, would light the way down from the mountains, burning out just as they got to the bottom; the other torch would light the way up. They would get back home from midnight mass about 2:30 A.M., and at 5 they would start down again for 6 A.M. mass.

After they left, we went out on the balcony of Krawatten, facing the northwest wall of mountains across the valley, the wall that the *Lawine* had hit the year before. The night was glittering with all the stars, and we could see the line between the peaks, and the sky. Across the valley, just below the peaks, were little lights, hundreds of little lights, hanging all over the mountain wall, some of them in winding lines, some in pairs, and some single. The little lights, in lines, pairs, and single, began to come down the mountains across the valley.

"Mostly," said Ingeborg, "there are no real paths like ours."

The little lights came lower, lower down the mountains, and the pairs and singles merged with the winding lines as they approached the bottom. Then as the lights reached the bottom, they went out, and we could hear the bells begin to ring.

Grandma says I ought to have my head examined. That's *her* opinion. *My* opinion is that *she* ought to have *her* head examined.

I'll say one thing for Grandma, she's broad-minded. She says that everybody has a right to his opinion. But I've got her there. If she's entitled to hers, I'm entitled to mine.

Grandma is always meeting a lady who is telling her something. It's never true, but Grandma has great faith in ladies she meets. Once, when she was just plain Ma and I was one and a half, she met a lady who told her the reason I didn't walk was that there must be something wrong with my spine.

"You ought to have his spine examined," said the lady.

Grandma jumped on the trolley with me and told Dr. Abt he ought to examine my spine.

"Who told you that," asked Dr. Abt, "a lady?" "Yes," said Grandma.

"That's all there is to it," said Dr. Abt. "If a lady told you, that's all there is to it. Here, you poor little fellow," he said, taking a lollypop out of his lollypop jar and throwing it down the hall. The hundred yards down that hall was the best century I ever ran — eleven flat.

Another time she had me and my big brother Howard out in Washington Park, and she met a lady who told her that those were two fine looking little boys. Grandma said the older one never gave her a bit of trouble, but the younger was a little devil.

"It's probably his diet," said the lady.

From the *Progressive*, January, 1949.

Grandma hot-footed me to Dr. Abt and said I ought to have my stomach examined, and Dr. Abt asked her if a lady told her that, and Grandma said yes, and Dr. Abt said, "He ought to have his bottom examined with a razor strap."

"It would kill him," said Grandma.

"It would half-kill him," said Dr. Abt, "which is just what he needs."

Grandma has never lost her faith in what ladies tell her, or in what Dr. Abt tells her, or in what anybody tells her except me.

"Look, Grandma," I say, "I'm happy. Aren't you glad that I'm happy?"

"How can you say you're happy," says Grandma, "when you're always attacking people?"

"For instance?"

"Well, there's the *Chicago Tribune*. Why do you always attack the *Tribune*? If you can't say something nice about people, why do you have to say anything? Why don't you write about things that make people happy?"

"For instance?"

"Well, take Mrs. Homyonum. It was her seventy-eighth birthday last week, and it was a beautiful occasion. Every one of the children was there."

"Including Henry and Herman?"

"No, of course not. You know that Henry got into some sort of trouble over his income tax, a terrible misfortune, and Herman never was any good."

"I know about Henry. I've been thinking of writing an article about him, but —"

"Don't you dare," says Grandma, "do you want to break his poor mother's heart?"

"Look Grandma, it isn't *me*, it's *Henry* who broke his poor mother's heart. But why wasn't Herman any good?"

"You know perfectly well," says Grandma. "His father gave him everything that money could buy and a nice interest in the business when he turned twenty-one, and Herman chucked it all up —"

"For a *shicksa*?"

"No, he never got married, though that little Schmiddleberger girl was crazy about him, and she was an only child, with millions on both sides of the family. A wonderful catch."

"What did Herman pass her by for, and his old man's business besides? It must have been something pretty nifty."

"Oh, I don't know," says Grandma. "Mrs. Homyonum never speaks of him. He never was any good. They say he left home to join the Red Cross and then became a Socialist or something. Spent every cent he had on some sort of Armenian orphan home."

"Didn't his family ever hear from him?"

"Only once," says Grandma. "He wrote them a letter saying that he'd come back if his father would give his — Herman's, that is — share of the business to the employees. They never answered him. That letter almost killed his father. In fact, he died the following winter, at Palm Beach."

"I suppose I really ought to write an article about Mrs. Homyonum," I say.

"I wish you would," says Grandma, "but you don't need to mention Henry or Herman. Remember, a little kindness goes a long way. If you can't say something nice about a person, don't say anything."

"Look, Grandma," I say, "there's a lot that's wrong with the world, isn't there?"

"Yes," says Grandma, "but where did you ever get it into your head that you were brought into the world to set it straight?"

"Never mind about that," I say. "Just answer me. Is there or isn't there a lot that's wrong with the world?"

"Of course there is," says Grandma, "but it's the only world we have, and we have to live in it."

"Not necessarily."

"Oh, shut up," says Grandma. "Here, have another piece of *Bundkuchen*."

"Listen, Grandma, there are millions and millions of people in the world who haven't had *one* piece of *Bundkuchen*."

"There are lots of people who don't like *Bundkuchen*," says Grandma. "Are you going to try to make everybody like what you like?"

"Look, Grandma," I say, "what was the last article I wrote that you *really* liked?"

"The one about Mother of Comptons, in the *Reader's Digest*. That was a beautiful article."

"And what would you say if I told you that the two sons of the Mother of Comptons turned out to be bums?"

"Why," says Grandma, "you said in your article that they were both university presidents."

"So I did," I say, "and so they were and are. But they're bums, too. What's to keep a university president from being a bum?"

"Oh, get out," says Grandma.

"Grandma," I say, "those two Compton boys are the *momsers* that made the atomic bomb."

"You should be so brilliant."

"Brilliant, my eye. Do you know what those two boys did with their atomic bomb? They killed a hundred thousand defenseless women and children with it. How do you like *that*?"

"Why don't you let Mr. Truman run the country?" says Grandma.

"Because he doesn't know how. He's running it into the ground. He's spending 80 per cent of your taxes on war. How do you like *that*?"

"I never mix in politics," says Grandma. "I believe in live and let live."

"But, doggone it, Grandma —."

"Don't you doggone *me*," says Grandma.

"I wasn't doggoning you, I was doggoning *it*," I say. "I was doggoning it because, because — doggone it, I forgot what I was going to say."

"You ought to have your head examined," says Grandma.

"I've *had* my head examined," I say. "There's nothing *wrong* with my head. You just tell me what's wrong with my head. I suppose some *lady* you met told you there was something *wrong* with my head."

"They all tell me," says Grandma. "They all tell me my son ought to have something better to do with his time than attack the Jews in the *Saturday Evening Post*."

"But I wasn't attacking them, Grandma, I was telling them to be better than the Gentiles. I was berating them."

"Berating, schmerating," says Grandma "you ought to hear what Rabbi Mann said."

"Rabbi Mann ought to hear what Amos said."

"Amos who?" says Grandma.

"Grandma, stop listening to the ladies, and stop listening to the rabbis. Do you know what Jesus said about the rabbis?"

"Jesus wasn't a Jew," says Grandma.

"He *was* a Jew, and everyone knows it."

"I'm not everyone," says Grandma, "I'm just your foolish old mother."

"I didn't say you were everyone, and I didn't say you were foolish. I said Jesus was a Jew and I say Moses was a Jew, and I say God handed down to Moses the Law of the Jews, and one of the laws is, "Thou shalt not kill," and these rabbis of yours kiss themselves in on every war and violate the Law of God."

"Well, I don't know about that," says Grandma, "but I do know that people ask me why *their* sons should fight for their country while *my* son calls himself a conscientious objector and stays home."

"Grandma, do you want me to kill anyone?"

"Of course not," says Grandma, "but you wouldn't have to. You could get a nice job in Washington or somewhere, the way the rest of them did. Why, a boy with your talents —"

"Grandma, I'm not a boy, and I haven't any talent that I'd be willing to use to help kill anyone or to get anyone else to. I'm not a killer, and I'm not a pimp."

"I don't know what you mean," says Grandma, "but the whole world can't be wrong."

"Why not?"

"There's always been war, and there always will be. That's the way people are, and you can't change them."

"But I can change *myself*, can't I?"

"Mr. Big-Head."

"I'm *not* Mr. Big-Head. The people who think they have a right to kill other people are the Mr. Big-Heads."

Grandma Ought To Have Her Head Examined   309

"Why," says Grandma, "don't you leave well enough alone?"

"Because it's not well enough."

"There you go again," says Grandma. "Everybody's out of step but you."

"Grandma, I once heard you say you'd rather see your son dead than in the Army."

"But you wouldn't have to go into the Army. You could get yourself a nice —"

"Grandma, wouldn't you be ashamed of me if I got myself a nice job in Washington while the other boys, as you call them, were risking their lives on the battlefield?"

"But you have your family to think of."

"I think of them day and night, Grandma. I don't want them to have to be ashamed of me."

"Well, they will be," says Grandma, "as long as you think the whole world's wrong and you're right."

"Grandma, you brought me up not to steal, and not to lie, and not to cheat, and not to kill, didn't you?"

"I tried to," says Grandma.

"Well," says I, "I don't steal, or lie, or cheat, hardly ever, and I never, never kill. Don't you think I'm wonderful?"

"Well," says Grandma, "everybody's entitled to his own opinion."

"But aren't you proud of me?"

"I'd be proud of my two sons, whatever they did."

I say Grandma ought to have her head examined.